EVERYONE IS AN

ENTREPRENEUR

ALSO BY GREGORY V. DIEHL

Brand Identity Breakthrough: How to Craft Your Company's Unique Story to Make Your Products Irresistible

Travel as Transformation: Conquer the Limits of Culture to Discover Your Own Identity

The Influential Author: How and Why to Write, Publish, and Sell Non-Fiction Books That Matter

The Heroic and Exceptional Minority: A Guide to Mythological Self-Awareness and Growth

EVERYONE IS AN ENTREPRENEUR

SELLING ECONOMIC SELF-DETERMINATION IN A POST-SOVIET WORLD

BY GREGORY V. DIEHL

IDENTITY PUBLICATIONS

For permission requests, write to the publisher at contact@identitypublications.com.

Contact the author at www.gregorydiehl.net.

Library of Congress Control Number: 2022904096

Orders by U.S. trade bookstores and wholesalers. Please contact Identity Publications: Tel: (805) 259-3724 or visit www.IdentityPublications.com.

ISBN-13: 978-1-945884-59-7 (paperback)
ISBN-13: 978-1-945884-68-9 (hardcover)
ISBN-13: 978-1-945884-69-6 (ebook)

First Edition
Publishing by Identity Publications (www.IdentityPublications.com).
Cover design by Irina Danilova.

DEDICATION

Knowledge is the prime source of wealth in the world. The knowledge promoted by this book represents my best attempt to temper the problem of inadequate wealth to sustain human comfort and thriving, otherwise known as poverty. It is how I wish to contribute to a state of ample opportunities among all people, which we can think of as greater wealth. Consequently, this book is dedicated to humanity.

ЧТОБЫ СТРОИТЬ-НАДО ЗНАТЬ,
ЧТОБЫ ЗНАТЬ-НАДО УЧИТЬСЯ

,,

In order to build, one must know. In order to know, one must learn.

TABLE OF CONTENTS

PREFACE

I HAVE WRITTEN this book for the man or woman who is intensely curious about how the world works and how they can improve their working worldview. It is for the person who is bold enough to question their beliefs about what value they can offer the world and, in turn, receive from it. These words are for those who do not accept limitations at face value, automatically believe what others believe, or follow rules for the sake of following them regardless of where they live in the world or the forces currently controlling their choices.

There may be some who open this book expecting tactical advice on improving the sales or management of their enterprises, cutting costs and increasing profits, and the like. Or perhaps they are seeking motivational prose for people who pursue lifestyle and financial freedom by becoming their own bosses. Such readers might overlook the purpose of the broader examination of entrepreneurial principles and world culture contained herein. They may miss the point of anecdotes featuring villagers trying to maximize the productive output of their dairy cows, the scarcity and necessity of a commodity called hay in winter, and the dynamics of baking and selling bread in a tyrannically controlled economy. They may not see the direct and principled connection between the choices they make in their own lives and the choices made by people the world over with superficially different lifestyles.

What's written here was directly inspired by the need I saw for knowledge of the principles of entrepreneurship among the rural residents of a scenic but underdeveloped village called Kalavan in the Gegharkunik province of the far-Eastern European (or far-Western Asian) nation of Armenia. It is a place where, beginning three years ago, I decided to make a home for myself. At that time, I purchased an old house in disrepair and began to gradually improve the state of my domicile and my social presence within the community. What began at first as an early retirement plan and the opportunity to explore Armenia, my maternal grandmother's nation of origin, turned into an on-the-ground examination of how this former Soviet nation has adjusted to the freedoms and responsibilities that come with the economic self-determination that followed the collapse of communist control.

In my observation, it is people in this transitionary state (in what economists might call frontier or emerging markets) who have the most to gain from learning to see the world as entrepreneurs. Fortunately, they now have the freedom to do so for the first time since near-total authoritarian control began over the economy and culture a century ago at the inception of the USSR. Despite how it is popularly depicted, entrepreneurship is not confined to offices or boardrooms, university lecture halls, startup garages, or trendy online membership forums. It does not require the hiring of employees and the turnover of millions of units of whatever asset someone manages to take to market. Entrepreneurship is a mindset, a revolutionary way of seeing the world that applies equally to people in all cultural and economic circumstances.

Take particular note of the fact that the title of this book is not "Everyone *Should Become* an Entrepreneur." It's "Everyone Is an Entrepreneur." There are none who do not fall under this description, except perhaps infants, the braindead, or the unconscious, who are incapable of making choices and performing willful actions in the pursuit of conscious goals. There is no escaping the fundamental principles of how intelligent human beings strategize to interact with reality to produce and manage the things they consider valuable: Not artists, doctors, teachers, laborers, farmers, homemakers, scientists, or any other category of service you can imagine, irrespective of age, nationality, race, religion, or gender. There is no one whose life cannot be improved by learning how to think this way and applying the logic of these principles to all their choices.

Entrepreneurship, like science, is at once a submission to the truth and the determination to squeeze out every emergent property the truth can offer. Everyone is an entrepreneur to the extent that they seek to interact with reality on its own terms in order to change it to be more satisfying to them. To cease being an entrepreneur would be to give up entirely on the idea of a principled approach to life, to willfully deny oneself the pursuit of one's own values. It would be to adopt a magical way of thinking that demands reality change to meet human expectations without first changing human understanding and actions to meet reality as it is.

Adopting and applying this paradigm of self-determination is what this book aims to help the reader accomplish, no matter where they live or their present level of material wealth and professional experience. Even lacking direct, explicit, and organized education, someone with an entrepreneurial way of seeing things can pick up on relevant patterns and principles, so long as they have the opportunity to observe them and the freedom to apply them. That's the point of willful entrepreneurship: To stop feeling like a victim of circumstances and instead believe in our reasonable ability to direct the outcomes of our lives.

Gregory Diehl
Kalavan, Armenia

THE STIFLED FLOWERING OF ENTREPRENEURSHIP IN A POST-SOVIET CULTURE

IF YOU ARE a Westerner who has grown up in a predominantly free society, you have had your paradigm for interacting with the world formed primarily by the opportunities afforded to you by your and your neighbors' abundant liberty. It's something often taken for granted: The freedom to, in large part, determine your own values, your own philosophical identity, your own role in society, the information and activities you will fill your own life with, and how you will pursue your own highest sense of happiness and purpose. It might be difficult or even impossible for you to imagine what life would be like if such essential choices were withheld from you, determined for you by a centralized authority that claimed the right to make them on your behalf and enforce your compliance through threats of imprisonment, forced labor, or execution.

That bleak depiction is precisely what life was like for millions of people living in one of the 15 nations under communist rule in the Soviet Union until just 30 years ago in 1991. The communist system collapsed after 71 years, and the citizens of previously dictatorially controlled nations were free again to do what they saw fit with their own lives, according to whatever best served their interests. Despite the fundamental economic, educational, and political changes that have emerged since those dark and directionless early days of independence, the methods many such people learned to live by continue to be carried over in their lives (and the lives of their children and grandchildren) now, even long after they gained the freedom to make those choices for themselves. Concepts related to business, wealth accumulation, self-fulfillment, and the conscious pursuit of meaningful goals that might seem to be common knowledge and in the best interests of all people continue to be overlooked—**not because people are too unintelligent or oblivious to understand them, but because they have been conditioned by generations of restricted freedoms and fear-based incentives away from such proactive ideas.** In the oppressive world they grew up in, such concepts were irrelevant or even dangerous to consider, so it's no wonder that there is still lingering reluctance in post-Soviet cultures to think about entrepreneurship proactively.

In the command economy of the Soviet Union, control over providing the basic necessities of life was taken out of the hands of individuals, so those individuals never developed paradigms that would have empowered them to take care of their own needs. Whatever they needed was provided for them in a bare minimum fashion without any possibility of disagreement or choice about what was proclaimed the best possible manner for the good of Soviet society. And when the State inevitably failed to adequately deliver the necessities it promised, there was no recourse or alternative avenues available to acquire what was needed. Even if individuals were clever and ambitious enough to devise alternative means of production and economic exchange outside the tyrannical rule of their Soviet leaders, they faced harsh and violent treatment from the penal system for doing so. It was illegal to even think or speak ideas that were counter to communist ideals, as an anti-Soviet mentality was classified as a mental disorder by the State. Contributing to "propaganda" that weakened Soviet authority or defamed the Soviet State was punishable by up to a decade behind bars.

Why was it inevitable that the centralized planners running the show and determining who needed what goods and services and in what quantities would fail integrally at their task? Why was the Soviet Union doomed to collapse from the outset? The answer is simple, and it is the same answer that explains why any intentional effort can fail to produce the intended outcome: The methods employed were incompatible with the reality being dealt with. No one can ignore the laws of economics because they seem unfair or inconvenient and expect a positive outcome. They likewise cannot ignore the laws of physics, even if being stuck to the ground or the inability to phase through solid objects is a bit inconvenient, or that two and two make four just because they prefer the sum to be five. They cannot succeed in these defiances against reality even with the full might of the Red Army to support their opposition.

If the ideal outcome of the economy is to meet the maximum amount of its participants' needs for the minimum costs required from them, only the millions of individuals participating in the Soviet economy could have adequately expressed what those needs were and how much of their time, labor, capital, and other assets they were willing, as individuals, to invest in acquiring them. The authorities forcefully commanding the Soviet economy made the same mistake that all authorities trying to make people behave in prescribed manners make: They ignored the actual priorities of the people and attempted to override them with their own under threat of violence for non-compliance and utopian indoctrination that required utter dependence on appointed leaders.

The fatal flaw was that the Soviet economic machine was never running according to natural and authentic inputs by the people seeking to meet their goals within it. It was, instead, elaborately and convolutedly constructed to produce the arrangement of goods and services that a small group of disproportionately powerful people decided would be in the best interests of everyone. Such an illegitimate representation of what consumers wanted could never begin to approach the optimal method of filling those wants. It also could not even produce its fabricated mandates in an optimally cost-efficient manner. The result was more and more costs required for less and less actual productive output, and what was produced was far from the optimal arrangement of what people actually wanted.

Under Soviet economic rule, both output and input were sabotaged from the start. There is no way for a Labor Department to organically calculate what productive roles people are best suited to perform and the ideal way to compensate them for their productivity without allowing them to make those choices according to their own priorities and abilities on an individual level. No generic and universal mandate can ever adequately approximate the vast confluence of what value is available to be supplied and what value is presently in demand, and the consequences of ignoring this fact only get more drastic the larger the scale of the economy.

What do you suppose the justification used by Soviet authorities for taking control over the arrangement of their economy was? In large part, it was a circular claim about individuals' inability to make those kinds of vital choices for themselves. It's easy for people to fall into the fallacy of thinking that the way something is presently done is the only (or best) way it ever can be. So, all a Soviet supporter needed to do to invent a justification for what an outsider would see as human rights violations and counterproductive economic policies was point to the visible occurrence of something as simple as the State providing bread rations for hungry people.

"See? We are feeding the hungry," they could claim. "Without us taking the extreme measures we do, these people would have no bread and quickly starve to death. The fact that any people at all are still alive is due to our direct intervention in the natural process of their starvation and the benevolence we gift them. If we were to stop forcing the production and distribution of bread to occur, there would be no bread at all."

This analysis leaves out an obvious yet unspoken premise: The only reason the State was the only producer of bread was that they employed violence against the bread-producing populace to ensure things worked out that way. There was generally no flour available in stores because the State controlled the production and distribution of flour. If any individual figured out a better way to produce grain and offer bread outside of State control and attempted to offer it on the market to hungry people, there would quickly be efforts to remove these private producers from the economy. Their choices and mentality would be seen as threats to all the people who depended upon State-produced bread. They would be considered profoundly selfish for taking matters into their own hands and caring foremost about their own benefit at the expense of the collective need for bread. That individuals continued to risk death by State mandate in order to find their own under-the-table methods of feeding themselves, their families, and their communities is a testament to just how bad the State was at meeting these essential needs for them.

This simplistic centralized economic model of feeding people also completely overlooks the fact that there are countless varieties of staple foods beyond mere bread, and there are equally untapped strategies for producing enough calories and micronutrients to sustain large populations of human life. In the West, where more varieties of food now exist in greater abundance than any other time in history, many people even elect to omit bread and other grain foods from their diet, which is something that would have seemed impossible to Soviet citizens who principally depended upon bread to meet even a basic level of nourishment.

It is now so easy to feed people in the West, in fact, that we have created the inverse problem of starvation: Far more people now die from eating *too much* than eating *not enough*. This is a beautiful form of irony that perfectly demonstrates what can happen when artificial restraints to production and consumption are removed and entrepreneurs are enabled to serve their vital function in society. More problems are solved in a greater variety of ways when you have more people free and incentivized to solve them. But a single centralized body can never take into account all the possibilities outside the linear models it has adopted as the singular means to solve what it perceives as singular problems.

Over the last 15 years, I have traveled from one economically developing country to another, living, working, or teaching among the local populations in more than 50 nations. I began my journey where I grew up in California but ended it in a rural village of Armenia, where I have lived the last three years. In many ways, the cultural mentalities regarding how to organize the productive pursuits of life could not be more different.

But what has always stood out to me is how often many of the poorest residents of a nation, notably those who live in villages or small communities away from major cities, are quite competent and talented in a range of important lifestyle skills. Their isolated lives require them to be. If they need to repair parts of their homes to protect themselves from poor weather, there is no handyman to call to give them an estimate and a timeline for the job. If their cars break down in an unfortunate spot, the burden is theirs to provide for themselves and support each other in fixing them with whatever is available. There is simply a problem, with real consequences, that they need to figure out how to solve as soon and as efficiently as possible.

Even without access to modern schooling, books, or the internet, as is often the case, they manage to pass wisdom and skills among their communities, from the old to the young and neighbor to neighbor. But what they rarely seem to learn is how to apply their knowledge and skills in tactical and systematic ways to take control over their ability to produce, manage, and leverage value in their favor.

The cause of this strategic shortcoming seems obvious. When people grow up with one particular paradigm for how they are allowed or ought to interact with reality, they will usually carry that paradigm forward for the remainder of their lives, no matter what changes around them. Likely, they will also pass their limiting beliefs on to their children, even if it is evident to an outsider that the world their children live in is radically different than the one they adapted to. While this unfortunate bias applies to all of us, it is of particular consequence to cultures undergoing rapid and massive changes in political and economic practice. The rules of the game that previous generations learned to play by as they were coming of age are outdated and often counterproductive to the aims of their progeny.

One conversation I had with Mery, a young Armenian woman from the capital city of Yerevan working as an English teacher in a village neighboring mine, comes to mind. She introduced me to her young students as a "business author" and then described her ideas about what business is to them in a way fairly close to how I would describe gambling. **"In business, you need to risk everything you have to start something new. And you might be very lucky for a little while and make a lot of money, but then the next day, you could just lose everything and go out of business."**

What sticks out to you about this description? To me, it reeks of a sense of having zero control over the outcome of being involved in business. Perhaps such people get into business for the wrong reasons and under the wrong impressions about how it will work. Perhaps they view it as a guaranteed get-rich-quick vehicle that is bound to bring hundreds of eager patrons with cash to burn to their doors. And maybe, just maybe, such people happen to be in the right place and at the right time with the right product so that they find some modicum of success at the start. But they are not capable of telling the difference between what they are doing right and what they are doing wrong, and, sooner or later, their mistakes catch up to them. The success (or the illusion of success) they start with quickly crumbles, and they are left with only the cold reality of a non-sustainable business model. They don't know what they did wrong, so they can't even blame themselves. They only blame some nebulous concept of business itself or the market conditions under which they failed to find success.

That's why such people prefer the apparent certainty of a guaranteed paycheck, however meager it may be and however unrewarding the work required to earn it. At the very least, they know their job won't just crumble beneath their feet for reasons they can't identify. This outlook is, of course, only an illusion of security. Any job in any organization can disappear at any time for reasons either in or out of their control. But a job creates the appearance of comfort, security, and a place to belong in the world, and that appearance is all some people have. They prefer it to the unknown uncertainties of trying to make it on their own.

It's quite ironic that laypeople tend to think of economics as a dull or impractical subject to learn about or discuss. In my paradigm, economics describes the sum total of willful human behavior on this planet. It's fascinating for me to consider everything it encompasses and how every choice people make interacts with and affects every other choice.

Economics is also one of the subjects that the average person seems to be the most ignorant on and, more than that, ignorant even of the fact that they are ignorant of it. Whereas someone who does not study biology or mathematics likely won't profess to understand very well how they work or form strong vocal opinions about them, it seems that just about everyone insists on some particular view of how economics does or ought to work, as though its objective nature were somehow malleable to popular opinion and the culture of the day. I've often pondered why this might be the case. The best answer I can come up with is that most people have never been taught that the science of economics even *has* an objective nature at all, most likely because it is the study of human choice, and humans have free will after all. Therefore, so they seem to think, economic models should operate however we freely will them to.

What this unvoiced analysis misses is that economics is the study of human choice applied to an objective and finite reality that functions according to hard and fast rules. It is a discourse on how we interact with reality to get what we want from it and change it to how we want it to be. There is no way to do this without first acknowledging the natural laws and qualities of reality, including the topics we call economics and entrepreneurship. **An entrepreneur, in principle, is merely someone who produces or manages wealth in the form of subjective value.** It is impossible to consciously live without doing this.

Many of my Armenian countrymen and other post-Soviet citizens still live today in a culturally derived state of unconscious fear about the concept of freedom and personal responsibility. Having lived under the control of dictators for so many decades, many have lost the natural and innate sense of pride that comes from taking charge of one's own life, deciding for oneself how that life will go, and achieving through intentional effort what one wants for themselves. The transition to a system of relatively greater personal freedom at the termination of Soviet control and the new paradigm required by it was not easy for them. Many among the older generations continued to believe that dictatorship and economic enslavement were preferable to the unprecedented burdens that are inherent to acting willfully within the world that they faced for the first time. They preferred a powerful and imposing figurehead or State agency to make choices for them about their production and management of wealth.

This pathological fear of freedom prompts parents and grandparents here in Armenia to teach their children to avoid unnecessary risk, which also means cutting them off from the possibility of emergent gains. The predictable result is that many talented and creative young individuals found great incentive to leave the limitations of Armenia for foreign lands that could provide greater freedom and opportunity to pursue their ambitions. And without its most entrepreneurially minded forward-thinking youth, Armenia's progress toward economic sustainability and abundance remains stifled.

Money is exchanging hands every single day all around us. Everyone decides all the time that there are countless things they would rather have than money, and that's why they make the exchanges that they do. Through this lens, it's really a wonder that anyone has any trouble finding at least one way to make money at all. Monetary exchange defines our modern way of life. The number of ways to *spend* money grows every day, and, by corollary, so does the number of ways to *make* money. After all, for every dollar, euro, yen, or dram spent, there must be a dollar, euro, yen, or dram received.

But people rarely think this way. They, of course, see the obvious range of options for giving their hard-earned money away. We are inundated with advertising and the other effects of consumerism that encourage us to spend, spend, spend on everything under the sun, including things we might not have even previously known existed, let alone that we should want. But when people think about the opposite side of the equation—the options for *making* money—they tend to view the world through limited and rigid structures pertaining to acceptable career paths.

So, why the imbalance? Why have we accepted that opportunities for spending money are abundant and freeform, but opportunities for making it are scarce and must adhere to strict dogmatic rules and be forced to occur under the limiting eye of bureaucratic social institutions? The answer is not physical or even intellectual in nature; the answer, of course, is cultural. And, fortunately for those who struggle the most to make a living in the world, culture can change. To be an economic success, all anyone really has to do is produce more than they consume. The ways they can arrange their choices and actions to accomplish that are as endless as the forms of wealth that exist for them to produce or manage in the first place.

You may already be critical of my premises and approach to this much-debated subject. **Accordingly, you should accept the arguments I make throughout this written work *only* if you agree with the premises and definitions I present and see the logical connections I make between them.** It has been my endeavor to be as clear and consistent as possible with the key terms I use; to that end, you will find a principled glossary of entrepreneurial terms at the end of this book that elaborates on exactly what I mean within the confines of this book and in the context of economics.

More than that, you should be able to extrapolate beyond the isolated, anecdotal examples I give here and apply them to whatever is going on in your own life and the cultural and economic conditions you are in. Only then can we say that the principles I endorse are universal and that they are not applicable only in a particular nation, economy, or at some arbitrary level of personal wealth and education. They apply to the most impoverished and least educated third-world residents just as much as they do to the rich and credentialed residents of the most developed countries on Earth.

I have never been one to let cultural associations with how things are *supposed* to work (or how people would *prefer* that they worked) stop me from figuring out on my own how they actually *do* work. And, in the end, that's all anyone needs to be a successful entrepreneur at any scale: The willingness to try new things, question established practices, and think for themselves about the best way to accomplish their goals according to only the hard and firm rules of reality. Anyone who tells you differently is trying to affirm the limitations of the paradigm they've learned to live by... or perhaps they're just trying to sell you something.

SECTION I:

_____

WHAT WEALTH IS AND WHERE IT COMES FROM

ALMOST EVERYONE ALIVE today is wealthier than almost everyone who lived in previous generations. Analyzing the validity of that bold claim requires us to first have a useful understanding of what wealth is and the natural hierarchy of how it comes into being. What most people think of when they picture wealth in their heads is actually only a facsimile of it, the map that points to the genuine territory it is supposed to be representing. Even those who most people consider to be professionally successful might not understand the nature of their material wealth and where it comes from.

Is seeing a large number in your bank account balance wealth? How could it be? It's just a series of numeric symbols on a screen or a piece of paper. Of what utility is that? What about the paper cash you carry in your wallet? Is that wealth? After all, it's just colorful paper (or plastic polymer, depending on what country you live in) with some cryptic designs and portraits of long-dead leaders.

Are precious metals like gold and silver wealth? What about diamonds and precious gemstones? Is Bitcoin wealth? It's just a bunch of computer code. But then again, so is every computer program ever written. Is owning stock in a successful company wealth? The company is certainly wealthy.

Is having completed a bachelor's degree, master's degree, or doctorate at a prestigious university wealth? They sure are expensive, so they must somehow correlate to the acquisition of wealth, right? Is knowing advanced calculus wealth? Or how to change a flat tire?

Are 1,000 rolls of toilet paper stockpiled in your basement wealth? How about a toolbox full of various hammers, saws, and drill bits? Does such an analysis depend at least partially upon your knowledge of what to do with such tools and your skill related to building or fixing things with them?

Wealth is something that every person in the world both produces and consumes every waking day of their lives. Yet, for something so ubiquitous, we seem to have a lot of misaligned ideas about what it is, how it works, and the best ways to procure and grow it.

All wealth derives from creation, and creation is the result of our choices and intentional actions. We use our knowledge and our skills to create things that we find useful. Utility is whatever is objectively capable of delivering value to an individual. But what you find useful might be very different than what I find useful or what the man down the street or on the other side of the planet finds useful. Value is whatever will bring an individual to a higher state of subjective satisfaction. What is subjectively valuable will change throughout a person's life and even moment to moment with the passing moods of each day. How two people prioritize all their values will never be completely identical.

This is the principle that allows a free society, a massive conglomeration of strangers working harmoniously for mutual benefit, to function. **Our differences in preference and ability allow one individual to pursue their own values by helping someone else pursue theirs and vice versa.** If everyone wanted the same things to the same degree (and they were equally capable of acquiring them), commerce as we know it could not function. All people would work to pursue the same arrangement of knowledge, skills, and material goods. It is our differences that enable us to specialize the application of our thoughts and labor to produce specific things that other people will want enough to exchange the specialized products of their labor for. We get something we want that we could not or would not have produced on our own, and so do they.

A wealthy person is one who has an abundance of options, a broad array of opportunities for utility. They have many avenues to acquire what will bring them satisfaction. They have more ways to solve the various problems of living than people of lesser wealth. They have more security, so long as they manage their wealth strategically, because there are fewer catastrophes that they are not prepared to manage or could not find a way to recover from. Wealth is ownership of assets that deliver subjective value; it is selective dominion and control.

That is why we can confidently say that almost everyone alive today is wealthier than almost everyone who lived in previous generations. The cultural ubiquity of modern technology in almost every part of the world today, such as plumbing, electricity, internet access, and cheap and accessible smartphones in some of the most impoverished places, affords opportunities to nearly everyone that could not have existed in generations prior. The common person today has more choice and available actions than royalty of ages past could neither have dreamt of nor exchanged every stone, horse, and servant in their kingdoms to acquire.

The generations that preceded us made it possible for us to enjoy our material splendor by gradually innovating new knowledge and technology for harvesting and refining the natural resources of the planet into useful commodities. Those commodities have been turned into goods that enable us to pursue goals that seem ordinary to us but that would have seemed like magic to anyone from a time before. Our economies and networks of exchange have developed to a point where we can find ways to buy almost anything we want that we cannot produce ourselves, so long as it exists somewhere on the planet, because we can communicate with other producers across barriers of language and culture and overcome logistical difficulties across any distance or terrain. And we can offer something other producers will find valuable in return for whatever random or esoteric product they happen to be capable of providing, even if what we give them is just a numerical representation of real wealth.

And because we are so blinded by our modern opulence, almost all of us forget what it is like not to have so many options from the time we are born. We can hardly imagine what it would be like to live in a society where we would have to find ways to provide all the things we consume by ourselves or from a small local community because they aren't instantly and universally available. So, we forget where things come from and what it means to be someone who plays a part in creating the visible splendor we associate with a high standard of living. But all the while, the truth remains that it is ordinary human knowledge, skills, and technology that are the foundation of everything we consider to be wealth.

CHAPTER 01

KNOWLEDGE AND SKILL—

INFORMATION AND ITS USEFUL

APPLICATION

FREQUENTLY, WHAT PEOPLE assume to be the most critical component of wealth and security is the willingness to work hard. It's a very linear equation in their minds: If you want to get wealthier, you have to work harder at it. And there are, certainly, tasks that must be done where this linear analysis is quite appropriate. If there's a large and heavy boulder in the road you're on (and no other paths are available), you're not going to get anywhere until you've found a way to move it, which will undoubtedly involve some amount of physical exertion. But even within this controlled micro-analysis, your ability to move what blocks you does not come down to your willingness to work hard alone. Certainly, all other things being equal, a larger and stronger person with high endurance will have an easier time pushing a boulder than a smaller and weaker person with low endurance.

But your success will also depend on your knowledge and ability to assess the situation and the resources available to you in your environment that might give you leverage and amplify the effectiveness of your actions. If you are extremely clever and resourceful, you might even be able to improvise tools on the spot that allow you to get the task done faster and with less exertion. If you are a good manager of people and can convince even complete strangers to help you in your task (with each focusing on what they are best at), what seemed like an impossible challenge might suddenly become quite manageable. With enough study, you might improve your powers of observation so much that you see obvious solutions that were there the whole time but which you had overlooked because you thought pushing as hard as you could was the only way to move the boulder.

Simply throwing yourself, body and soul, at the boulder until the end of time like Sisyphus is not the most efficient way to work. The knowledge of how to use (and, if necessary, improvise) tools that will multiply the effects of the force generated by the muscles in your body will ultimately contribute more to the moving of the boulder than mere brute force alone.

In the chain of value causality, knowledge of how reality works is the prime mover. From our knowledge, all our choices spring. By understanding what to do or not do in order to achieve the outcomes we want and avoid the outcomes we don't want, we become capable of performing useful actions. If wealth is valuable utility, it is our primary priority to become educated on what is valuable (both to ourselves and to others) and how to access or create it.

It may take some paradigmatic adjustment to begin to see the world this way, but nothing that exists in nature actually has any utility in its default state. Without some kind of deliberate action upon it to make it useful, it remains only a raw, unrefined resource with the *potential* for utility. Its inherent potential, however great, still relies upon a human mind attuned to recognizing the value in it that will acquire and act upon it.

Consider the history of the planet. The vast majority of natural resources that exist today on Earth have existed in roughly their present forms for millions of years. Various woods, metal ores, and fossil fuels have been around longer than we can imagine. Even the modern plants and animals we cultivate as our primary foodstuffs have ancient equivalents. If their value has been the same all this time, why is it that only in recent decades and centuries do we see their value being put to use in a scalable sort of way? Our earliest primitive ancestors and every non-human animal should have had access to the same levels of wealth as modern humans if the value truly exists inherently within every resource in its natural state.

But clearly, that is not the case. There is a major discrepancy between what we are capable of accomplishing with natural resources now and in the recent past than at any time before or what any creature of lesser intelligence has *ever* been capable of. The difference is knowledge of what to do with our abundance of potential.

If any of us were to venture out into the rawness of nature, away from civilization, modern technology, and the abundance of man-made possessions we are accustomed to, we would quickly realize the true nature of wealth and value. Would having a lot of money be valuable to us in the uninhabited tundra, desert, or jungle? Perhaps, if we wish to burn it for warmth, but certainly not for its intended function as a medium of exchange. What use is a medium of exchange when you have no one to exchange with?

Would having a lot of raw, unprocessed resources be valuable out in nature? In an ordinary forest, where life is teeming in all directions, we would already be surrounded by more lumber in the trees for shelter construction, plant fibers for weaving, meat and vegetation in the wildlife for food, water from the rain or lakes and ponds for drinking, hides of animals for tarps and clothing, and stone for tools than we could use in a lifetime. But none of this natural abundance of resources has any utility unless we have the knowledge, skills, and technology to harvest and process it into useful forms.

Under natural conditions, trees do not fell themselves or divide spontaneously into wooden planks of uniform dimension, and those planks do not arrange themselves into the form of a cabin. We need, at the very least, hand tools like axes and saws to cut them, and we need the knowledge of how to join them together so that our cabin will protect us from the weather and other dangerous elements. Under natural conditions, wild animals do not just wander over to a campfire, skin and gut themselves, and cook what remains to our liking. We will need some manner of hunting weapon, such as a knife, spear, or bow and arrow, and the practiced skill of using it effectively to catch our prey and prepare it for the fire.

Under natural conditions, someone who has knowledge of the principles of their environment, has practiced basic productive skills, and has even a single versatile tool such as a lowly hatchet will survive better than the richest person in the world who has none of these. In time, they will learn how to apply these starting assets in ways that allow them to acquire more and more. After enough time living in the forest, they will discover where new sources of food and water are. They will locate additional natural resources that they can harvest and use more effectively to ensure their comfort and survival. They will build new tools. They will practice using these tools until they are highly skilled and have many options for creating new kinds of wealth out of the rawness of nature.

If we were to remake the modern world from square one, that is how we would do it—by starting with our knowledge of how things work and expanding naturally to produce wealth from there. The more you understand about how reality works, the more you are capable of doing in reality. This is why it's advantageous not to limit education to just a single specialized area that is cut off from the rest of what we can know about the world. While becoming a hyper-specialist might make us more capable within that field, it prevents us from seeing all the innumerable other ways we might combine our broad knowledge of things in ways that no one before us has done. Special value often comes from uncommon arrangements of many distinct practices, not just phenomenal precision in a singular applied task.

This is why the wisest investment in present and future wealth and security does *not* lie in the end products commonly associated with wealth, such as currencies and commodities or even luxury goods like cars and real estate. **The greatest security in life comes from useful knowledge, as from that, we can go on to produce everything else that is considered valuable, including new things that no one yet even knows to consider valuable.**

Fortunately, there has never been an easier time in history to get educated about almost anything you could wish to learn. Education is *not* restricted to universities, degrees, or any form of formal schooling. It's not even limited to what you can be trained to do in professional trade schools. There may have been a time where those were the best places and avenues to learn more useful knowledge about the world, but it simply isn't true anymore. What such places *are* likely still the best for is acquiring degrees and certifications for your knowledge, which may still be very useful depending on how you plan to use your knowledge.

How can you get an education about something you want to learn about? There are only two ways: Personal experimentation or secondhand instruction. Of these two options, far more of what you will ever learn in life will come from the advice of other people than will come from your own direct experience. There is far too much to know and not nearly enough time for you to infer it all directly. Yet, sometimes trying something yourself and forming your own conclusions is still the best (or only) way to learn what you seek.

Secondhand instruction is everywhere and comes in countless different ways. This book is a form of secondhand instruction from me to everyone who has the opportunity to read it. A parent answering their toddler's incessant questions about why common things work the way they do is a form of secondhand instruction. That same parent showing their teenager how to drive a car is a form of secondhand instruction. A video of a skilled craftsperson performing their trade and explaining how they are doing it as they go is secondhand instruction. Anyone who knows enough about anything and can adequately articulate or demonstrate it is a secondhand instructor. Instructors and opportunities for learning are everywhere in the modern world, but you might not notice them until you've made the conscious determination to learn something.

When we apply our knowledge through our targeted actions, we start to call it a skill. Skills are choices made manifest as strategic actions for the purpose of achieving valuable goals. In the Soviet Union, professions were predetermined by a primary skillset that would go on to define a limited number of repetitive productive actions people would perform under the command of the Labor Department throughout their productive lives.

But looking at the world through the entrepreneurial paradigm, the concept of a mono-tradesman is a mostly outdated one. It was the result of the limited avenues once available for being educated and (if necessary) certified in a particular domain where people could trust your work enough to pay you money to perform it. Not only is it profitable now to learn a second, third, or fourth marketable skill, but anyone can exponentially increase their earning capacity by acquiring skills that strategically complement each other. This is frequently the path a tradesman takes to become a full-fledged business founder. To run any business effectively, you need at least a passable understanding of not just the primary source of the value sold to customers but everything related to it as well. You need to know how and why people make the choice to purchase one option over another in your field. You need to know about the implementation of the products or services you peddle, including everything that can go wrong and other areas of life that might be affected by owning or using them. No trade exists in a vacuum.

So, although you do not need to be a bonafide expert in every tangentially related area of life to your primary area of study, learning at least the basics elevates you to a position where you can far more effectively offer people a broader range of what they want. It gives you the perspective to evaluate a larger range of situations and the type of help required in them (and whether or not you alone can deliver it). It makes you better able to find, hire, and manage people who might specifically specialize in the areas you prefer not to focus on because, at the very least, you will be able to judge their abilities and the quality or appropriateness of their work for what you intend to deliver.

Holding a variety of skills, even ones that aren't obviously complementary, is analogous to diversifying your monetary investment portfolio. Remember that everything new you learn how to do is an investment in yourself, as you will be able to move forward from that point in time doing that thing in ways that are valuable to yourself, your loved ones, and even complete strangers who might be willing to pay you money to do it or offer you something else of value in return.

Any economic environment is subject to shifts in what is in demand. When you are the "owner" of many commonly valuable skills, it is unlikely that all of them will simultaneously fall out of demand for very long. All you need to do to adapt to changing circumstances is shift what skills you put your focus on promoting and performing depending on what you see is receiving the most popular response at the time (and therefore will likely generate you the most income). You are the only manager of the business that is your life. Your products are your abilities.

Skills are more difficult to acquire than mere knowledge. Knowledge is intangible. It exists in its own theoretical world of logic, concepts, and symbols, a vacuum not affected by the physics of reality. Whereas, any skill requires training our bodies to perform specific, often highly precise, actions that use our knowledge in a tangible way to create something real. The body can't change its ability to operate instantly. Its muscles retain their own memory through their repetitively performed actions.

Even if we can have something explained to us and understand it as a concept very quickly, it takes frequency and recency to train the relevant parts of our bodies to work the way we want them to on command. For some difficult tasks, we may need many months or even years to develop both the strength and endurance required to do them reliably and effectively enough to include them in our portfolio of income-generating activities. That's one reason why it's not generally a good idea just to wait and see what skills are in demand right now and then begin to learn them. We want to already be in a position to capitalize on what we can do when the opportunity is there.

All other things being equal, the best skills to acquire are those that arise from a natural passion for the craft. You will have a much easier and more pleasant time learning them. As a bonus, the skill itself will be a joyful reward even if you never have or need the opportunity to apply it professionally. Find out what you like to do and what you have a natural aptitude for now so you can begin the lengthy journey of building a skill-set around those things. This is one of the best ways you can invest in your future wealth and security. So long as you are alive and mentally and physically capable, you will still be able to capitalize on those intangible assets that are now part of you.

Learning new skills teaches you how to solve problems you didn't know you could before, perhaps even problems you had just accepted must have no solution or problems you had not even realized were problems. When your default response to any problem is to assume that there must be a solution some-where and you just aren't seeing it, your entire approach to it will change. You won't just be analyzing your life and opportu-nities on the level of analysis you are accustomed to. You will actively be looking for other perspectives at all times. You will ask yourself what you would assume the best way to resolve this problem might be if no one had ever told what the only solution was or that there was no solution at all.

As well, once someone, anyone, has accomplished some-thing previously unknown, it's relatively easier to observe their work and reverse engineer it than to figure out how to do it from scratch all over again. Even knowing that at least one vi-able method exists makes it possible to focus on the solution more than when you were just playing with possibilities. If you can watch someone perform a difficult skilled task, even if you don't know exactly what they are doing and how they are doing it, you will intuitively begin to deconstruct what you can observe of their technique and begin to map for yourself what changes you would have to make to your own approach to more closely approximate theirs.

CHAPTER 02

CAPITAL AND CONSUMPTION GOODS—TECHNOLOGY FOR PRODUCING WEALTH AND SATISFACTION

TOOLS OF ANY kind are the physical instruments that help us be more efficient at accomplishing a given task and the attainment of the goal sought by the success of that task. It is often not the task itself and the labor we must put into it that we find rewarding but the delayed satisfaction we will receive upon its completion. A capital good is anything we use as an intermediary means to attain the long-term value we seek, as opposed to satisfaction that comes immediately from consuming something. It is wealth that we combine with our time and labor to produce greater amounts of wealth. The ability to give up a relatively small amount of something we value now for the possibility of receiving a larger amount of something we value more later is one of humanity's defining features. Indeed, it is characteristic of every choice we ever make.

So, if you've determined what kind of value you are best suited to produce based upon your education and abilities (not to mention, your interests) it is only reasonable that you should figure out what tools will help you be more efficient at those forms of production. Furthermore, you should realize that your tools of production are actually the most important material possessions you own, as they are what enable you to acquire all the others.

Among the population of my village here in Armenia, I feel confident in making the claim that I am the laziest and least hardworking able-bodied adult here. Yet, I probably also produce the most wealth and make the most money. Why is this? How do we explain the inverse correlation? My highly skilled neighbors, due to having lived through many years of long hours of hard labor, have developed a level of physical endurance that I can only be envious of. Their culture and lifestyles demanded this of them since the time that they were teenagers.

And what was I doing when I was a teenager? Experimenting with ways I could convince strangers to pay me to perform small tasks for them. Helping my wealthy retired family friends sell their old designer clothing and collectibles online, where I had to learn the optimal way to photograph, price, and describe items I knew little about. These activities were physically unstrenuous and rarely even mentally demanding for me. Many of them were entertaining. But they were slowly contributing to my knowledge of how markets worked, how to use modern tools and technology to perform tasks I would never bother or be able to do by manual means, and how to interact with people in ways that would get me what I wanted.

The enormous difference between what people in any trade could produce just a few hundred years ago and what those same people can produce today can be explained by both superior intangible factors (in the form of the aforementioned knowledge and skills) as well as tangible factors (in the form of superior tools and technology). The education and technology of today enable modern people to multiply their output many times over. The industrial farmer of today is not limited to the productive output made possible by mere ox power, sickles, shovels, axes, and plows. They can produce thousands of times more viable food for human consumers from the same land and manage a far greater amount of it with less manpower because of modern powered tools like tractors, backhoes, chainsaws, extensive automated irrigation systems, and climate-controlled indoor greenhouses.

What kind of productive output would be possible in your trade or profession using only the tools available before the Industrial Revolution? Could your industry even exist at all? Tools increase our ability to produce and our ability to want new things we previously could not have fathomed, which, in turn, leads to the development of new industries and new opportunities for producers to profit. This is an entrepreneurial way to think about the nature of the work you do and the most strategic way to choose how you spend your money or apply your actions.

I was very surprised when I first started hiring a small team of my neighbors to begin renovating the old home I bought here. I quickly learned that most of them did not own many of their own tools, even though they had been doing various kinds of construction work for decades, taking jobs here in Armenia or abroad in Russia whenever the opportunity came up to work on a large project for a few months. In all those cases, they had been provided tools to work with by their employers for the duration of the job. So, they naturally expected me to do the same for them, which I ended up doing. Currently, I am the person in the village who owns the most tools and has the least amount of experience with them. This is, again, another strange inverse correlation and one that can be explained by the differences in our culture and perspectives.

I purchased thousands of dollars in premium power and hand tools like a table saw, cordless drill and impact driver, sledgehammer, and many others when I moved here three years ago because I foresaw that I would be able to produce greater wealth by having them than the money required for the investment of purchasing them. Some of that foreseen wealth, I can produce myself by learning to use the tools for basic household tasks and projects. For most of it, though, I hire people more knowledgeable and skilled than me to build things that I am not presently able to build for myself. The combination of their valuable skills and my valuable tools to multiply their productive efforts leads to a tangible increase of my wealth in the form of a nicer house and furniture and a tangible increase of their wealth in the form of the money I pay them.

Even now, though, after employing them for a few years at a rate much higher than what they are used to being paid for this type of work, they don't have a compelling answer when I ask them why they haven't used some of the money I've paid them to purchase their own tools. It appears to me that they are still stuck in an old cultural mentality that instructs them to hide away whatever money they manage to make for fear that in the future, they might lack an income source and need to survive on it. They don't see the simple truths that are obvious to someone from a culture where entrepreneurship is taught to and celebrated by almost everyone: That the tools they hesitate to spend their limited resources on would allow them to take control of how they apply their skills to produce more wealth for themselves.

Eventually, it was explained to me by younger Armenians that this present hesitation to invest in tools of production for entrepreneurial use is related to the fact that under Soviet rule, capital goods were the explicit and exclusive domain of the State, which officially managed all choices related to sanctioned economic production throughout the USSR. Somewhere still lurking in the subconscious of many Armenian people is the belief that it is not their place to be in charge of owning and deciding what to do with the means of production because a State-designated authority figure should be playing that role for them. They grew up and got used to a boss figure telling them exactly how to apply their skills and providing for them the means to do it exclusively within the designated capacity. As a result, they are not accustomed to thinking creatively about rearranging reality to attain greater wealth because doing so would have gotten them arrested or worse by Soviet economic planners who portend to know better.

Still, today, they believe it is taboo to own much more than what they will personally consume in the near-term future. To me, this tragic state of affairs is tantamount to debilitating trauma via years of psychological abuse and brainwashing. It almost totally nullifies their ability to plan long-term into the future or build complex models of causality in their minds. Such visionary work is only appropriate for a State-appointed manager of industry, or so they have been conditioned to believe.

It's important to remember that tools or technology of any kind cannot tell you or anyone else what to want; they just help you get what you want better. If someone wants something immoral, reprehensible, or self-destructive, they can employ tools to optimize the output of accomplishing as much of that as possible for the least possible input. The tool, in and of itself, is entirely neutral. It is only how we apply it that gives it virtue and association.

The assets we acquire for the purpose of producing other forms of wealth (i.e., to accomplish some goal other than the experience of consuming it) are capital goods. What then of the assets we acquire for the direct experience of consumption? Those that represent end goals in and of themselves and immediate satisfaction from use?

This description applies to most of the "stuff" ordinary people buy and use in their daily lives. We perceive a lack of some kind and seek to acquire something that might fill it. We are hungry, so we seek food to consume by eating. We are bored, so we seek televisions to consume by watching. We are curious about new subjects, so we seek books to consume by reading. When used in these ways, these assets are not intermediary steps in a larger plan to produce more wealth or achieve a greater delayed satisfaction. They are terminal goals—ends in and of themselves. They remove some manner of subjective dissatisfaction and promote satisfaction that is unique to the individual's evaluation at the moment of experience.

Consumption goods that we buy with the intention of repeat consumption (such as clothing we will surely wear more than once) are based upon our history of understanding our own recurring preferences, which, while not ever perfectly knowable, are also not random and tend to occur within fairly predictable cycles. It's unlikely you will wake up tomorrow and find that all your tastes in aesthetics, music, sports, cuisine, and leisure will be totally different than they are today, even if they are always somewhat evolving.

If wealth derives from what you find to be subjectively valuable, it behooves you to learn your own principal preferences and spend your money in accordance with them to the furthest practical extent. There is no tactical advantage that comes from buying only as much as you immediately need of something aside from the momentarily smaller amount of money you will be spending. But as you'll see, that frequently means forcing yourself to spend more in the long run and subjecting yourself to great inconvenience and insecurity. It is frequently wise to spend more money to secure a medium- or long-term stockpile of the things you use most or that are most vital to your lifestyle.

I was surprised to learn how absent this mentality is (and not just among Armenian villages). My early assumption was that since these people have grown accustomed to not always having the convenience of a corner store or gas station to run to any time they needed something, they would learn to keep stockpiles of whatever goods they could not easily produce for themselves. After all, you don't want to be living half an hour from the nearest gas station when you suddenly realize you forgot to fill up the tank the last time you were out and now don't have enough left to make it into town.

One of my neighbors remarked to me, upon seeing that I kept in storage at my home what I considered a reasonable amount of household consumption goods like spare light bulbs, knives, flashlights, extra t-shirts, shoes, and so forth, that my house was like a marketplace. He had never seen one place with so much extra stuff lying around, not in active use, unless it was intended to be sold. I tried to explain to him that I like to buy most of my regular needs in bulk quantities because it was just more convenient for me to know I had enough of those particular things and didn't need to think about them the next time I went into town on a shopping trip. Besides, it was frequently cheaper to buy in bulk than to buy individually, and life in a fairly remote village means that I can't always plan on regularly being able to get the things I need as soon as I need them. What if something like a car accident or a landslide happened to block the only road going into town on the day I planned to do my shopping? What if I got into town and the specific store I planned to go to happened to be closed or out of stock that day?

Then in 2020, the COVID-19 pandemic and ensuing national lockdowns came to Armenia. Suddenly, even the somewhat spotty access I had had to modern commerce became utterly unreliable. The policies pertaining to when, where, and how I was allowed to go into populated areas were changing on a weekly basis. During one phase of the coronavirus lockdowns, I was blocked in the road by police from going to the super-market I usually patronized because it was located across an imaginary line in a different region of the country, and they were prohibiting non-essential travel across regions. So, I could only drive back an hour in the opposite direction and buy from supermarkets located in my same region, which left me with far fewer options.

During those peak times of uncertainty, I was especially glad that I had developed the habit of saving more than enough basic consumable goods to sustain my comfortable lifestyle for several months if needed. Besides the stuff I bought and stored, I was also already producing much of my own food through the rabbits and ducks I raised for meat and eggs and vegeta-bles from my garden. Nowadays, when someone in the village needs a bit of extra gasoline because the single liter they bought to fuel their chainsaw turned out not to be enough to get the job done, they come knocking at my door because they know I will probably have a spare 20-liter container of it kept in storage for emergencies and inconveniences.

Remember: The nature of wealth is the subjective value an individual applies to objective utility. The physical goods you have a long habit of buying and using should be obvious indicators of that quality for you. And it is how you principally use the assets you own that determines what category of wealth they fall into.

If you are a music teacher, your guitar and piano might be your primary tools of production of the service called music les-sons. They are part of a strategy for attaining the goal of greater knowledge about and skill for playing music for the students who hire you (and the attainment of the goal of money for you). But if you simply enjoy playing music, a piano and a guitar would be considered consumption goods. The value they produce for you is the immediate satisfaction from leisure, entertainment, challenge, and artistic expression.

The different ways you use any type of present capital good can instantly change it to a consumption good or vice versa. The clothes you wear might be vital tools in your profession. Your television might help you conduct research that you apply elsewhere to produce greater wealth. Even the very food you consume can be seen as an investment of calories and nutrients in your body for the purpose of fueling it long enough to produce something you value more. The value does not exist within any of these assets themselves but within your interpretation of how you wish to use them—either for the experiences in and of themselves or as intermediary steps toward the attainment of more.

CHAPTER 03

COMMODITIES AND CURRENCIES— INTERCHANGEABLE AND REPRESENTATIONAL FORMS OF WEALTH

IN EARLY SOCIETIES, if there was something that everybody participating in a local economy wanted on a consistent basis and that could easily be transferred from owner to owner, that good became a commodity among its users. Prevalent examples in the past have included salt, spices, nuts, seeds, cattle, and other things that were ambiguously preferable in their respective contexts. Stockpiling commodities worked as a store of value because even if you didn't really need any more salt for personal consumption, you could be very confident that most of your neighbors would need it sooner or later, and they would be willing to exchange other types of goods you needed for it. Commodity goods were the first things to take on the characteristics of money.

Depending on their form and intended function, commodities have different lifespans and storage requirements. Metals are obviously desirable because they generally have many applications, are durable against damage, don't degrade any discernible amount with the passage of time, are malleable and easy to work with, and are compact and easy to store even in a limited space.

Other categories of commodities might not fare so well, though. A barrel of oil is highly valued all over the world for its energy potential as various forms of fuel like gasoline. Few people want the oil itself; they want the universally useful things the oil can be made into. But that barrel will weigh over 136 kilograms (300 pounds) and take up an impractical amount of space for most people to conveniently store. As well, oil is hazardous to keep because of its flammability and noxious fumes. Consequently, if you wanted to buy commodities as a store of value, it probably wouldn't be a good idea to try to store mass amounts of crude oil in your home.

How much unprocessed lumber or cotton do you think you could keep on hand? These things are certainly going to be in demand for a long time to come due to their plethora of practical uses, but they are inconvenient to store and subject to deterioration. The average person could, however, easily find a safe and practical way to store several kilos of their favorite metals without them losing the physical properties that enable them to perform their functional utility.

Commodities, though predictable in their subjective value and objective utility, can still shoot up or down in price over time depending on technological and market factors. Aluminum, a lightweight and corrosion-resistant metal that is so commonly and casually used today that most people's primary association with it is in the cheap soda cans they throw into the trash or recycling bin every day, used to be one of the rarest and most expensive metals on the planet. It was so difficult to find and refine in its natural state that it was initially more expensive than gold by weight. Eventually, new chemical refining methods made it exponentially easier to refine huge quantities of the once-rare metal. Additionally, aluminum is one of the most recycled materials in the world, so the available supply barely depletes with use.

Today, even with an explosion of industrial market demand for it since its early days, a kilo of aluminum costs only about $2 USD, whereas a kilo of gold costs more than $60,000. It's strange to think that this common and disposable metal was once considered more precious than the world's oldest and most famous form of money, something which is commonly used as a representation of the concept of wealth itself. Still, this stark historical example shows just how arbitrary and subjective evaluation really is.

Cheap and common commodities can also do the opposite of what aluminum has done—shoot up in value many times over, becoming rare and expensive. Fine silver was once so cheap that Americans carried it around in their pocket change and probably lost countless tons of it over the decades due to sheer negligence or being too lazy to pick up a dime or quarter once dropped. Today, with silver being highly valued and hoarded by collectors and investors the world over, this seems like an absurd proposition.

What we call "waste" is any commodity produced that lacks known and desired utility. A banana's peel provides the utility of storing and protecting the sweet edible center while it ripens and until it is eaten. After that point, though, we consider the banana peel a waste product because we generally can't think of anything useful to do with it. The same is true with the cellophane and Styrofoam most of our modern packaged goods come in. Their function is necessary and highly valuable up to the point we remove the product from its packaging, and then they immediately become burdens we must deal with. Their previous utility switches almost instantly to a proportional degree of disutility.

Under present technological conditions (at least until artificial lab-grown meat becomes the norm), we cannot produce beef from a cow without also producing several other byproducts. Some of these, such as entrails, organ meats, and pelts, we humans have found alternative useful applications for. We have found contexts in which to derive subjective value from them. But everything else the cow exerts through its necessary metabolic processes during its life cycle up to the time of slaughter also counts as a waste product. Since cows must eat an awful lot of grass to grow so big and produce so much meat, they must also produce a lot of urine and feces along the way, for example. It's hard to think of a more literal interpretation of the term "waste product" than actual cow crap.

But remember the adage that one man's trash is another man's treasure and the subjective nature of value. Even feces cease to be waste the moment some human innovator has a stroke of genius that allows them to employ them toward some valuable outcome, such as fertilizer for plants they wish to grow. Similarly, the carbon dioxide we and other animals exhale with each breath, while a waste product to us because we cannot breath it, is a valuable commodity to the plants that use it as part of photosynthesis and that, in turn, expel wasteful oxygen for us to consume. And since it's valuable to plants, it's likewise valuable to the entrepreneurs who cultivate those plants.

Is it possible that, someday, most of the things we consider the most egregious waste products of modern urban lifestyles and industrial production such as car exhaust, spent nuclear fuel, and non-recyclable industrial scraps will be valuable commodities worth seeking out and keeping? Under such conditions, there would be no reason to try to limit our productive capacity or the byproducts of it, as there would no longer be any significant harm to us or the environment. All that needs to change is our knowledge and technology for how to use what we currently consider to be waste.

The difference between commodities and currencies is that the perception of what commodities can do for us is based on their objective utility—physical properties that enable them to perform specific functions according to the inherent laws of nature—whereas what we perceive that money can do for us is entirely speculative. Money's material value is that of the paper it is printed on (if it exists materially at all and not just as computer code).

From the time we are children, we are trained to cherish the pieces of paper we call banknotes. It's an emotional tradition built into our minds from our most impressionable stages in life. We feel like we understand how money works because we've been surrounded by it our entire lives, and we've received advice from experts about how we are supposed to earn it, save it, invest it, and spend it.

But the strangest thing about money is that even though nearly all of us think we want it and are willing to work hard to get it, it's not actually the money itself that we want. **We want what we perceive money can do for us.** No matter how much we want money and how much we are willing to sacrifice to get it, there are always things we want *more* than money. If this were not true, we would never buy anything. We would never spend any of our money because we would repeatedly make the subjective value judgment that it was better to keep the money than use it to acquire any of the countless things people regularly offer us for money. Money is meant to be the ultimate means but not an end unto itself.

Money, by itself, is only a number denoting an imaginary unit. It is only as valuable as the rest of the world collectively determines it is by their actions. Whereas a well-made shovel remains just as capable of digging a hole and a healthy sandwich remains just as capable of providing calories and nutrients no matter the general opinion of them, money is wholly dependent on subjective opinions to perform its function.

Money is unique among forms of wealth in that the more of it that exists, the less utility it has. There is no other objectively useful type of property for which this is true. Your car does not become any less capable of getting you to work and back if millions more of the same model are put into production. If the manufacturer of your car offered to give you an extra one for free because they suddenly made a million more, the utility of both the first and second one would remain the same. It is true that the price at which you could sell the car on the open market would be negatively affected by buyers' perceptions of the available supply, but there is nothing a manufacturer can do to make your car work worse than before merely by making more of them.

But the same is not true with currency. **With any pure currency, there is no objective utility beyond its exchange function in sales and purchases.** If your salary goes up, your wealth is not necessarily increasing because the utility of any given dollar depends upon the total supply of them. Every new dollar makes every old dollar less valuable as a medium of exchange for other types of wealth. So long as the money supply goes up faster than your ability to make money, you are losing objective utility. In effect, your money is always being "resold" on an open market where the supply available to its "buyers" is always increasing.

Historically though, coins were minted from valuable commodity metals like gold, silver, and copper so that people had some finite and tangible basis to evaluate their worth upon. Bronze (an alloy of primarily copper and tin) has countless productive applications, but more importantly, it can easily be weighed so that its exact quantity can be determined. It's divisible, which means that owning one whole ounce of bronze is just as good as owning two half ounces of bronze. It's fungible, meaning one ounce of pure bronze is, for all practical purposes, identical to another.

Because people didn't want to have to test the weight and purity of their metal every time they bought or sold something, governments issued coins and other molds of metal that symbolized their authenticity and could not easily be faked or forged. The face on a coin became a symbol of its legitimacy and value. You weren't just appraising the value of money by its material components of metal but also by the reputation of the people or entities endorsing it.

Today, all major world currencies are fiat in nature, meaning that their function as representations of wealth depends upon State enforcement to make people use them as such. That's why paper US dollars today contain the words, "This note is legal tender for all debts, public and private." It's not just a promise of the money's utility to represent wealth; it's also a threat. You *must* accept this as money if you wish to sell on the open market in the United States, or else prepare to pay a hefty fine (denominated in US dollars, of course) or go to prison.

Until 1971, the US, like many other countries, tied the value of its currency to physical stores of fine gold. The gold standard ensured that every paper dollar in circulation represented a tangible quantity of a naturally scarce, universally in-demand commodity. When the US, like other countries, abandoned the gold standard, it gave them the ability to freely print on paper or digitally manifest as much money as they wanted and arbitrarily deemed necessary for the economy. With the money supply free to expand at an arbitrary rate, it made rapid inflation (i.e., devaluation) of the currency a foregone conclusion. With each passing year, every dollar in your wallet or bank account can purchase fewer and fewer actual useful goods and services because there are more and more of them in circulation.

Similarly, until 1965, the US continued to mint its dime, quarter, half-dollar, and dollar coins in an alloy containing 90% fine silver, the world's second most popular commodity money. This effectively guaranteed that the coins would always be worth at least as much as the quantity of silver they carried, and their sizes and weights were chosen specifically to contain the correct quantity of silver to reflect their face value. That's why an old silver dime (10 cents) weighs 2.5 grams, a quarter (25 cents) 6.25 grams, a half dollar (50 cents) 12.5 grams, and a dollar (100 cents) 25 grams. Their silver weights are perfectly proportional to the wealth that is represented by their designated face value. Today, the material value of those coins minted before 1965 in 90% silver is about 20 times greater than their face value.

Because modern currencies are based on nothing but mass speculation about their value and the expectation that everyone else is speculating the same way you are, they are historically insecure and unstable. This works out well for the governments that produce, manage, and enforce the use of their fiat currencies among their citizenries; there is no need for any State to be fiscally responsible or perform their various functions in an equitable and sustainable manner (i.e., at a profit) because they can always produce an arbitrary amount more money to compensate for the losses of their inefficient strategies. Accordingly, rampant inflation causes almost every major world currency to depreciate with each passing year. A country's currency is quite often tied to its political fate and the state of its government. So, while currencies can be quite convenient for everyday economic transactions, they tend to be one of the worst ways you can store your wealth long term if you care about preserving or growing it.

To fall in love with the representational wealth of money is to get caught up in an illusion and forget what is real and why the money matters at all. Many currency-rich people fall into the trap of not even caring where their money comes from or what they have done to earn it. They care only that they have it and the power to spend it as they please. They seek only reward without responsibility. Their money becomes an arbitrary numeral to denote to the world how important they are and how much power they feel they deserve.

SECTION II:
_____

HOW ENTREPRENEURIAL THINKING LEADS TO WEALTH ACCUMULATION

WITHOUT OUTSIDE INTERVENTION, the organic path from a state of relatively low wealth to one of relatively high wealth is to acquire knowledge and skills that inform and enable better choices and actions. We use strategies and tools to generate wealth for ourselves or others in increasingly more efficient manners, and that is how the world becomes wealthier with time—by producing greater value with less effort at a rate faster than what we lose through entropy, accident, and consumption. This is the essence of efficiency. There is no escaping this chain of causality any more than there is escaping momentum, gravity, and wind resistance if you wish to build a machine capable of sustained flight.

So, ironically, the best way for someone without much money to begin to acquire more of it is to break away from the mindset that places money as the primacy of wealth acquisition. It should be clear by now that mindset, which is a combination of knowledge and skill, plays the most important role in our ability to produce. All the money in the world won't help anyone if they don't know how to spend it effectively by exchanging it for knowledge and material possessions of real wealth that have the capacity to grow into more over time organically.

And though I've deliberately downplayed the importance and utility of money so far, I mean that only in relation to all other forms of wealth that can be accumulated. Money, properly implemented, is a fantastically useful tool and one of humanity's greatest inventions. It is essential as a medium of exchange to the functioning of a modern, complex economy with large numbers of individuals producing a wide variety of different kinds of value, the market demand for which is constantly changing.

Money is useful because it is often the easiest way to convince people to do something you want them to do. That's the entire point of its existence. Money is supposed to be the thing we all universally value, an impressive but imperfect attempt to objectify the infinite different subjective wants between us all. You don't have to give people exactly what they happen to want in order to get them to do something for you because you can assume they will want money, which they can use to acquire other things they want (either now or at some point long into the future).

Money simplifies the calculations required for mutually beneficial exchange to occur because the only variable becomes the amount of money it takes to incentivize someone to perform a given action, which changes from person to person depending on how much money they already have, how much of it they perceive that they need, what other opportunities they have to make money, and the relative discomfort they would have to suffer in order to do the thing you want them to do for you.

Yet, many people still take the unconscious view that money is something of a necessary evil, a burden forced upon them by an artificial consumerist society. Oh, how much easier life would be if we never had to think about how much things cost or our ability to afford them! People who take this downtrodden view of currency and its function are either living in a society that forces them to use a very poorly designed currency (i.e., one that does not perform its function of a stable medium of exchange well), or they have not been taught how to make and spend money in ways that are vastly easier and more efficient than trying to acquire all the things money acquires via other means.

By 1991, hyperinflation caused by the Central Bank of Russia's rapid expansion of the supply of Soviet rubles combined with sharply declining productive output from workers had made money largely non-viable as a medium of exchange in many Soviet communities. This contributed heavily to the development of a black market barter economy that people depended on to acquire and distribute the basic requirements of life. Under those conditions, it was legitimately easier to directly exchange commonly available and universally needed goods like clothing and food staples for each other in some standard equivalent quantities than to try to introduce a hypothetical numeric denomination that was constantly losing value anyway. Commodities and consumption goods once again took over the function of currency, just like in primitive societies that stockpiled and exchanged salt, because they were legitimately better at it.

Consider the immense irony here. Currency, a tool invented specifically to obviate the inconveniences and inefficiencies of direct bartering, was so poorly designed and managed that it was actually *less* efficient to use it than not use it. Imagine a power drill so poorly constructed that it was actually easier for you to just go back to a simple hand-powered screwdriver than to try to make it work or a car that moved so slowly, consumed so much fuel, and broke down so often that you'd rather just walk everywhere.

That's one reason why people in former Soviet Union countries like here in Armenia might not be highly incentivized by money. The toxic and non-viable relationship they were conditioned to have with money under Stalin's oppressive rule and counterproductive economic command policies incentivized them to innovate other means. By constantly introducing new money to the supply, the State could only temporarily create the illusion of actual wealth production. Ironically, by doing this, they were only losing what little ability they still had to incentivize better results and output from the working class, who were forced into arbitrarily chosen work conditions with arbitrary success metrics.

While those days have been gone for three decades now, the unconscious distrust of money (even with the current Armenian dram currency that officially replaced the Soviet ruble in 1993) still lingers for many, especially among the older generations. For some, the distrust manifests as an obsession with cutting out all unnecessary expenses and converting as much of their wealth as possible into foreign currencies like dollars or euros for long-term saving. It is common, as well, for larger purchases like cars or houses to be priced in thousands of dollars instead of millions of dram because the fluctuations in the dram's purchasing power are too erratic to rely on. Of course, depending on a relatively stronger foreign currency only pushes the problem back, as even the most robust fiat currencies are not safe from devaluation or collapse.

Other Armenians seeking to extract value from their earnings may opt for the opposite instead: Spending as much money as possible on unnecessary things with no long-term value because they do not feel they can be sure of what tomorrow will bring, so they might as well enjoy what they have right now. It's a shame that both extremes of people, those who hide away in the apparent safety of long-term storage and those who maximize short-term consumption, are missing out on the systemization, efficiency, and scaling benefits that would come from learning to think of the value they buy and sell in consistent numerical terms, even with a less-than-optimal fiat currency like the dram.

To adopt an entrepreneurial mindset about systemic wealth accumulation is to step away from the limited paradigm of money as a necessary evil for acquiring the short-term necessities of life and instead look at everything we ever produce and exchange as part of a cumulative package. The ways we spend our money are just as important as the ways we make it. Every purchase and every strategy we make is an attempt to either grow new wealth or protect our existing wealth from loss.

CHAPTER 04

PURCHASING AND INVESTING—THE STRATEGIC TRANSFORMATION OF MONEY INTO GREATER WEALTH

IF MONEY IS a medium of exchange of various types of subjective value, one of the most obvious principles anyone should be able to grok is that every dollar (or any other unit of currency) ever spent should garner something of value for the spender in return. That much seems clear. But what many people miss is that the different types of value have different degrees of effect and vastly different durations of effectiveness. Additionally, value is always dependent upon the context of what one already owns or has access to in order to determine what most they need next. The nicest furniture in the world does not offer much utility without a dwelling to place it in, for instance. Its value is quite low until such a dwelling is acquired, and then it increases suddenly and dramatically.

Sometimes, value, though significant, lasts only moments, like when we purchase a delicious and nutritious meal when we are hungry. It's a necessary expense, for, without food, we would, of course, quickly grow uncomfortable from hunger and eventually die from starvation. But though the enjoyment we get during the moments we are consuming our food and from the feelings of satiation that come immediately after may be great, it all quickly passes. Our bodies are biologically locked into cycles of recurring discomfort that require regular resolution, and there is little we can do to systematically alter that. We can only address the symptoms. To live, we must continually reacquire the short-term values required by life.

Sometimes though, the value we acquire with our purchases can last many years or even more than one lifetime. A well-made piece of furniture will serve its purpose with little depreciation in function for decades, so long as proper maintenance is undertaken. The potentially large amount of money we spend on a great table or couch on the day of the purchase is an investment in those many years of utility. To a person with a long-term mentality of value and whose ongoing cost of living is lower than their earning capacity, it is easy to justify the large up-front purchase.

There are even forms of value that multiply and return more value to us over time. These are often the hardest to conceptualize because they are the least intuitive form of value to spend money on. The value of food when you are hungry is obvious. Every beast in the wild lives or dies by it. The value of a sturdy oak table is clear if you are the kind of person who has many uses for a table, appreciates such craftsmanship, and can reasonably predict that those personal conditions will continue to be true for the foreseeable lifetime of the table. But seeing the value in things that, through proper time and application, might produce more value (and therefore money) for us requires many more layers of conceptualization and projection across time, factoring in many unknown variables and conditions. It requires an entrepreneurial mentality that is not common in most parts of the world, including the ability to see sequences of profitable interactions as machines with moving parts that can be understood and consciously improved.

While none of us can predict the future perfectly, there are certain reasonable constants that we all have come to depend on and structure our lives around. We know that we will need to eat regularly until we die. We know this because all humans have always needed to eat. However, what we eat and the ways we eat are subject to change with new technology, culture, and economic and ecological variables. How accurately can you predict a year from now what kinds of foods you will want to consume and have access to? If you feel confident making such a guess, what's stopping you from investing some of your money into a year's supply of your primary non-perishable foodstuffs? Buying in bulk will certainly be cheaper than buying in individual quantities, and the price may rise anyway over the next year due to inflation and other marketplace factors. If you buy what you know you will use at the current lower price, you will be saving that money you would have lost by buying it at higher prices later.

Can you predict what kind of house you will want to be living in for many years to come and where in the world such a house should ideally be located? Or can you at least predict what kind of materials you will need to make it out of if you plan to build one yourself from scratch? These kinds of purchases, if made at the right price, are an investment in your future utility—your ability to live in the way you find most pleasurable and meaningful. The better you can predict your own wants, needs, and subjective preferences, the smarter the choices will be that you can make about how you spend your money on acquiring value for yourself.

However, we cannot expect to just keep endlessly acquiring more and more of the same narrow range of material goods and reap the same level of value. There are diminishing returns to the assets we acquire. Past a certain point, they even become liabilities. The stress of protecting them from loss, theft, degradation, or damage and maintaining their functionality eventually becomes a greater burden than the value they provide for us.

It is never wise for any of us to haphazardly spend whatever money we have on whatever incidental objects catch our attention and seem to be able to offer at least some temporary value to us. Yet, that is precisely what many of us have been trained to do with our earnings. We own less and less of things that provide reliable long-term value for us and more and more frivolous junk that long ago lost its utility in our lives. Or, perhaps we dispose of what is called our "disposable" income on shallow immaterial things like entertainment and quickly fading experiences that do not contribute any lasting value to our memories, personalities, knowledge, or abilities.

Though these short-term pleasures are necessary to each life in some quantity, they are the least important form of wealth to own and accumulate if the goal is to achieve wealth security and increase our productive capacity. We all have to eat, but the value we derive from our food disappears nearly as soon as we finish a meal. We all need to relax, but there are only so many ways a large television will enable us to produce more value than we did before—unless we are clever and driven enough to employ our television recreation for that end. There are only so many Friday nights we need to spend bar-hopping with our friends before we've derived the maximum novel value from that experience and the returns diminish completely. **All other things being equal, it is a logical certainty that if we switch our buying habits away from short-term depreciating value toward long-term stable value and (even better) value that appreciates and returns on us more than what we put into it that we will increase our wealth over time at a rate faster than we did before.**

Recently, while waiting an indeterminate amount of time for a broken laptop computer to get repaired, I quickly reached the conclusion that it would be an equitable investment for me to drop the equivalent of about $500 USD on a new one that I would be able to use while the old one was unavailable. I had not been planning on spending that amount of money on a new computer at that time. But it was a perfectly justifiable choice and viable strategy in my mind—an investment with as close to zero risk as one could expect. I could make this calculation because I knew that without daily access to a computer (which is my current primary tool of production), I wouldn't be able to maintain most of the work I do and get paid for. My sources of income that require me to have access to my computer would diminish until my laptop was finished being repaired, which could take weeks. As well, all my writing projects would have to be put on hold, which did not equate to an easily calculable short-term monetary figure but would have represented a major lost opportunity for me. Accordingly, I did not hesitate to spend $500 on a new computer, even if I would only end up using it in the short-term future because I knew that I would make more than that amount of money by having access to it. As a bonus, I would be able to keep and rely on the new computer as a backup in the future in case my primary one ever stopped working again, even if only for a short time.

However, in my village neighbors' eyes, spontaneously buying a new computer (something they considered to be a luxury expense that they could only ever justify owning a maximum of one of at a time, if even that) was just an indicator of how spoiled and wealthy I was that I could make such a grandiose and unnecessary purchasing choice on a whim and without serious long-term consideration. They could not see the invisible economic calculation going on that made it a clearly equitable purchase in my situation. In the paradigms brought about

by their upbringing, spending large amounts of money unnecessarily is to be avoided at all costs. To them, it would have
been better for me to just wait patiently until my laptop was
repaired and resume my work at that time, going into a defen-
sive non-spending mode until I was sure I had a reliable source
of income again. It's not their fault they think this way. It's how
they've lived most of their productive lives, jumping from one
short-term and unreliable opportunity to make money to another when it emerged and always adjusting their spending habits
to match the amount of money they happened to be making
at the moment. They had not developed much of an ability to
think systemically and entrepreneurially about how they apply
their knowledge and skills through the use of specialized tools
to produce wealth for themselves in the long run.

The entrepreneurial mind that views its material possessions
foremost as tools for greater and more efficient wealth production determines quickly when it is wise to fortify the tools most
crucial to how it happens to produce its most important value. Intentional redundancies in the knowledge, tools, and systems we
most rely on are a form of an insurance policy that any of us can
implement, personalize, and remain in control of by thinking critically about how we acquire what we need most and other ways
we might accomplish the same or an equivalent process. It begins
with knowledge of how else we might acquire the fundamental
requirements of our comfort, whether they be biological necessities like food, water, and waste disposal or idiosyncratic luxuries
that are more personal to our present sets of expectations.

In my case, in addition to gladly paying extra money for
a second computer that I will be able to rely on if my primary
workstation is unavailable, my insurance policy of intentional
redundancies extends to the 4G mobile wifi internet connection
I pay for at home. Internet speeds are certainly better than I expected they would be in such a remote location as my village.

But there are still occasional service outages with a given pro-vider that last anywhere from a few minutes to several hours, during which time I will have no access to the internet. To my neighbors who view internet access as a luxury or, at best, a mere convenience instead of a necessity like I do, these short periods where they may be unable to get online are not a big deal. They are hardly even noticeable in the context of the fre-quency with which they go online or the relative importance of the tasks they need the internet to perform in the first place.

It's a totally different subjective value analysis for me, how-ever. I use the internet every day of my life to make money, research important topics, write my books, participate in my social life, and entertain myself in an unending variety of ways. Sometimes, I need to be online at specifically designated times to meet with people in order to begin or perpetuate a series of actions that will lead to massive amounts of value creation for myself and the other people involved. So, under the wrong circumstances, even a little internet downtime could lead to cas-cading losses of productivity and wealth for me, in exactly the same way that a carpenter's only hammer or saw breaking in the middle of a complex job or his only supplier suddenly run-ning out of lumber might lead to cascading losses of productiv-ity and wealth for him.

For that reason, I am quite happy to pay the equivalent of about $20 USD every month for an extra wifi connection with a separate internet provider, even though I only use it a small fraction as much as I use my primary connection. The proba-bility that both connections will cut out at the same time for unrelated reasons is not zero, but it is substantially smaller than that either one of them will cut out at all. Even if it only happens once a month that my primary internet connection goes out and I am able to generate at least $20 of value from that time that I otherwise would not have been able to work, my insurance policy of redundant internet access is already paying for itself with the loss of productivity it is protecting me from.

Systemic insurance policies like this are ultimately about retaining as much control as possible over the material uncertainties of life. On the opposite end of the control spectrum, people with little established wealth-producing capacity tend to be attracted to things like the lottery and gambling, systems where they have little control over a favorable or unfavorable outcome because they perceive that they have little control over how they make money in all other areas of life too. This is, of course, excluding people who are addicted to such activities or just genuinely enjoy them as pastimes.

To have any degree of control over how you make, spend, and invest your money, you need knowledge about what you are doing with it and its relevant contextual factors. You need a decent degree of skill pertaining to these elements as well to ensure that your actions result in the outcomes you intend. You need to understand how the other people you forge synergistic relationships with will perform their roles in the chain of value creation and exchange you are participating in (including how those roles complement yours). That is the only way to exert your influence enough to steer whatever you put your money into toward a state of higher value, thus ensuring that your investment pays off instead of draining into nothingness.

When you purchase any asset for long-term personal use, you are speculating about your own future value preferences. When you purchase any asset to generate wealth that you will sell to other people, you are speculating about the capacity of your own productive skill and what other people will find valuable enough to buy from you. When you purchase any asset to resell to other people at a higher price, you are speculating that other people (either soon after or at some point long into the future) will view it as more valuable and be willing to pay more for it. This principle is true no matter what class of asset you are dealing with, tangible or intangible: Precious metals, antique furniture, real estate, cryptocurrencies, livestock, consumable goods like foodstuffs, or anything else.

To make such a prediction accurately, you need to understand both the fundamental qualities of the asset and how they are generally valued by the people who buy and use them. Further still, your predictive abilities need to be better than those of the general market, at least in regard to where you choose to spend your money. If everyone interested in an asset is as skilled as predicting its future value as you, they will already be purchasing it too, and the price will already be at the place everyone agrees it is heading. Suppose everyone in the lumber market knows with the same degree of certainty that the price of lumber will double next week. In that case, they will all be buying as much of it as they can at half price this week, either with the intention of reselling next week for a 100% profit or saving it for their own eventual use. That rush to the market would, ironically, invalidate the expected timeline and instead cause the price to rise now instead of next week.

The same applies to everything put into a business in the hopes of returning long-term profit. A working business model requires the investment of time, energy, and capital into a variety of tangible and intangible assets under the presumption that you will be able to transform them in some way to increase their value on the market. Remember that even the labor of people you hire constitutes a product that you must arrange in a particular way to make it worth more than the price you must pay to acquire it. If you don't understand the type of products you will be working with, the labor and resources that go into producing them, and the factors that affect how buyers perceive them, you will have a very hard time ensuring the higher evaluation (and, therefore, the profit) you are seeking.

But still, aspirational entrepreneurs frequently fall into the trap of chasing after popular business models they have no specific knowledge of or passion for, merely because they heard somewhere that they were foolproof or easy to make money with. But how could anyone verify the truth of these claims without first gaining an intimate understanding of the market mechanics and finer production details? Perhaps the people who find success and generate the hype for these kinds of easy copy-and-paste business models can only do so because they understand subtle things that newcomers will not, invisible but crucial details that might be difficult to quantify and qualify for someone who doesn't have the familiarity they do.

A friend in the village called Artur who, perhaps inspired by my frequent discussions of entrepreneurial ideals, expressed to me a keen interest in starting a local cheese business. I was initially surprised by this because I was not aware that he had any particular knowledge about making cheese or the mechanics of distributing and selling it to his intended local market. I did not even know that he particularly liked cheese at all.

However, it turned out that Artur had not really put any thought into the possibilities for the types of cheese he could produce or who his intended market of buyers would be. Upon further questioning, I realized that pretty much the only reason he thought to start a cheese business at all was that he owned a lot of cows, and his primary source of income was selling their milk to local cheese producers. He was business savvy enough to realize that his milk would be worth more if he had the machinery and staff necessary to turn it into cheese before selling it. It was simply the most direct way he could see to increase his earning capacity with the assets he was already used to working with.

And why do you suppose Artur acquired all those cows and got into the business of selling milk in the first place? For no other reason than that it was what he saw other people in a similar position doing and finding a moderate amount of success with. His cows had become his most valuable tools of production, creating a regular supply of the commodity milk that he could sell for a predictable price on a daily basis to entrepreneurs who would use it to produce the consumption good called cheese. However, as fortunate as he was to have that independent source of income, I could tell there was no real passion behind the acquisition of his cows or any specialized knowledge that gave him any particular advantage with livestock or dairy.

I made it my mission to challenge Artur's line of thinking a little bit and open up his mind to more possibilities for the types of income streams he could generate and businesses he could run. I told him that, sure, he could go into the cheese business with the milk he and his neighbors were already producing. But it would probably cost him many thousands of dollars in startup costs for the machinery he would have to purchase and all the certifications he would have to acquire from the State before he could start producing, not to mention the work that would have to go into packaging and branding his product before he presented it to consumers.

Artur hadn't even considered the consumer end of things because he was accustomed to selling his milk in wholesale quantities to businesses that would handle all that when they made and sold their cheese. He hadn't even thought about what kind of cheese he would produce and how it would be different from what was already cheap and plentiful on the market, including what would make it superior in the eyes of at least one category of cheese consumer. In short, he was woefully underprepared to upgrade from his relatively simple and linear business model of taking care of his cows and selling their milk wholesale to the much more complex and multidisciplinary model of turning that milk into cheese, branding it, and finding a market for it.

Knowing this man and his interests fairly well at this point in our relationship, I proposed a completely different and unexpected entrepreneurial path to him, one that seemed obvious to me but would probably never have occurred to him. I had observed Artur and his habits over the course of many months. He had been present at my house a few times when I had had furniture delivered that I purchased from department stores in town, most of which was generic and mass-produced but affordable and functional. I noted on those occasions how much attention he paid to the pieces I bought, how much I paid for them, and where I would place them in my house, commenting on what he liked or thought could be improved about their construction and design. From those observations, I realized that he had a strong passion for the craftsmanship that goes into furniture. And, based on his handiwork I had seen on some local construction projects, I figured he probably had the necessary carpentry skillset for it too.

Based on that information, I asked Artur why he didn't consider going into business with something he understood better than cheese, something he had a natural passion for and would therefore better enjoy learning how to overcome the challenges associated with it... Something for which increasing his knowledge and skillset through experience would be genuinely enjoyable as well as financially rewarding. When he answered me that the reason he couldn't go into furniture making was that he lacked the tools he would need to do it, I knew something was broken in his mentality.

How was it that Artur had been fully prepared to risk thousands of dollars on starting a cheese business, including all its costly machinery and supplies, but considered it out of the question to spend considerably less on the equipment he would need to start making furniture? I realized that the answer, as usual, had something to do with the ideas implanted in him by his culture. No one had ever given him permission, whether implicit or explicit, to start a furniture business. He did not see anyone in a similar position to him attempting to do it, so it was not part of his paradigm. His perspective of opportunities was starkly limited by what he could directly observe, not what he could infer might be possible. There would be, of course, many questions he would have to find answers to before he could confidently assume that making and selling furniture would be profitable and that he would easily recuperate the costs required to get started. But they are all questions he could have found the answers to if he had been encouraged to think like an entrepreneur throughout his life.

My budding entrepreneurial friend was on the right intellectual track. He at least had enough entrepreneurial ambition to want to improve his earning capacity in a way that was a logical expansion of what he was already doing. Whatever you produce, it is always worthwhile to ask what you can do to improve its perceived value and how easy it would be for you to implement those actions. After all, there is no asset that cannot be made somehow more valuable through superior processing, refinement, and/or transformation. Nothing exists in a perfect state. It's only a question of whether continuing to invest further resources into it will produce an equitable appreciation in value or whether you're better off just releasing it onto the market as it is and taking what profits you can. This principle is true for every work of art, every consumption good, and every new idea ever dreamt up by humans.

CHAPTER 05

ASSET SECURITY—PROTECTING ACCUMULATED WEALTH FROM THE INHERENT RISK OF LOSS

ALTHOUGH PEOPLE FREQUENTLY shy away from conventional ideas about entrepreneurship because they do not want to expose themselves to the risk inherent to it, what they frequently fail to see is that there is an inherent risk in everything. As we do not know everything, there is never any guarantee that what we do will result in the outcome we desire by doing it. We just come to rely on layers upon layers of redundant systems that make it all the more likely that life will continue to go the way we have come to be accustomed to. We turn our keys in our ignitions expecting our cars to start. We show up to work expecting to receive regular paychecks. We go to the grocery store expecting to see an unlimited supply of the foods we love best. But these outcomes all depend upon physical processes we cannot control.

Those living in lesser-developed economies are less likely to take their dependence upon these modern conveniences for granted because they may have lived through wars, supply shortages, closed borders, hyperinflation, and failing infrastructure that prevents the economic machine from turning as it is supposed to all the time. That is part of the reason why they tend to rely more on their own skills and those of their immediate neighbors to accomplish the things Westerners automatically outsource to places unseen and disregarded. There is a keen awareness of the fact that things can go wrong at any time for any number of reasons. The power can go out when you are expecting it to be available. There can be an accident or other obstacle that blocks the only road to where you are expecting to be able to go. So on and so forth, ad infinitum.

These uncertainties matter because everything we ever do carries a cost, even if it's not a cost we usually consider to be significant but just a normal part of living. Transportation consumes fuel (which may be quite expensive) and puts wear on our vehicles. Even the very act of solving problems in our heads induces some level of cognitive stress, which is something each of us has a finite tolerance for. Putting those solutions into action, likewise, induces some level of physical stress on our bodies and carries the possibility of accidental injury. There is nothing that does not consume some measure of time, which none of us can ever get back. Whatever we choose to do, it is a choice against everything else we could have chosen to do and every opportunity we could have pursued. And even when we know with theoretical certainty what the outcome of a physical or chemical process must be according to the relevant well-established scientific laws, we cannot perform these processes in a vacuum that is immune to unanticipated interference or with perfect control over our actions and the materials we work with.

So, it is clear that, in the most literal sense, we are all risk managers. We willingly incur these losses and the possibility of many others because we foresee the probability of disproportionately greater gain according to how we personally view what a gain would be, which changes from individual to individual and the changing moods of the day. The people we call professional entrepreneurs are those who have learned to scale this natural risk-management process we all necessarily participate in to higher and higher levels with potentially much greater wealth returns (monetary or otherwise). All that is really needed is a proper understanding of what we want, what we are willing to give up to get it, and roughly what the chances of our plan working out the way we envision will be.

This is another part of why it is so important to get involved with businesses we actually understand and not just follow obvious and visible trends of what appears to be profitable for other people. **We cannot begin to assess what risks are worth taking without being intimately familiar with the processes that determine the outcomes of those risks accurately.**

What is the single greatest loss of material wealth you could suffer with your life set up as it is right now? The answer to that depends on what forms your material wealth takes and what its vulnerabilities are. Cars, being the complex multi-faceted devices that they are, are prone to breaking down and, thus, require regular maintenance to provide their transportation utility. If an important and expensive part of your car stops working, it could effectively negate its ability to provide its intended value in your life for a long while. If the cost to repair it is greater than the value of the car itself or a replacement part is inordinately difficult to find, it's going to equate to a massive loss in material wealth for you.

Houses and other forms of real estate might seem like one of the safest and most reliable forms of material wealth. Even if the housing market in a particular area crashes and the price you could get for selling your property is much lower than you anticipated, it still retains its objective physical functionality as a shelter. You still have a place to live that will protect you from the elements and (presumably) be a comfortable and enjoyable place for you to reside.

But houses are still vulnerable to material loss in many forms. Earthquakes and other natural disasters happen even in places not known for them. Careless mistakes lead to housefires that can grow out of control even with smoke detectors, fire extinguishers, and a nearby fire department. Improperly protected pipes can freeze and burst in winter, leading to flooding that causes untold amounts of water damage. There is even wanton vandalism to consider, as there is nothing guaranteeing that someone senseless looking to cause trouble won't spontaneously decide to throw a rock through your window.

In my situation in the village, I even have to actively consider the threat to my house posed by Armenia's neighbors on either side that have openly expressed intentions of territorial expansion into many regions of Armenia, including specifically the province where my village is located. If the infantry of Azerbaijan or Turkey follows orders to cross international borders, march up the road to my house, and force the evacuation of my village at gunpoint, I will have little choice but to accept a total loss of the material wealth of my home here, including all the possessions I cannot physically carry with me and the many thousands of dollars' worth of home renovations I have paid for.

Do you prefer to keep your material wealth in cash? That's what my neighbors tend to do with what money they accumulate. Their reasonable lack of trust in financial institutions means that most of them don't maintain bank accounts. Their cash gets stuffed under a mattress or behind a bookcase somewhere in their homes whenever they accumulate more money than they can spend at one time upon completion of a job.

But paper money faces obvious threats of destruction and degradation from mere exposure to the elements. Most paper bills only last a few years in circulation under ordinary conditions of use. Kept in storage, there is water rot, damage from pests, and fire to worry about (not to mention theft or careless misplacement). If you keep your cash in the bank, it will almost certainly be safe from those common household threats, but that does not mean it will retain its value as a medium of exchange.

Inflation is a problem with every fiat currency in the world. It means your money is all but guaranteed to lose value over time as more of it gets printed out of nothing and enters circulation without an equivalent increase in the products and services it is supposed to represent. Usually, this happens slowly and predictably, but it can also happen quite suddenly when irresponsible monetary policies are put into effect arbitrarily by the people commanding a nation's money supply. What $1,000 USD put in the bank can buy when you decide to withdraw it ten years later will probably be significantly less than what it can buy when you first put it in, even if the material value of the paper and ink remains exactly the same. If the goal is to defend material wealth against loss, currency devaluation must be accounted for.

Of course, this whole analysis depends on the assumption that you actually own the wealth you are trying to protect in the first place. Another observation about the difference between buying habits back home in the United States compared to most of the developing world is how hard Americans work just to try to be able to own a little bit more than what they can actually afford. For reasons I have never fully understood, borrowing and living in debt are basically ways of life in America. Taking out loans from the bank and building credit scores are a normal part of the cultural education of living there.

I know how strange this sounds to people living in other parts of the world who commonly only make enough money to cover the basic costs of living when they consider that Americans tend to make significantly more money than they do already. Why would they need to borrow even more money and go into debt when they already have so much? Why not just spend the money they have on something they can afford? In most cases, I see no other reason than primarily that it is what they are trained to do by their cultural paradigm, and going into debt becomes necessary to maintain the high standard of living they grow accustomed to.

Living at a level of material consumption even slightly beyond your ability to produce creates enormous stressors that people who only spend money they actually have never encounter. Going into debt locks life into a game of perpetual catch-up, always having to work harder and harder to meet the standards you have prematurely decided to live by. It makes it exponentially harder to accumulate capital and invest it in ways that will return profits or even just hold their value. Yet still, the Western way of life often amounts to sacrificing the young individual's systemic ability to make and spend wealth efficiently for the temporary comfort of getting something material they lust after in the moment. There is no such thing as a free lunch, and you cannot get something for nothing. Everyone pays their dues, and all accounts are balanced in the end.

The way people view risk changes quite dramatically once they have a foundation of confidence and control to operate from. When they don't believe in their ability to reliably produce wealth from their knowledge, skills, tools, and relationships, they apply a scarcity-oriented mindset to whatever they *do* manage to produce. Everything is precious because they are not sure of how they can replace it once it is consumed or lost. And remember: Everything can be lost. Some things can be lost much more easily than others.

Realistically, if everything is under threat at all times from some form of loss of value, what is the greatest amount of security in their wealth a person can have? Everything physical is subject to accident and entropy. Food spoils quickly. Clothing wears out. Tools and appliances break with regular use. Even houses fall apart or are destroyed by untimely disasters.

What about intangibles, then? Your knowledge and skills are part of your mental and physical conditioning. They are subject only to the health of your body and mind. So long as you take care of yourself, you should be able to rely on your knowledge and skills throughout your life (though even the body and mind do eventually fall apart and are subject to the same accidental tragedies as everything else physical, so nothing is truly secure). Relationships too exist in the minds of the people participating in them. They exist until we die or let them degrade through poor treatment or loss of positive reputation.

Understanding this, doesn't it logically follow that the greatest possible amount of security in life would come from investing foremost in our *intangible* assets? The more knowledge, skills, and relationships we forge throughout life, the more wealth we will always be able to produce, even in uncertain times when our tangible forms of wealth seem unreliable.

Think about how rapidly fortunes can be made or lost, often due to factors that have nothing to do with human error. Market crashes happen in all areas of commerce. If you hold the bulk of your wealth in a market that suddenly becomes worth a lot less, you might feel like you've lost everything you've worked your whole life to build for yourself and your family. This is because you associate your security with the tangible products or symbols that represent wealth. You believe you will be able to rely on liquidating them at some future time when you need money, which itself is just another symbolic representation.

It might take decades the first time around to acquire enough money to afford a nice house, a car, a stock portfolio, or several ounces of gold buried in the backyard. But if you lost all those things simultaneously through some tragic series of misfortunes and had to go back to square one with zero tangible assets, how long do you think you would need to get them all back and more? The answer is a much shorter period of time than you needed before.

Why? What's different between the first and second time around? **Even without everything tangible and symbolic that you consider wealth, you would still retain the causal assets that you relied on to build that wealth in the first place.** See, what you were actually acquiring for most of the years that you were working was not the money and the possessions; it was the knowledge of how to acquire them and the experience required for your relevant skills. Depending on your line of work, you were probably also developing relationships with other people whose knowledge and skills were complementary to yours. Through that, you earned for yourself a positive reputation (a personal brand, so to speak) that made it far easier for you to conduct business with new people who otherwise might be reluctant to trust in your expertise and ability. With all these factors still in place, it should be relatively easy for you to restore every tangible and symbolic form of your wealth again.

These factors explain a lot about the psychological differences between people who have earned substantial amounts of wealth compared to those who acquired theirs through chance or accident, such as lottery or jackpot winners or people who just happened to buy the right stock at the right time. People who come into incidental windfalls of wealth tend to treat their good fortune as scarce because they have no foreseeable way to replace it once it is spent or lost. It is causally disconnected from their productive actions. Every dollar that comes off the stack represents the lessening of a finite supply.

But people who have their roots in the proper understanding of *how* to produce wealth through their own knowledge, abilities, relationships, reputation, buying habits, and other intangibles that cannot be easily extracted from them will have a totally different psychological disposition. For one thing, they will be much more willing to take calculated risks and spend their money in ways that will return even greater amounts of wealth back to them. They will see their wealth (currency or otherwise) as extensions (i.e., the branches and leaves that emerge from their roots) of who they are and how they interact productively and proactively with the world. No matter what happens to the branches, so long as the roots remain intact, the tree can grow again.

Knowledge (and, to a lesser extent, abilities) are the most secure forms of wealth you can have because they are the ones that are most intrinsically connected to your life itself. You cannot guard all your physical possessions at all times, no matter how careful you are. You cannot even pay active attention to most of them. But your knowledge rests solely in your mind, and your abilities are functions of your body's motor skills. If you keep your mind and body safe and healthy, which you should already have plenty of incentive to do anyway, you can protect your knowledge and abilities better than you protect anything else that you own. So, not only are they the most important assets you own, but they are also the most reliable.

To be sure, you can be permanently injured both physically and mentally. Anything you were once adept at can get weak or rusty with time. You can forget valuable information you used to know. You can, of course, die at any moment from any number of causes. It goes without saying that once you are dead, any forms of wealth you had while you were alive will lack all utility and value for you. So, if you're going to spend your life acquiring something, what makes the most strategic sense to make the primary focus of your acquisition? Paper money? Consumable goods? Useful tools and machines? Or the knowledge and ability required to make all the aforementioned valuable?

CHAPTER 06

EDUCATION CAPITAL—LEVERAGE FROM THE LEARNING ECONOMY OF SCALE

ANYTIME YOU ENCOUNTER a problem that you perceive needs solving, you have an array of predictable options for dealing (or not dealing) with it. Picture, for example, a scenario where a button has come loose from the coat you are wearing. The functional utility of the coat has now been somewhat compromised because it cannot close all the way, which leaves you somewhat exposed to the elements. The coat's aesthetics and social utility have also been negatively affected by the loss of this solitary button because you now look a bit disheveled and unprofessional walking around in public with a missing button and a coat that does not close as intended. In the wrong context, it might contribute to a negative social impression that costs you job opportunities, or perhaps it will leave your date less than impressed with you and ruin your romantic ambitions.

You have a few options you must choose from to resolve this problem:

1. You can ignore the problem and continue to wear your coat in its present state of nonoptimal function. Perhaps the weather is not so cold that your partial exposure to it is not a serious discomfort to you. As well, perhaps you are not in a social position to be negatively affected by dressing inadequately. Perhaps you simply do not mind the missing button enough to do anything about it.

2. You can throw the coat away and not replace it. Maybe you don't really need to be wearing a coat at all, and its loss is not a significant detriment to your comfort or style.

3. You can buy a new coat. Maybe you didn't really like the coat all that much to begin with and were just waiting for an excuse to replace it with something you consider subjectively better. Maybe it already had several little tears or stains, and this additional minor problem of the button coming off was the straw that broke the camel's back and made it equitable for you to replace the whole damn thing. Maybe you have more money than time, and you are in a situation where it is just simpler and easier to grab a new one as you pass by a coat shop than to figure out a way to repair it.

4. You can get someone who has the tools and materials necessary (at minimum, a needle and thread) and knows the proper sewing technique to fix the button for you, perhaps a friend willing to do you a favor or a professional seamstress who will charge you a small and reasonable fee for their service.

5. You can fix the button yourself. You will need to acquire the tools and materials and study the technique required to do so if you haven't already. Maybe you've

never sewn anything in your life before and need to start from a completely novel state of knowledge and ability. Maybe you've sewn simple things like small tears but are unfamiliar with the technique required to replace a button. Or maybe you are an expert button tailor already, and this will be a breeze for you, requiring you to learn or acquire nothing new at all.

How you arrive at the optimal solution to this problem will depend on several factors, some of which will be in your control and some of which will be out of it. You probably can't do much to affect the weather or the social expectations of the people around you, for example. You can't do much to change the available options for purchasing a new coat or hiring someone to fix the button for you, but you can do a lot to improve your awareness of what those options are (such as by researching the shops that are near you).

But, by far, the domain where you have the most control is over your ability to improve your knowledge and skill in order to accomplish a given task. Even in a situation where you seem to have no educational opportunities like instructional books, DIY videos, internet articles, or even someone in front of you to show you how to sew a button, you always have the age-old method of trial-and-error at your disposal. Given ample thread, a determined mind, and a long enough period of time, the intended outcome will eventually be reached by first trying many things that do not work. And then it will work every time after that. It is only a question if all that effort will be worth it merely to achieve the goal of sewing a lowly button.

The first time you do something new, you are operating at your lowest state of personal efficiency. If you know you will need to accomplish the task you are trying to learn only once or even just a few times, it will almost certainly be more equitable for you to get someone else who already has the necessary tools (e.g., a sewing needle), materials (e.g., sewing thread and a re-placement button), and knowledge/skills (e.g., the technique for sewing a button) to perform the task for you. The startup investment requirements for almost any valuable productive pursuit only begin to make sense at a certain scale.

We use the term "economies of scale" to describe how com-panies become more efficient by producing more and more units of output from the same or a comparatively small increase in required input. But we frequently fail to see how the same logic applies to our personal choices and the repeated series of inten-tional actions they lead to. When I say that the greatest wealth security resides in developing the intangible side of yourself first, it is because those traits are analogous to the physical ma-chinery we are accustomed to seeing big companies factor into economic calculations—just like the cheese-making machinery my village friend was willing to invest thousands of dollars into on the assumption that it would enable him to make more than that amount of money back over time as he produced endless amounts of cheese to sell.

If you focus on how difficult or expensive it is to do some-thing new the first time, you're going to miss how much easi-er and cheaper it might become once you know what you are doing and have the resources in place to optimize the process. It's like this every time we learn something new, and it's one of the primary points of psychological resistance that prevents us from expanding our capabilities. It's automatically more tempting to continue doing things we already know (and have therefore become easy to us) than to force ourselves through the learning curve of a new discipline, where our actions will feel arduous and inefficient for the longest time before we can start to see equitable output from them.

It's the same form of analysis we must go through when deciding whether or not to invest some of our hard-earned capital in a new tool that we don't necessarily have substantial immediate use for. Is it worth it to buy a sewing machine for hundreds of dollars if you only plan to use it to mend a few pieces of clothing? Probably not. The value of the repairs to the clothing just isn't enough to justify it. Even if that shirt or dress happens to be really expensive or impossible to replace, you could almost certainly just hire someone to do the repairs for you at a fraction of the cost it would take you to purchase your own sewing machine, not including the time value of the labor you'd have to put into doing the repairs yourself and the other sewing paraphernalia like needles and thread you'd have to maintain a supply of.

But suppose you felt comfortable predicting that you would need to make many repairs to your finest clothes throughout the multi-year lifetime of your sewing machine. And suppose that you could calculate that the cost of hiring someone else to do these repairs would quickly outweigh the cost of the machine and the value you place upon your time. At a large enough scale of output, the one-time cost of the sewing machine becomes equitable.

To see this, you need to be capable of applying a long- or even just medium-term outlook to your thinking and future needs. And, unfortunately, people who perceive themselves to be poor and in desperate situations are accustomed to only ever seeing what is right in front of them. The next job. The next paycheck. Just making it to the end of the month and getting the bills paid. Scrounging up enough cash for the critical part of your car that suddenly needs to be replaced. And so forth.

Imagine being so bold as to apply this scaling mindset beyond just your own needs. Maybe you feel confident that you could sell at least one shirt or another article of clothing you could make if you had an expensive sewing machine, but the profit from one shirt won't be nearly enough to justify the machine's high cost. But if you were bold enough to take the risk and could predict the long-term existence of many customers, even if their individual purchases were small, the investment cost of the sewing machine would obviously seem equitable.

This all seems a bit like gambling to the inexperienced, which reflects how Mery, the English teacher in my village, prematurely saw the principle of running a business: Betting big effort and money on the possibility of a future outcome over which you have little control. Maybe if you buy that sewing machine, you'll get lucky and find a healthy stream of clients right away. Or more likely, maybe you'll rarely ever find anyone at all who needs you to sew for them, and that machine will sit on your table as a monument to your failure as an entrepreneur. But the more you learn about the mechanics of markets, the more control you will be able to exert over the likelihood of your own success, no matter what business you go into.

Instead of dumping the whole of your effort and resources into one Hail Mary play and praying it works out, you can take a more tactical approach by starting with a multitude of small related activities, each one requiring very little risk and investment from you, until you have experimental evidence of what actually has the potential to work. Any individual project turning out to be a loss will not matter much, so long as at least one or a few of the others end up paying off. Better still, if your projects are related enough in nature, you might be able to combine the starting costs of each of them, making it much easier to justify the cost of branching out into something new. Or maybe you already have the tools and other resources you will need for them because you acquired them for personal use and other purposes. Can you adapt your mind to see the latent entrepreneurial value of the knowledge, skills, and various tangible assets you already own?

My village neighbors are frequently bewildered to see how impulsively I will purchase new tools and toys due to what they must assume is my irresponsible American consumerist mentality. Just spend, spend, spend on whatever shiny objects catch your attention. Cost supposedly doesn't matter. But I know that nearly every purchase I make is something that will offer me the chance to explore how interested I really am in a new subject, skill, or entrepreneurial opportunity. Many of the material possessions I buy might eventually end up being forgotten about, sold, or discarded, but some minority of them will become gateways to new passions for me. Some of them, I'll even be able to apply in conjunction with my other existing assets to increase my productivity and income.

The inevitable waste that accrues from following my whims in a principled way is well worth it to uncover the interests I would otherwise never have known were within me. After all, I wouldn't want to spend the remaining decades of my life only playing the same musical instruments I learned as a child or commit to writing books as my only profession just because I happen to know at this moment that I can do them. I hope I never stop growing in my hobbies and entrepreneurial endeavors.

For me, it's not much different than impulsively buying books on subjects I suddenly discover an interest for. Many fervent readers can relate. My reading habits are sporadic. Sometimes I only end up reading a chapter or a few of a book I am very intrigued by before losing interest or getting distracted and never returning to it. Sometimes, I never get around to reading a potentially great book at all. The inevitability of some "wasted" books that I add to my collection but never finish reading is the cost of playing the game. Because I have enough capital to work with, I don't worry too much about taking a similar approach with various tools and toys that might cost a few hundred dollars each and that I may only end up using a few times before realizing my interest isn't actually that strong. A select few of them will end up becoming mainstays in my life and provide incredible value to me that far surpasses the losses of indulging my other curiosities.

As a spontaneous serial entrepreneur, I've fallen into a similarly reckless habit with micro-business ideas. The question of whether I can find a way to ethically derive a profit from something without too much risk or effort is always in my mind. It might be as simple as buying something I think is probably undervalued and finding a buyer for it at a price closer to the going market value. This is just me taking advantage of basic market arbitrage—the relative difference in personal interpretations of value. An entrepreneur is someone who understands that different people will evaluate the same things to different degrees and who works to correct the imbalance.

Sometimes, the entrepreneurial mindset manifests as looking for ways to combine the knowledge and skill sets of people who are already profitably employing them in linear ways into something emergent and more valuable than what any of them can accomplish on their own. This is the "whole being greater than the sum of its parts" phenomenon as applied to human production. An entrepreneur is someone who sees unrealized avenues for value creation and acts on them, and sometimes their most valuable contribution to wealth production is merely to oversee and manage what other people contribute in the most efficient manner possible.

There is no real reason to even see lifestyle habits as sharply divided into arbitrary opposing categories like work and play, professions and hobbies, or labor and leisure. There is no reason to see any assets we own as strictly useful as capital goods we employ for long-term wealth production (i.e., "work") or consumption goods we employ for immediate satisfaction (i.e., "play"). We can always be looking for new and interesting ways to apply the totality of our knowledge and skills efficiently and profitably. An entrepreneur is someone who understands that with the right mindset, any activity (whether inherently pleasurable to them or not) can be turned into a form of subjective value for themselves or others, and you can always be finding more kinds of activities to participate in that might be equitable for you. Education is the increase of one's working knowledge about how reality works, and every new activity offers the opportunity to do that in some regard.

Yet, it still boggles me how few people living here in Armenia see things this way, even the brightest and most capable ones. Due to the poor, centrally enforced Soviet schooling experience of yesteryear, intelligent and capable people fail to see acquiring new knowledge and skills through the same lens an entrepreneur applies to acquiring new tools that they will go on to produce disproportionately greater amounts of value with.

Even the children and young adults who are coming up in the world and undergoing their primary education today are still suffering the fallout of the retrogressive educational policies of their forefathers. Like with many other aspects of Soviet society, it was easy for proponents to select the most visible and isolated metrics like general literacy and showcase them as evidence of having forced a high-quality education system into existence for the masses who would otherwise have had no options for education.

Do you recognize this cliché false alternative yet? **"Without us forcing our particular manner of what we determine to be a good education upon you, you would have no education at all."** It is the same fallacious argument, in principle, that could be applied to anything the Soviet State did to (not for) its people without their input or consent.

While it is a historical fact that the percentage of people who could read improved significantly once the Union of Soviet Socialist Republics took control from the tsar of the feudal Russian Empire that preceded it, this statistic is practically meaningless on its own. The ability to read in isolation does not constitute a healthy education any more than bread in isolation constitutes a healthy diet. Reading and writing are highly useful skills, to be sure, but their utility only comes out when they are consciously applied in valuable situations in conjunction with the right tools. As it happens, the primary motivation behind ensuring a high literacy rate among the Soviet populace was to make them easier to indoctrinate with communist propaganda, which is something that should be considered an extreme disutility and counter to the goals of freedom and free thinking.

As skills, reading and writing are no different than the abundant abilities my neighbors have had their whole lives but still frequently fail to find productive outlets for. **This is the inevitable result in an authoritarian education model where habits and conclusions are memorized under threat of punishment and orders from a central authority about exactly how to apply what one learns.** There is no room for creative or critical thinking without curiosity and self-interest in learning. It makes as much sense to learn how to read and write while lacking the perspective to be able to apply these skills in pursuit of your own educational goals as it does to fill a library full of books you cannot understand and call yourself educated because of it (which is another bad pseudo-educational habit I'll cover shortly).

Even today, every Armenian schoolchild undergoes years of mandatory English language training that amounts to little more than memorizing bulk paragraphs of obscure information solely for the purpose of regurgitating it at the time of exam. Yet, few of these children graduate being able to functionally apply their knowledge of the English language to produce value in their own lives or anyone else's. The entire prolonged process is an exercise in demonstrating the futility of bureaucratic approaches to education, and the opportunity cost for all Armenians is tragic and enormous. It creates the appearance of real progress in the form of test scores, grades, and diplomas with no meaningful effect upon the actual production of wealth. Output is still chosen and measured arbitrarily, just as it was under bureaucratic rule throughout the Soviet Union.

Real education, foremost, requires an open and curious mind, which is often the first thing to degrade when children are compelled to learn things they are not interested in through a manner not conducive to their individual temperaments. But what the Soviet Union called education largely consisted of memorizing what Soviet authorities commanded and being trained in repetitive physical tasks because they considered it useful for their goals for Soviet society. As a Soviet citizen, you did this until you reached the age they deemed you worthy to begin working in a profession they assessed, with their limited perspective, that the economy was in need of, with productive outputs for your actions already determined. Understandably, this did not lead to a culture rich in critical or creative thinking, personal fulfillment, or even the meeting of the basic physical requirements of human life.

This is especially unfortunate today for the Armenians who still struggle to acclimate to the principles of an entrepreneurial paradigm. The ability to think independently and assess the merit of one's own actions are vital to any free individual who operates without a central agency dictating the production and consumption in their economy. The institutional practice has largely stripped individuals of the intrinsic human ability to spontaneously learn new things that interest them or that they can at least see a long-term personal benefit to knowing. Just as the entrepreneurial mind does not wait for external authorities to come along and force productive actions from it, it also does not wait for orders about what it should be learning. It sees opportunities for education everywhere, and it knows there are more useful and valuable things to learn than it ever could learn with the time and resources available to it.

You will see the disastrous effects of this, to varying degrees, in every part of the world. How many intelligent adults have you known who instantly insist that they cannot learn something they are interested in because they are no longer in school or of schooling age? How many young people have you met who decline to study subjects or practice activities that are not part of the curriculum allotted to them by the path their school has given them permission to specialize in? How many people believe that it is impossible or at least unlikely that someone could understand a complex subject without having studied it in a formal school setting or without having acquired a degree or some other form of official certification designating them as an expert?

The common dynamic among all these narrow ways of thinking about the act of learning is that if it does not happen through sanctioned channels or in a specific centrally condoned manner, it does not count. It is not real unless our masters declare it so. And so, people who would and should be lifelong curious learners taking advantage of an ever-growing abundance of options for increasing their accurate knowledge of how reality works have their progress defeated before it ever really begins. They lack confidence in their own learning ability and fail to see the opportunities for knowledge accumulation all around them. It is a direct parallel to the stunted and artificially limited way that the economy will develop and wealth will accumulate among individuals when it has been violently forced to happen in only a certain arbitrary way. Whether it's opportunities to produce wealth and exchange with others or opportunities to expand our minds and bodies, we no longer see what is right in front of us because we have been trained not to.

ANTI-ENTREPRENEURIAL BIASES, MISINFORMATION, AND OBSTACLES

FORMERLY SOVIET-CONTROLLED NATIONS like Armenia have been mostly free for 30 years to begin reshaping the economy according to the genuine demands of their people. The tyrannical State that locked up or murdered entrepreneurs for the egregious sin of participating in commerce of their own accord no longer reigns. The single biggest obstacle to self-determination by economic means is not in play anymore, but that doesn't mean that the people suddenly have what they need to embrace entrepreneurship wholeheartedly and wholemindedly.

A whole new generation has risen up out of the dark times and despair that their parents endured. But still, even though these young adults were born after the collapse of communism and never directly experienced the persecution their parents did, they are likely to carry forth the same psychological baggage of generations prior. Parents and grandparents unconsciously pass along outdated strategies for living that they were conditioned with. Most of them derived from chronic expectations of insecurity, low opportunity, and the lack of freedom to choose their own goals. As such, paradigmatic concepts related to producing and accumulating wealth, setting lofty ambitions, and taking strategic risks for the possibility of greater gain are heavily discouraged in Armenian culture.

Individual ambition had little place in the USSR. For Armenians living under Soviet control, upon graduating from mandatory university study, the State would assign jobs according to what it deemed they were best suited for and was in the best interest of Soviet society. You took what was thrust upon you, and you didn't complain, or else you faced the potential loss of your social standing and access to amenities like healthcare and education that were supposed to be guaranteed by your glorious communist leaders.

Sadly, this addled anti-choice mentality spilled over into most areas of personal life too. Early marriage, for instance, was an essential part of finding security and getting along in Soviet society. Most often, you were matched up by your parents with someone in your local area and got married when they decided it was the right time. Many of the young Armenian women I know now are very grateful to have been born after the collapse of the Soviet Union because they know how much worse their lives would have been in that era for this reason and countless others.

Living in Armenia these last few years, I've seen countless differences of perspective between parents and their teenage or adult children about what kind of educational and professional goals they should be setting for themselves. Parents typically insist that their offspring place job security as the highest priority, well above superfluous things like passion, fulfillment, opportunity, and meaning. It makes sense; they grew up in a world where the key to staying alive was keeping the boss and the State at least minimally happy so that they would be allowed to continue to exist in their society. Western ideals about increasing your earning capacity through commissioned instead of salaried work, freelancing online with clients all over the world, or starting your own small business have gradually made their way here, but these ideas must compete with everything that parents have been teaching their children since the '90s.

This line of thinking is often used as an excuse by people, like many modern Armenians and members of other developing nations, who perceive themselves to be poor, underprivileged, or disadvantaged in some way to give up quickly upon trying to improve their situations if they don't immediately find success in entrepreneurship. They have been programmed by cultural dogma to accept that wealth and success are just not possible for them. At the first sign of failure, they take it as confirmation of the myth about their lot in life. It's a debilitating cycle. As long as they believe that their circumstances are beyond their control, they have no reason to try to change them, and it's always easier to blame some nefarious outside force than to take accountability for one's own life.

It will always be true that some people begin life more fortunate than others. Some people will always have more access to resources, education, and opportunities. But none of that changes the fact that the best way to improve your situation in an absolute way, however relatively good or bad it happens to be, is to apply the principles of entrepreneurship in a systemic and systematic way over whatever you *can* control. Lamenting all day about what you *cannot* control will not help you. Focusing on what you can actually change is how you will accelerate from a position of relatively low wealth to one of relatively high wealth without relying on luck or coercing wealth out of the hands of others.

Imagine this self-defeating line of thinking being applied to any other discipline in life. If you were new to woodworking and wanted to be able to build a decent table from scratch, your very first efforts might consist of cutting and nailing a few pieces of wood together in a haphazard way that did not at all resemble what the table should look like in your mind. If you had been programmed to believe that it was impossible for someone like you to become a skilled carpenter, you might take this early failure as confirmation of the obvious truth and give up on the process. Your bias would be quickly confirmed by the first and only evidence available to you.

Alternatively, you could adopt a more realistic outlook and realize that learning how to cut and join wood properly is merely the first step you will need in order to get proficient at the skill and eventually wind up with the end product of a table, one micro-process out of many you must practice. To give up on entrepreneurship just because your first attempt at making money on your own (as so many intelligent and skilled people tragically do) is like expecting yourself to be able to make the exact piece of furniture you want when you've had no previous exposure to the principles of carpentry. It's a discipline that requires study and practice, but one which, when mastered, will enable you to combine its components into a variety of known and unknown ways to get the result you want.

In a marketplace set up to enable entrepreneurial interaction, the people who apply the appropriate principles will systemically grow their wealth, while the people who fail to apply them will systemically lose theirs. Regardless of the place they arbitrarily happen to start from and the other advantages or disadvantages they may face, they will move up or down in accordance with the choices they make.

For people who grow up and are educated in "developing" countries or who live under enslaved economic conditions, much of what has been taught about the nature of the economy is misinformed. Much of it may even have been outright deception. It was taught by people who themselves hold only the limited and flawed understanding of the teachers who came before them and the cultural influences they were raised under—or even by people who had explicit agendas of keeping the working class under their control. That's why it is such an advantage to be exposed to the ideals of the entrepreneurial paradigm, this whole way of seeing the world and the possibilities for willfully interacting with it, as young as possible like Westerners typically are—before the faulty cultural programming sets in completely.

While it's not impossible for an older person to forget the bad ideas they have inherited about how producing and accumulating wealth work, it will typically be more difficult because they have so many more bad thinking habits to undo than young people. The more identified someone becomes with the way they see the world, the more likely they are to experience inordinately negative emotional outbreaks, like allergic reactions of their ideological immune system, to definitions and ideas that contradict what they already believe. "Ideollergic reactions" function much the same way physical allergic reactions do by causing us to treat harmless unfamiliar substances as aggressive foreign invaders. That is the primary reason why it can be so difficult to convince people of new ideas or even to question the merit and structure of their old ones. It is much easier to educate those who are still young and curious because they have no settled paradigms to compete with better information as it emerges.

Ironically, many of the aspects of entrepreneurship that communist States like the Soviet Union have tried to promote to their citizenries as selfish and evil are, in reality, the principles that make it uniquely empowering to individuals and civilization. A dictator like Joseph Stalin or Vladimir Lenin will always have their own agenda for telling you that entrepreneurship is inherently counter to the pursuit of a peaceful and fair society because it forces neighbors to compete against each other when, clearly, they should be working together for the common good. Promoting the common good is what he claims he is accomplishing by dictating who should be working where and in what manner to produce what goods and services that only he and his close associates, from their elevated position, can say are in the best interest of society.

In the communist paradigm of how reality works, when an entrepreneur makes their own choices about what they will value and produce because they perceive there to be an opportunity, it harms everyone else for solely the lone entrepreneur's benefit. But those of us who have always lived in mostly free economies know how backward and contrary to the actual outcome this way of thinking is. When an entrepreneur enters an industry because they see an opportunity for profit, that is another way of saying that they see an opportunity to give consumers more of what they want in a more cost-efficient manner. Profit is the reward for figuring that out, which benefits the entrepreneur as a direct consequence of benefiting others. And the best part about this natural correlation between producing more wealth for oneself by producing wealth for others is that there is no ultimate cap to it. So long as you are alive, thinking, and employing your skills through the material tools of production you acquire, you can continue to scale up in the efficiency and effectiveness of your output.

Many, perhaps even most, of the limitations that we've accepted as real are, indeed, only social constructs carried by our cultures about what the acceptable, correct, or official ways to do things must be. The paradigm that Soviet communist society required for survival was one focused on holding onto the minimal securities the State promised instead of thinking of ways that you, as an individual, could find to improve upon the fulfillment of those basic services. Rather, we should say that the State pretended to promise these basic services, as history shows how fragile those basic securities actually were under State management. The functioning of the entire system depended on the suppression of individual ambition or even individual values. The intergenerational emotional effects of this have been severe and are still readily apparent in the culture of Armenia and other post-Soviet States today.

CHAPTER 07

ENTREPRENEURIAL BLINDSPOTS—
OVERLOOKING EMERGENT
OPPORTUNITIES FOR WEALTH

THE LINGERING COGNITIVE and perceptual limitations of anti-entrepreneurship show up in countless harmful ways. I noticed it shortly after buying my house and moving in here. Every resident of my village produces a variety of goods or has cultivated a variety of skills, most of which are strictly applied for their own family's consumption. They grow vegetables or raise animals to feed themselves. They build their own furniture or work on their homes as needed with their potpourri of construction-adjacent skills. They milk their own cows and goats, ferment their own yogurt, press their own juices, and distill their own vodka. They have a plethora of self-reliance home skills that would make most people who grow up in the West, where almost everything comes in a package from a supermarket shelf, feel envious and incapable by comparison.

So, I was shocked and somewhat saddened as the response to my attempts to help organize these valuable assets into some kind of entrepreneurial strategy and maximize the profit these people could receive on the impressive things they already do was at once unilaterally rebuked. Operating from their non-entrepreneurial mentalities, the community leaders could not understand why I was asking them to do seemingly useless exercises like make lists of all the present goods and services the residents of the village were capable of offering. They couldn't see the massive potential for exchange with all the people who didn't have but might want the things they were currently producing for only themselves. They couldn't see how we might organize and brand these things with a recognizable label and identity that would make it easier for the rest of Armenia to start to hold a positive reputation in mind of the village and its producers. **They didn't see how an overhead perspective on all these complementary skills and resources might yield an awareness of new opportunities for synergistic arrangements in which they had not previously been combined.**

When I made a suggestion as simple and as obvious (to me, at least) as opening a small shop in the center of the village where everyone who lived here could sell the things they produced like fruit, vegetables, vodka, wine, meat, eggs, and milk to each other and the tourist visitors that they wanted to come stay, it seemed that no one could understand why that might be a good idea. "Gregory, everyone here already knows who grows which foods or raises which animals. We know whose houses to go to if we need something from them. A shop would just be for you because you don't know these things yet." I tried to expound that sometimes if you give people easy and convenient options for buying things, even things they might not have realized they wanted until they saw the convenient opportunity to acquire them, you increase the chances that they will buy those things, but I saw my words were quickly losing my audience's interest.

That's why we call them "convenience stores" in the West. There are usually other ways to get the common goods sold at convenience stores (and usually even at slightly cheaper prices), but the location and selection offered make it far more convenient for people to just grab the few things they need at the little shop on the corner. They are also designed to appeal to our latent demands—things that on some level we recognize we want or need but that we might not be actively thinking about acquiring until a convenient opportunity suddenly presents itself.

Over the next couple of years in the village, I would go on to have private conversations with tourists who came to stay. Almost all of them would gush over the beautiful scenery and the appeal of the quiet village life. Still, they would confess to me how inconvenient it was that they had to bring all the food and other consumable goods they needed with them for the duration of their stay because, despite being surrounded by food producers, they didn't know where to get such things in an easy fashion. More than once, some actually cut their intended stay in the village short for simple and easily avoidable reasons like that they ran out of cigarettes and fresh vegetables and didn't know where to get more except to drive an hour back into town. At that point, it was easier just to end the trip than to deal with the logistics of making back-and-forth trips to grab things they had reasonably assumed would be available here.

So, not only did the people in my village who saw no reason to open a central store lose the opportunity to make money by selling consumption goods to people who visit the village (and to each other in an optimized fashion)—they also lost the other revenue they would have received by the extra days the tourists would have paid to stay in their guesthouses and adjacent goods and services like tours, souvenirs, and meals that they might have bought during that time. Complementary forms of value like this always carry the potential to create synergy, generating more than any of them are worth on their own. By having an organized approach to solving one common and predictable problem for people, you then also create the opportunity to solve other problems for them. And every problem you solve potentially represents more profit.

In the villagers' shared paradigm, the totality of all possible supply production was already underway, and the totality of all possible demand was also already being met. They saw their local economy as entirely cyclical and predictable, which is exactly the way the Soviet State tried to force it to be on a national scale. It's a very uncomplicated way to live: They need something, so they acquire and consume it. Their lack of entrepreneurial vision, however, prevents them from extrapolating even a little bit to consider that if one person (themselves) wants the things they produce, it might be reasonable to assume that other people (whether they are in the same village, within Armenia, or anywhere else in the world) might also want it and that they could create far more value for themselves by systemizing and offering these things to them instead of merely tending to the requirements of their own immediate consumption.

It's yet another manifestation of that same basic fallacy that has been used to justify countless communist atrocities against people who just wanted the basic freedom to take care of themselves: **To assume that the opportunities you are aware of or the way you are doing things must be all the opportunities that exist or the best way to do them—to overlook what you don't know that you don't know.** It's thinking like this that keeps people stuck in the same unfulfilling jobs they've always known but have never really been satisfied with. It keeps them dating the same types of people they know they will never have fully fulfilling relationships with. And it keeps them from see-ing how they could apply the processes they are familiar with in unfamiliar ways or even from learning new and wildly un-familiar processes to begin to apply productively to life. The source of the problem is the limited scale of their perspective, both in magnitude and across time.

Why do shopping marts exist, anyway? It's not like they actually produce the goods sold there. Farmers, resource har-vesters, and various manufacturers do that. Doesn't it seem unnecessary that we waste the immense fuel, manpower, and other resources required to deliver them to middlemen that do nothing more than just resell them to the people who will ulti-mately end up consuming them?

The errors of this reductive argument should be apparent. A supermarket facilitates the exchange between producer and end consumer through the convenience of a centralized loca-tion and standardized buying experience. As well, the entrepre-neurs responsible for managing the store are tasked with opti-mizing and maintaining the value of all the assets stored and sold there, which is an enormous burden requiring knowledge, skill, operating costs, and risk.

It is obvious that consumers, by and large, would not go out of their way to purchase most of the individual products they want from each respective producer of said products if it were even mildly inconvenient to do so. Some won't even both-er walking to the back of a store to get what they want if it's too far from the entrance. The shopping experience also provides the opportunity to market products to consumers that they may not have even known they would want to purchase when they initially set out to buy something. Online retail sites perform the same function on the internet, saving consumers the trouble of having to search for and complete separate transactions for every little thing they want to order. My village has plenty of producers but no standardized middlemen to make the buying experience convenient for potential consumers. And so, the producers assume the consumers must not exist because if they did, they would already be going through the trouble of buying from them.

It may sound shocking to Western mentalities because of how ingrained and celebrated the concept of young entrepreneurship is in our culture, but developing economies all over the world do a great deal to impede their own opportunities, each shooting themselves in the foot by actively discouraging entrepreneurial ideals in the young. In many cultures, the concept of working for money is still shrouded in cultural superstition. It is seen as an inescapable demon—a necessary evil that the adult men of the household subject themselves to for the sake of providing for their families. A child's place is to be studying in school, doing chores at home, or playing innocently with their friends. A lifetime of work awaits them later on when they have their own families and are old enough for the burden.

In Armenia, there is even a saying that speaks directly to this superstition: "*Փող ձեռքի կեղտ է:*" (p'voghy dzerrk'i keght e)—"*Money in hand is evil.*" **Many Armenians believe that their kids will become greedy and mercantilist if they start to interact with money early, which is a similar judgment that the Soviet State applied to them when they were growing up.** So parents hide money away from their children like how parents in the West might attempt to censor violence and sex. They are trying to protect their children from a perceived evil, which makes it less likely those children will ever be able to see money for the fantastic tool of exchange that it is.

Meanwhile, in the West, it's practically a rite of passage for young children to set up lemonade stands on sidewalks near their homes or go door to door offering to mow their neighbors' lawns for a dollar. We almost universally view this behavior as endearing. We admire the ambition and ingenuity of young children who undertake efforts to offer something of value to the world and ask a small fee (which we are happy to pay) for it. It may not seem like a big deal, but this kind of early positive reinforcement primes the children who are exposed to it to form certain associations with the concepts of making money ethically and especially with finding creative ways to do it.

On one occasion, my neighbor's children, with whom I had had many positive interactions, came to my door asking if I could hire them for any job. They had become aware that I was hiring a few of the adults in the village to work on the restoration and refurbishment of my house, and some mixture of natural curiosity and self-interest impelled them to see if they too could take advantage of the opportunity to make money that I was providing.

Not wanting to disappoint their burgeoning entrepreneurial ambitions, I gave them gloves and told them I would pay them the equivalent of $1 USD each (500 Armenian dram) if they would do about 15 minutes of outdoor chores for me. This was a task that would be genuinely valuable to me because it would save me time that I could use for tasks I produce greater value from. The work was completed quickly, and I paid them the agreed amount. They seemed excited and pleased by this arrangement, and I felt good about encouraging them to think proactively about helping themselves by offering to help others.

Imagine my surprise when the next day, the father of the children showed up at my door quite upset about the arrangement he learned I had made with them. It was initially difficult for me to understand what the problem was due to the culture and language barrier between us. My first thought was that he must have been angry that I had engaged his children in potentially strenuous physical labor, but I quickly realized that wasn't it. He wasn't mad about the type of work his children had done for me or even necessarily that they had done any work at all. He was mad that I had *paid* his children for the work. He just kept repeating, "They are too young. They are too young."

"Too young for what, exactly?" I wondered. I knew that he and the rest of the village didn't think they were too young to do these kinds of chores at home. I knew no one thought the children of the village were too young to interact with me, as I frequently volunteered to work with them at the school. The only new variable in this equation was the payment of money, which their father interpreted as somehow demeaning to his family. Money was to be made by the father alone and later the adult sons when they too would be old enough. Children going off to work, in his mind, was surely a sign that they were destitute and desperate for a handout. Their cultural beliefs, which were, ironically, designed to keep them from feeling poor, were setting their children up for the continuation of their lifestyle of lack of material wealth.

Imagine a scenario where these children actively rebelled against their parents' wishes for them to refrain from learning useful skills and making money until they were adults and ready to submit to lives of real labor. Imagine that they became inspired by exposure to Western ideals of entrepreneurship and, by the time they were teenagers, already started reliably earning more money than their parents through unconventional means beyond their old cultural paradigm. What do you think their parents' reaction to that would be? In my opinion, the probability is that they would feel threatened and be very unapproving of their children's aberrant behavior regardless of the objective benefits it would lead to. **They would do whatever they could to discourage or outright ban their children from making these kinds of beneficial choices, which is strikingly reminiscent of the tactics employed by a communist State**

seeking total control over the ambitions of its people. And their children, in turn, would either submit to their parents' coercive and counter-progressive tendencies or make it a point to oppose them even harder, driving an irreparable rift between their culture of origin and the more capable people they would be growing into. That is the terrible choice facing many young people who somehow manage to break out of the psychological prisons they were born into—alienation from their home or success at levels beyond what their culture could ever have enabled them to dream of.

Now imagine the opposite scenario. Imagine that these village children had parents who, despite not having much direct experience with it, saw the obvious potential benefits of encouraging their children from an early age to find ways to get what they want by helping others. Imagine that they did not feel threatened by the prospect of their children going on to adopt values and live lives that might be starkly different than their own but that made them happier, healthier, and more personally fulfilled? What might those boys go on to accomplish as adults? Sadly, we might never know. Not in this generation, anyway.

Thanks to natural curiosity in the young, however, not all hope is lost for radical cultural evolution regarding entrepreneurship. It wasn't long after this negative incident with the children that teenagers from around the village started showing up at my house to monitor the work they too had learned I was hiring adults to do. For most of them, it started as just general curiosity about me and some of the uncommon choices I was making for the new amenities to my house, which was gradually taking on a more modern look and shape.

Noticing their curiosity, I asked the teens if they would like to get involved with work on the house, too, for which I would pay them a slightly lower daily rate than the adults (due to their lesser experience). Well, it turned out that even if they could get their parents' permission, that wouldn't work for them because most of them had a lot of other obligations between school and chores at home. They couldn't devote whole days to doing things like basic landscaping and construction work around my house because their schedules just wouldn't allow for it. But I didn't want to lose this opportunity to actualize their interest for what might only be a fleeting window that it had risen to the surface.

I proposed a different, more entrepreneurial deal to them: They could show up at my house any day or time they wanted and get to work on any of the various established projects going on. I would pay them a fixed rate for every hour they participated. I would let them decide their own hours and what type of work they were most comfortable with or qualified for, which meant that they would have to think a little creatively (i.e., entrepreneurially) about the work. It wasn't like a regular job with a boss commanding them to follow strict and repetitive orders for a designated block of time five days a week. They could show up for a couple of hours on a Saturday morning or an hour in the afternoon after school if that's what worked best for them. All that mattered to me was that they put in an honest effort and make reasonable progress on whatever they felt confident working on.

What started as a couple of stragglers coming now and again when they needed a little extra cash to buy something essential soon turned into some reliable regulars showing up for at least a few hours every day. Very quickly, they saw the relationship between how much they were willing to do to offer value to me and how much they would be compensated in return. As they were the ones in control of how and when they would offer it, their work ethic was consistently strong. They knew there would be no point in showing up to work when they were too tired or unenthusiastic to get anything done, so they only came when they were in the mood for it and their labor would be efficient. It's no different than how a modern self-employed freelancer or work-from-home employee is free to manage their own time and working schedule because there is no reason for them to show up to an office and force themselves to work at less-than-optimal productivity simply for the sake of maintaining a regular schedule and being easy to manage by their overbearing employer.

When the teenagers finished the small projects that I had initially hired them to work on, they were quick to propose other things they could do for me around the house, such as building a larger outdoor pen for my rabbits, clearing brush and making footpaths, or building retaining walls outside my home. When I asked if they had done those things before, they admitted that they hadn't, but they felt that they could easily learn how. And indeed, it was easy for all of us to learn. Merely by watching a few short instructional videos online, asking a few of the more experienced adults for some pointers, and doing a quick stock of what building materials I already had or would need to purchase, they were able to extend their entrepreneurial employment with me to new forms of value that neither I or nor they had been aware would be equitable for me to pay them for.

The teens didn't realize it, but they were essentially participating in a sales process with me as their customer. They successfully convinced me to spend money on services I had not, at first, realized I wanted to spend money on. And it was all motivated by their self-interest in making more money and their curiosity to learn how to do new useful things (i.e., develop their knowledge and skills). We both profited greatly from the establishment and maintenance of this new working relationship.

CHAPTER 08

PSEUDO-ENTREPRENEURIAL FAÇADE—RESULTS LACKING RISK OR RESPONSIBILITY

THEN THERE IS the case of programs designed to mimic the appearance of entrepreneurship and the wealth it generates but that ultimately fail at their stated missions because they lack the prerequisites of genuine entrepreneurship—namely, knowledge and individuals being accountable for their choices.

In many of the villages around Armenia, government grant programs have given out the equivalent of many thousands of tax dollars to villagers who agree to use the money to renovate their houses and turn them into lucrative guesthouse accommodations for tourists. The goal is to incentivize tourism out to these remote regions, at the same time providing the locals sustainable ways to support themselves with their own businesses built upon one of the material assets they already own: Their homes. And from what I can see, the first half of these well-intentioned programs has worked pretty well. Many villagers have been able to turn parts of their old homes into nice and modern-looking tourist accommodations.

But that's where the story ends for most of them. Now, they own complex businesses thrust upon them by the State, businesses they have zero personal experience with or knowledge of how to run effectively or even at a profit. Most of them have never traveled far outside their own home regions and have, thus, never even been patrons at guesthouses. Consequently, they can't envision things from the perspective of their intended customers. They don't know the first thing about attracting the right people to come stay in their nice new accommodations or what they should do to adequately meet their needs and expectations once they are there and paying for a certain kind of experience. So, many of these new guesthouse owners will freely admit that the only people who have actually come stay in their upgraded homes are their own friends and relatives who wanted to visit them anyway—not as paying tourists, mind you.

Do you see the inherent problem with this short-sighted attempt to kickstart entrepreneurship? Their government gave them tools and resources but no education about how to use them effectively. All the brand-name power tools and premium lumber in the world won't help you build a table without first learning how to use them effectively. You can sit around and wait for a table to spontaneously emerge from the pile of potential you've stumbled onto, but it won't happen without your strategic action. And that's essentially the equivalent of what most of these non-functioning guesthouse owners are now doing—**sitting and waiting for paying patrons to emerge from out of nowhere and offer them money merely because they have assets that represent potential value in the form of guesthouses.**

By being given access to tangible assets they do not know how to use, these villagers have bypassed the natural causal hierarchy of wealth creation. Whatever potential their guesthouses might have had to become thriving businesses is almost entirely squandered. But what do they care? Their homes are nicer now. They walk away having profited even if they never attract a single paying customer because they never assumed any risk or responsibility. And so, they remain psychologically infantilized because their pseudo-parents are incapable of teaching and encouraging them to grow up by embracing the responsibility of their ambitions. What natural incentive do these beneficiary pseudo-entrepreneurs have to ensure that their businesses actually deliver value at a profit in the marketplace? Because they did not apply their own discretion to open guesthouses and did not pay for the renovations to their homes, they do not feel the pressure of entrepreneurial risk that would compel them to overcome market obstacles to produce favorable results.

Imagine how different the situation might be for a villager who worked hard all year to save up $3,000 of their own money and did the market research necessary to arrive at the rational conclusion that a guesthouse in their village might be a good business model. Imagine them spending their own time to learn how to run such a business, how to brand it with a unique identity, what attractive features and amenities to implement that would justify a higher daily rate and a competitive advantage over more generic guesthouses, and how to promote it to the appropriate target market of tourists (whether local or foreign) who like to visit villages around Armenia. Imagine learning enough English and other common world languages specifically so that they could cater to foreigners who do not speak Armenian but still want to see the country in a convenient and comfortable manner. That's a person who would do whatever it took to see their investment of time, energy, and capital pay off many times over. That's a genuine entrepreneur.

Best of all, the knowledge and skills such a villager would garner from earnestly throwing themselves fully into the risks and responsibilities of this entrepreneurial endeavor would go on to be useful in any other businesses they might want to start in the future, regardless of how much monetary profit this first one might generate. Those intangible assets of knowledge and skill would be the real source of their sustainable wealth production, not the big beautiful building gifted to them by a benevolent benefactor. That is only the appearance of results without the foundation necessary to get and stay there.

There is a similar causality error that occurs in villages that are happy to accept huge State grants to establish libraries full of English books, with selections ranging from Dr. Seuss' *The Cat in the Hat* to James Joyce's *Ulysses*. The problem is that they haven't first bothered to implement effective English education programs for the youths that are meant to be reading these books.

Tangible developments like a beautiful library look great for the press. They tell a great story by creating the appearance of measurable progress in the metric of apparent English reading ability and the level of sophistication to their education model. **But without an effective methodology in place to teach the intended readers of these fancy and impressive books in their shiny new libraries how to actually read them, these assets are, essentially, little more than wall art.** Their functional value is reduced to mere aesthetics. They cannot produce their intended value as books. They cannot convey information by being read until they are in the hands of someone who knows how to read them and has the inclination to do so.

Lacking the incentive to produce results according to meaningful metrics, the people running these schools and libraries have no real reason to make sure their students get better at English, no reason to make sure they are actively reading these books and garnering the improvement to their intangible knowledge and skill that should come from doing so. English is objectively the useful language in the world because it has the highest number of speakers using it in the most diverse range of places and circumstances. Therefore, all other things being equal, shouldn't language learners subjectively value English quite highly for the various forms of wealth they realize that acquiring it as a skill could allow them to produce? What if everyone in these villages could see the causal relationship between being able to speak good English and being able to participate productively in countless professional and lifestyle opportunities that would bring them substantially greater wealth, happiness, and purpose throughout life? How much more incentive would they have to make sure that they and their children learn to speak and write well in English, even if they never have an impressive-looking library or famous American novels like *Ulysses* to display on their shelves? Further still, how much greater wealth in the form of English-related knowledge and skills would such a library and its impressive collection of books (i.e., English language tools) be capable of producing in the hands of people who have the methodology and the knowledge of causality in place to use them?

After the establishment of such a library, a piano was generously donated by a private party to the same school in my village. Though the piano was placed in a common area where it would be on prominent display, months went by without any attempts by the administration to get it into playing condition or to get the children involved in learning about it in any capacity. I offered to donate several hours of my own time to tune the piano and begin leading a rudimentary music education program to students who expressed interest in learning. I knew that I was the only person in the area who was qualified to derive any of the piano's utility and value as a music-making tool. Though interest was feigned, my efforts were rebuked. So, the piano sat gathering dust, books, and coffee mugs—an aesthetically pleasing piece of furniture but not a functional tool for producing music and expanding the minds of the musically inclined.

The unwillingness to take responsibility for acting upon the utility of tangible assets to extract their value is so extreme in some places that it seems hopeless and absurd to Western minds. Several times in my travels around other post-Soviet nations like Ukraine and Georgia, I ran into situations trying to rent apartments from locals, where I frustratingly realized they did not even possess the minimum entrepreneurial mentality required to put themselves in a position to profit from even this most basic form of transaction.

It is sometimes the case that people with little income—people Westerners would certainly consider poor—will own multiple homes or apartments that they either acquired very cheaply long ago or that were passed to them by family members who had been holding onto them for lack of something better to do with them. But does owning real estate—one of the expressed goals of the "American dream" and a bragging point for self-made people all around the Western world—automatically make someone wealthy? Does the property produce wealth and utility for its owners all on its own, merely by existing? Or is still some level of strategic activity necessary to derive its utility and value?

Someone reared with an entrepreneurial mentality will come to consider real estate both an income-generating asset and a long-term appreciating investment. But a strange sort of opposite perspective exists in many of the places I've been that lack entrepreneurial cultures. Unless actively occupying the property owned, the non-entrepreneurial mind is inclined to view a house or apartment as a burden. It's a liability that requires cleaning and maintaining, something to worry and deliberate about, and many of these unwitting owners prefer to just ignore their property and let it fall into filth and disrepair if they can't quickly sell it for cash.

On occasions when I've tried to rent apartments on a long-term basis from such people, it was often frustrating and difficult to make the transaction happen at all. If I tell them I need internet access in the apartment, they say they personally don't use the internet at home, so they don't see any reason to get it installed—yet another indicator that they aren't even thinking of their property as an asset that they are offering to someone other than themselves to use in exchange for monetary profit. I point out to them that the one-time cost of getting internet installed would be relatively little money compared to the hundreds of dollars I would be paying them every month in rent and that the difference between those two prices would be pure profit for them—an amount that typically was actually greater than what they earned working at their meager jobs (if they had jobs at all). Again, bafflingly to my mind, they were unable or unwilling to see the bigger, longer-term perspective beyond the one-time cost and inconvenience of getting internet installed. This usually would have amounted to little more than a phone call to the local internet company and a signed agreement that could be canceled with little notice, which would enable them to rent the apartment to me in the short term and recover the cost immediately. Furthermore, the internet-enabled apartment would then go on to be a permanent asset they could rent out to other tenants who required internet at home. Considering how few property owners bothered to make internet available to their renters at all in some of these places, offering it and advertising this fact would give them a strong competitive advantage among other rental properties, ensuring a higher rental price and a higher likelihood of keeping the property occupied with tenants.

Some of these landlords had mentalities so far removed from thinking systemically about their property and its potential as an asset to produce wealth for them that they were not even willing to clean their apartments before trying to rent them to me. I can't tell you how many dirty old apartments I looked at (that had obviously been unoccupied for years) with owners begrudgingly telling me to either take them as is or stop bothering them. They weren't willing to spend a few hours of their own time sweeping and dusting, and they certainly weren't willing to pay some trivial amount to a cleaner for a day of work to transform a useless old liability into a sustainable source of income that would instantly and substantially improve their standard of living.

If I hadn't experienced this surreal phenomenon and others like it so many times in developing economies around the world, I would assume that anecdotes like these were an exaggeration of the truth and not representative of general mentalities, just as you may be assuming this now, too, as you read these stories. Perhaps, eventually, the descendants of these people who never learned to see the larger perspective and enormous potential in the material tools and resources they let go to waste will be in a position to apply their newly acquired, superior, and non-dogmatic approach to improving the state of their own lives and the state of their societies. When that happens on a massive scale, we will quickly see the standard of living for all developing economies rise to meet and surpass even what we consider to be the most entitled places on Earth under present economic conditions.

CHAPTER 09

THEFT—THE COUNTERPRODUCTIVE WANT OF SOMETHING FOR NOTHING

THE UNSPOKEN DESIRE for massive output without the required level of input is largely responsible for what we in the West call a "get rich quick" mentality. It is a way of thinking that goes beyond the admirable attempt at optimal efficiency. It goes against the rules of reality by ignoring or denying that things have to be produced before they can be consumed.

For those whom have always worked hard for their wages and for whom there is no foreseeable way to organically increase their earning ability, the allure of something for nothing is understandable. It's ironic that the same people who can be so hardworking can also let the ugly side of laziness get the better of them and ultimately prevent them from taking real measures toward building wealth in the realistic, ethical, and sustainable way. But nothing ever actually comes from nothing. It only comes from someone else.

Modern scams often prey upon this weakness. Human judgment gets very screwy when it's biased by latent greed.

Inherently unrealistic promises are more likely to be accepted at face value when wishful thinking about easy money is at the forefront of the victim's attention. The same thing happens to traders who might make slow incremental gains in the market by following trends and meticulously analyzing when the ideal time to buy or sell a position is. Then, suddenly, they get carried away by the appearance of a massive bull run that they buy into at the worst possible moment—just before a correction and massive sell-off. They get so excited about the possibility of quick massive gains that they stop looking at the situation realistically.

The lust for output without input is always a mind killer, and it ruins many decent people's chances of actually earning a living because they never develop the discipline to see through its enticing allure. **The antidote to the get rich quick mindset is to learn the real principles of controlling your labor, creative output, and its identity in the marketplace.** And this applies not just to the knowledge and skills you develop for wealth-producing applications but also to the relationships you rely on for the profitable exchange of these assets.

I've heard countless stories of Soviet workers taking every opportunity they could to steal resources and supplies from their job sites in order to procure as much short-term gain for themselves as they could. From their perspective, it was one of the most reliable things they could do to secure at least a little guaranteed wealth for their families. In Western cultures, the analysis would obviously work out very differently. Why would a Westerner dare risk losing their good job, blemishing their professional reputation, and possibly sabotaging their career for life just to get something for free that they could otherwise buy for themselves at a reasonable price with their ample salary?

But Soviet workers had few long-term gains to worry about losing in exchange for the short-term ones brought about by stealing from State-run factories. If you knew there was a long queue to get some of the basic goods you required like clothing for your children, and you worked at a clothing factory, it was more advantageous for you to just steal what you needed from your workplace than to wait and hope that the State came through with the clothing it promised to provide you long ago. Even if you didn't have an immediate personal need for the things you had the opportunity to steal, you could be sure that some other Soviet citizen suffering from the same State shortages would happily barter other valuable goods for it.

One of the first workers I hired for my house renovations in the village proved that, despite how glad he was to have lucrative full-time employment with me, he just couldn't resist the opportunity to try to squeeze a little extra cash out of me through blatant attempts at trickery. Because I was new in the village, he thought he could take advantage of my ignorance by lying about the prices of various tools and amenities I was paying him to acquire for the work we were doing on the house. When I confronted him about the obvious discrepancy between the prices he told me he had paid and the prices on public display, he played dumb and tried to laugh the difference off, hoping to move on from the conversation as soon as he realized that he had been caught in his lie.

I stopped working with him shortly after that. He went from having a good job that paid more than anything else available locally to being unemployed because he wanted to get something for nothing at my expense. I also suspect that this is not something he would have attempted to pull over on any of his other Armenian neighbors. Is it possible he perceived that it was morally permissible to steal from me specifically because I had more money than he did? Did he presume that because it was relatively easy for me to make more money, I wouldn't care about or even notice the crude theft? Now, I have a permanently worsened opinion of him and will certainly not be hiring him for any additional projects or trusting him with money or valuable possessions.

Was my reaction to these incidental indiscretions too strong? From my point of view, the risks of continuing to hire him far outweighed the benefits. If he was willing to lie to me about such a simple and obvious fraudulent transaction, I have to assume that he'd be willing to lie to me about other less detectable transactions too. What if I'm not always able to monitor that he's actually showing up for work every day or working for every hour I'm paying him for? What if one of my expensive tools goes missing, and I have to wonder if he might have taken it since I know he does not respect my property or money? What if he lies about the cost of other, far more expensive supplies I depend on him to acquire for the job? His first minor indiscretions could easily lead to significant financial losses for me over the many months I'd be hiring him. Additionally, the extra time, effort, and capital (such as if I felt it necessary to install security cameras where he would be working) I would have to expend as a result of being suspicious of this man greatly diminish my incentive to hire him instead of someone I feel I can trust.

What was this man's entrepreneurial error? Why was he willing to risk his profitable relationship with me and his positive reputation in my mind just for a quick and easy score at my expense? Surely, that must have been an obvious losing proposition to him. It seems to me that he suffered from two primary cognitive blindspots.

First, he lacked the entrepreneurial mentality required to understand his own income-earning ability from a systemic overhead point of view. He was so accustomed to analyzing the world as a series of short-term opportunities to make a little cash at a time that he lost perspective of the long-term value of his working relationships. Besides the work I was already paying him for, he didn't consider that staying on good terms with me could lead to other opportunities down the road. What if I want to build a new house on my property or perform more renovations a few years from now? He should want to be the first person I think to call and hire if that time comes. What if other people move to the village and need recommendations from me regarding who they should hire? His name should be the first from my mouth. The same reputational principle should apply to the village as a whole as it attempts to make a positive name for itself with Armenia. Over time, those villages that best understand and implement the reputation principle will see their entrepreneurial opportunities increase and, therefore, their wealth too.

This man's second error was perceiving me as an exploitable resource, not a human being on an equal playing field with whom to make fair and mutually beneficial exchanges. This is a common view that residents of developing nations have of Westerners who come as tourists or expatriates to their countries, and it contributes to an impassible sense of class divide between them. The typical view rural Armenians have of Americans, in my experience, is that we are all born into wealth and are guaranteed good jobs throughout life because our government is so powerful (whatever that means). They see it as unfair that they have to perform hard labor for a meager living while people like me are practically swimming in money from what they perceive to be little or easy work.

These unfortunate people are aiming their envy and resentment in the wrong direction. It is their culture that has failed them by not giving them permission to think freely about how to participate with greater leverage in the economy, either locally or globally. Forming a positive professional relationship with someone like me who is in a position to offer greater professional opportunities could be a crucial first step to ascending out of the economic trap that's kept them stuck at the same level of wealth production and accumulation their whole lives. So, it becomes a sad sort of self-fulfilling prophecy. My dishonest worker, believing he can only rely on sporadic short-term opportunities to snatch as much profit as possible, makes choices that condemn him to a limited slate of opportunities corresponding to what he already believes. His dishonesty is the very thing that puts him in a position of having to continue to be dishonest.

An entrepreneur—someone who has no artificial cap upon the rewards of their productive actions—quickly realizes that the correlation between how much they produce for others and how much wealth they, in turn, accumulate for themselves gives them a strong natural incentive to be as productive, fair, and honest with other people as possible. They have good self-interested reasons to create as much value as they can with their life and be upfront with the people they exchange with. Whatever value they do not directly consume or keep for themselves, they can exchange with others for the direct products of their productive efforts. The chain of causality is very simple in a closed system of market incentives such as this.

But the equation changes quite dramatically when we introduce even a little theft. Even incidental, short-term thefts and cons have far-reaching systemic effects on culture and economy, but the individual thief never realizes this. When one person steals from another (and gets away with it), they get rewarded for something other than producing or managing value. The relationship totally shifts from one of win-win interaction, where one party profits from helping the other also profit, to one of win-lose interaction, where one profits from the loss of the other. Mutual symbiotes degrade into destructive parasites and their unfortunate hosts.

If stealing produces greater reward with less cost, the thief will come to have no incentive to produce and manage wealth — only to take what others produce through lies or force, thereby also ruining the original producer's entrepreneurial incentive. These are the kinds of unintended effects that sprouted from all the Soviet propaganda about how evil it was for anyone to have more material wealth than anyone else.

Sadly, this is the path that many habitual criminals fall onto. Many of them genuinely believe that they have no viable options to be productive in society because they either can't see a way to get conventional jobs, or the amount they would be paid for conventional jobs would be insignificant compared to what they know they can acquire through fraud. Some fraudsters, scammers, and con artists apply so much skill and ingenuity to their crafts and innovate such genuinely impressive ways of misappropriating other people's wealth that one can only wonder what kinds of unprecedented value they might have been able to produce for society had they found a viable means to apply their intangible assets as ethical entrepreneurs.

Imagine a whole society that becomes so broken and dysfunctional that there are more people stealing than there are people producing things to be stolen. Eventually, there will be nothing left to steal, and the few remaining entrepreneurs will have lost their incentive to continue to produce at all because whatever they create gets taken just as quickly as it is created. Such a society would be on the brink of collapse, and everyone's standard of living would quickly descend back to a state of raw interaction with nature.

When someone steals or allows stealing to go unacknowledged and unpunished, they contribute to the decay and downfall of everyone economically connected to them, which ultimately hurts them too. **Theft and fraud destroy the economic order of modern civilization, which strips away its sophis-**

tication and brings us all closer to a more primitive state of disorder where we are much less able to take advantage of the knowledge, skills, and tools of other people. So, taking pride in the wealth, security, and control you build for yourself by applying the principles of entrepreneurship in your life also means doing what is necessary to protect those things from misguided people who have not learned to value and respect them. It might even mean going out of your way to avoid interaction or collaboration with people who do not carry the same standard of ethical autonomy as you do or else risking paying the price for those associations.

Consider as well how even the mere threat of theft forces us to change our lifestyles and productive habits. How much money, time, and effort does the average person invest into measures for defending the wealth they have accumulated through their productive efforts? Locks on our doors, bars on our windows, safes hidden beneath our floorboards... even the keys required to start the ignitions of our cars. All of these are examples of technology invented and mass-produced to deter or counter the threat of theft to our most valuable material possessions. They are ubiquitously in use around the world in all but the safest of small trusting communities because there are people everywhere who would, if given the opportunity, prefer to take by force what they want instead of producing or exchanging for it. I'd guess that very few of these criminals do this out of some inherent sense of malevolence or a desire to harm others. For most, it probably comes down to convenience. They simply don't see any feasible way to engage morally and proactively with society that will net them the level of material reward they seek, and they are envious of the possessions that others have seemingly unfairly acquired.

Sometimes, I imagine what the world would look like if everyone with even a basic amount of useful knowledge and skill learned, from the time they were young, how entrepreneurial principles could be applied to capitalize effectively on their fundamental assets. Imagine these principles being integrated into cultures the world over and the eternal human problem of finding a way to make a living going away almost entirely. Anyone, at any age or in any part of the world, who could produce or perform something valuable for other people could find ample means to provide for themselves. In that kind of world, all of the time, attention, and money we all have accepted as necessary to put into protecting what we've built from people who would seek to take it would be freed up to be better spent on things we care more for—our passions, our hobbies, the development of further knowledge and skills to earn with, and the people we care to share our time with.

CHAPTER 10

BUREAUCRATIC MENTALITY—THE TRAGEDY OF THE "RIGHT" WAY OF DOING THINGS

A CONSEQUENCE OF looking to social authorities to override your wants and solve your problems for you is the rise of bureaucratic mentality, which is in every way antithetical to entrepreneurial mentality. And although it often appears to provide a solution to the problems it addresses in the short term, it ultimately destroys the ability to observe openly, think critically, innovate solutions, and implement them in the most efficient and effective fashion.

The goal of efficiency is minimizing input while maximizing output as you define those terms in each analysis. You can't measure efficiency by only the first or second half of the equation alone. Furthermore, you need to know you've selected an output actually worth measuring (i.e., one you actually value and are intending to accomplish).

At the height of the Soviet Union, a superficial analysis could easily have been made about the health of the economy and the livelihood of the citizenry based solely on inputs like how many people were working or how much money the State was investing into various industries. But who is to say what the value of those workers or money invested turned out to be? What were the prescribed goals of each job taken, each day worked, each ruble spent, and each choice made by a bureaucrat about how Soviet society ought to function? Certainly, no proud communist openly intended for millions of people to die of starvation, their currency to become worthless, or their great union to collapse due to unsustainable economic practices. There was a profound disconnect between the intention of the input and the output generated.

As an entrepreneurial mentality requires being able to approach every problem, every intentional pursuit of a meaningful goal with fresh eyes willing to figure out the optimal way to arrive at the outcome desired, it is incompatible with a bureaucratic one. **Thinking like a bureaucrat usually means focusing only on established procedures with zero creative conception about how things could be done better or, indeed, if they are even being done well at all in their present form.** It could also mean focusing only on one output while ignoring the inequitable costs that were required to create it.

There is a natural, universal principle that explains why bureaucracies are, by their nature, inefficient at best and counterproductive at worst. They are either bad at accomplishing their goals, or they actively accomplish the opposite of their goals. And this bureaucratic principle is actually the inverse of the natural principle that requires entrepreneurs to adapt, innovate, and get more efficient over time at producing various forms of value. It has something to do with the causal connection between the individual making a choice and the responsibility for the outcome of that choice. It has to do with the invisible economic calculation that goes on whenever we willfully set out to produce specific valuable outcomes that will require investments of our time, effort, and resources.

Imagine that you develop a passion for gardening and decide you want to grow your own tomatoes. But, being a particularly arrogant and impatient kind of person, you decide that you don't need to learn anything about the physical laws that determine what will or will not enable tomatoes to grow. In your underdeveloped paradigm of tomato-related causality, you've accepted that all that really matters is that you have a strong desire for the outcome of tomatoes being grown. So, you never read a single gardening book or even ask experienced tomato growers for some basic tips about soil composition, watering frequency, appropriate levels of sunlight, or the best season to plant your tomato seeds in (if you've even gone so far as to realize that tomato seeds are the first necessary step to producing tomato plants). You don't even humble yourself enough to acknowledge that there are objective principles that govern how tomatoes can and will best grow, and you certainly don't invest the necessary resources into trying to understand those principles so that you can make them work to your advantage and produce the goal you seek.

Without knowledge of the principles inherent to tomato growing, no matter how much time and effort you put into trying to make tomatoes grow, you will not end up with tomatoes. Or, at least, they will not be very good tomatoes. You may just get lucky enough and sprout some in spite of all your negligence through a random confluence of factors you did not intentionally cultivate.

While it's absurdly easy to see how true this is within a domain of discipline as commonly acknowledged and practiced as something like tomato gardening, the same applies to liter-

ally every other human endeavor, no matter how complex, esoteric, specialized, or removed from everyday concerns it might
seem to laypeople. You cannot build a working and optimized
system of coordinated actions intended to produce an outcome
without understanding the natural and objective principles that
apply to every relevant input of that system. This is why new
entrepreneurs fail at business, and it is also why hastily implemented bureaucratic programs do not accomplish their intended outcomes, no matter how noble the intentions may be, how
much public support they have, or the confidence and popular-
ity of the charismatic leaders who spearhead them.

In the hypothetical tomato-growing system you have attempted to implement, you are the one who has to face the
consequences of your failure or success at producing tomatoes
(i.e., the end result of having lots of good quality tomatoes, a
few bad quality tomatoes, or no tomatoes at all). Because you
will be directly positively or negatively affected by the output
of your input, you are incentivized not to waste your time, effort, and other resources on means that are incongruent with
the intended goal. The physical and objective reality you live in
has rules that cannot be broken, no matter how much you may
wish you could break them.

But what if the end result of the quality and quantity of tomatoes produced had no direct effect on the attainment of your
goals? What if the output was not in any way related to something you cared about accomplishing? What if the potential for
a bountiful harvest of plump, bright, juicy vegetables to feast
upon meant nothing to you? Further still, what if you never even
bothered to check the results of the work you were doing for the
ostensible purpose of producing tomatoes, and you never even
saw that your methods might be producing no tomatoes at all?

If you never directly observed the output or if the output
did not matter to you, you would do whatever you happened to

believe was the best thing for you to do. Or perhaps you would just do what was most convenient. Perhaps you would do what most people thought was the best thing to do (i.e., common wisdom or the "everyone knows" approach to solving problems). One of two fallacies follows from here. You may attempt to minimize the losses and discomfort required by your actions. You will do the least amount of work possible. Or you may make the opposite mistake of assuming that the harder you work, the greater your results will necessarily be. So you will waste epic amounts of effort attempting the hardest method of tomato growing you can envision, all the while ignoring that it has no measurable effect on the tomatoes you produce.

The tragedy of this kind of bureaucratic mentality is that it impels intelligent human beings to give up their capacity for critical and creative thinking to follow rules for the sake of following rules. They do what they are supposed to merely because they have been mandated to and not because they can see what result following such rules will accomplish and they agree that the result is desirable. Bureaucratic thinking requires its adherents to follow the strict letter of the rules outlined and never the intended spirit, even when it is obvious to anyone willing to look that operating even slightly outside the prescribed mandates would aid the goal that the rules were written for in the first place.

Bureaucratic thinking is what led Soviet overlords to funnel ever more money and other resources into whatever areas of their planned economy seemed to be failing most. In their bureaucratic paradigm, it was not possible that there was something wrong with their strategies when they failed to produce the intended outcomes. They simply needed to do more of them, faster, better, and harder. Ironically, this only incentivized counterproductivity, as the less you produced, the more you were rewarded as more money flowed to the least productive sectors of the economy and away from those where actual value was being created.

Perhaps the worst byproduct of living in a bureaucratized world is that intelligent, capable, and creative people end up not believing in themselves enough to take responsibility for their own productive efforts and what they perceive is possible for them to accomplish, as seems to have happened here and led to the present epidemic of post-Soviet self-defeatism. The subjects of bureaucracy rear into the world with an unconscious need to seek permission from authority figures (real or imagined) before they can take novel action or follow their own impulses. In their perception, if they cannot do things the commonly practiced ways, they should not attempt to do them at all. Worse still, they will pressure others to also follow the same difficult or inefficient paths because it makes them feel like their hardships are justified.

Imagine the personal embarrassment of having to admit that there has been a better way to do things all along. Imagine perceiving that other people have an unfair advantage over you because they figured that fact out before you did because they did not need to seek permission or do things the "right" way and trusted their own ability to choose instead. Forced adherence to tradition and other forms of cultural elitism are forms of bureaucratic thinking. Any time you catch yourself using "that's the way we've always done it" as justification for anything, you too are thinking like a bureaucrat.

People will continue to fight for their culturally accepted procedures even in the face of mountains of evidence that there are better ways to achieve the results they want. When I offered to volunteer my time and expertise to help teach English to the children of my village, I was ignored for years. No matter how many times I tried to convince the adults involved in the school administration (or even just the children's parents) that I could be a big help in their development of English conversational fluency, my offer was never considered because my methods did not align with the bureaucratic education model of the lone village schoolhouse. It did not matter how many compelling arguments I made about being the only native English speaker around and having taught and tutored English all over the world.

It was only after I had found community institutions in town that eagerly wanted the entrepreneurial approach to English education I was offering that my village neighbors began to receive the social cues that gave them permission to accept the objectively superior methods I had been offering all along — only by then, I was too busy with the other people demanding my services to be able to offer as much time to them as they needed. What might have been accomplished for the children of my village and the surrounding areas had even a single person had the entrepreneurial vision to recognize the long-term value and consequences of the rare opportunity my knowledge and skills represented? How many unnecessary hardships and obstacles will the exclusively Armenian-speaking children here face throughout life now simply because their bureaucratically minded parents and community leaders had stopped looking for better ways to achieve their goals and better goals to seek? How many opportunities will they miss out on because they will never even have the perspective to assess what could have been had they developed the skill of comfortable communication in English?

It seems absurd, but it's the same type of mindset people apply to their own knowledge and skill development. It's the same mentality they rely on to avoid ever attempting to start making money through their own means, no matter their objective qualifications. "Oh, I can't start a business. I don't have any training for that. I don't have a license. I don't have a storefront and a fancy logo. I didn't go to business school." These poor souls have been conditioned to believe that a business doesn't count unless it has achieved a certain arbitrary level of polish in its presentation, turns over a certain arbitrary amount of product, employs a certain arbitrary number of employees, maintains a storefront of a certain arbitrarily large amount of physical area, or generates a certain arbitrary amount of revenue. In reality, once you devise a way to generate profit through the creation or exchange of valuable goods or services, you *are* an entrepreneur.

An entrepreneurial approach to improving our goal-seeking strategies even applies to the everyday tasks we are certain we have already mastered. Our usual thinking goes that if we have made something part of our daily lives for years, how many more unconsidered aspects to it can really be left to uncover? How many ways can we really still optimize and improve it, especially if everyone around us does it the same way we do? We may think there are none, but it's usually people who are willing to ask these absurd questions and think deeply about the potential answers who end up innovating new tools or strategies that ultimately change the way we live and form our regular habits.

When the first winter hit after I moved into the village, my old house was hardly prepared for it. Since there is no gas connection in the village, everyone relies primarily on wood-burning furnaces to keep warm until spring. They dedicate an awful lot of time in the months building up to winter chopping firewood with simple hand axes. While it's a great upper-body workout (if that's the output you're looking for), it's also incredibly time- and labor-intensive. Yet, lacking any other significant source of heat, they have little other choice about having to provide this significant physical input every year before the cold hits.

Being the supremely lazy being that I am, I quickly decided that I did not want to put this much effort merely into splitting truckloads of wood when there were so many more lucrative and productive things I knew I should be doing with my time. So, I did what I always do when I attempt something new for the first time: I researched what, out of all the available options, would be the optimally efficient tools and strategies for splitting firewood. Within several minutes of searching, I learned some things about splitting firewood that none of my neighbors, who had been splitting firewood their whole lives, seemed to know.

As it turns out, an ax is *not* the ideal tool for splitting large pieces of wood. A typical ax is not heavy enough, and the angle of its blade is too narrow to effectively push the two halves of the wood apart with its downward force. What such an ax is best for is chopping down trees from the side with swift, lightweight repetitive swings or splitting smaller pieces of wood that do not require much downward force. What I actually needed was a different tool called a maul—the bigger and heavier two-handed fearsome lovechild of an ax and a sledgehammer. The head of a maul weighs many times more than the head of a typical ax, and its edge is angled wider. As a result, it pushes the wood apart as it penetrates with much greater downward force. Using a maul instead of an ax would clearly save me countless hours of needlessly repetitive chopping every year.

But to my dismay, I could not locate such an apparently superior tool anywhere in Armenia, even at the megastores in the capital city Yerevan. So, I had to import one at great expense, but the expense was worth it for the time and effort it has saved me every winter since. Even my neighbors were impressed with how many fewer strikes with the heavy maul it took to split even big, thick tree trunks and logs compared to what they had just accepted was part of the necessary struggle of heating their homes. It wasn't long before they began asking me how much I spent on my maul and how they could get one too. If only the maul manufacturers of the world could realize the huge gap in the marketplace that apparently exists among people who heat their homes with wood but still struggle with subpar axes to do it every year.

How did I, a complete newcomer to village life and firewood splitting, manage to improve upon the efforts of people with decades more experience and far more skill and strength than my own? I approached the task like an entrepreneur, with the same mindset I apply to every new business project I experiment with or hobby I want to pursue. I did not bureaucratically assume that the rules I had been shown must be followed under all circumstances and couldn't possibly be improved. I tried, instead, to determine what the most efficient way to accomplish the task would be according to all available information sources and with the resources I knew I could rely on. I even try to imagine, as often as I can, what solution I would come up with to a problem if I had no information available at all, which is often the case with unconventional issues for which there are not countless handy DIY guides and tutorials available online.

How do you think my neighbors (and presumably the entire population of all of Armenia's gasless villages) learned that the best way to split firewood was with axes instead of mauls? Likely the same way they learn almost everything they know: Cultural osmosis. They are born into a local culture where everyone uses axes, so they copy what they see. Their fathers probably show them as young men how to use an ax, and they continue their father's technique until they die, passing it on to their own sons because it clearly works well enough to (eventually) get the job done. As I had no culture of firewood splitting to be indoctrinated from, I had no ready answer to this new question I was suddenly obliged to answer. And since I have the temperament of a man who quickly grows weary of strenuous repetitive labor, I am highly incentivized to figure out a solution that does not require me to submit myself to it for longer than I can bear.

Simple opportunities like this for systemic entrepreneurial improvement are everywhere once we learn how to look for them. Life does not have to be defined by the constant re-solving of familiar problems. We can, with enough wisdom about the lifestyle patterns we fall into, set up systems that minimize the active input required to make it through each day and arrive at the next. That's how we create enough free space to set our sights upon the bigger picture of where we might go next, including how we can justify investing into long-term knowledge, skill, and tool development that might take many years to result in profit.

If one begins with an outcome as their goal, their mindset changes to optimizing the processes that will lead to that outcome according to their priorities. Priorities might include quick speed to completion, low monetary expenses, a high degree of quality or proficiency, flexibility in scheduling, or any of dozens of other factors that could affect how to go about accomplishing a task. But if a person dedicates themselves to a *process* with no consideration of what the *outcome* could be or other strategies that exist (even strategies yet undiscovered by anyone), they will prematurely limit what they can do and how they can do it.

Note that this analysis does *not* apply when choosing to engage in some laborious process because we enjoy or derive some other benefit from the effort of the process. Maybe it's cathartic to spend our Saturdays fixing up old cars. In measuring solely the output of repaired cars produced by our efforts, it might be far more equitable to just hire a professional to do the work for us. But what that analysis leaves out is that there is another form of output being produced at the same time as repaired cars: Our enjoyment of working on cars. It's a form of subjective entertainment or relaxation for some people, and only we can decide the relative worth of that form of output according to our values. There may be other intangible products too, like the improvement of our skill and knowledge related to car repair. If we do the work with a friend or family member we care about, it's a social bonding experience too. Everything we willingly choose to do is because we perceive there to be benefits (things we value) worthy of the perceived costs (things we disvalue). Therefore, our strategies for achieving our goals, if they are based in accurate paradigms of reality and we execute them perfectly, are always equitable.

When you find yourself in the position of repeatedly dreading having to complete a certain type of task that seems crucial to the value you want to produce, it is only sensible that you should make it a priority to consider all the ways you can ease or remove this burden from your process. Perhaps there is an unconsidered piece of technology that would obviate what you struggle most with, such as was the case with me realizing that I could chop my firewood at a fraction of the time and effort by switching from the common tool (an ax) to an uncommon but better-optimized one (a maul). Perhaps there is a slightly different but significantly better way to use the tools you already have. And if it turns out to be as simple as hiring someone else who will happily do it for a fee so that you can focus your efforts where you are better equipped to produce greater value, so much the better.

Laziness combined with curiosity is what motivates us to keep looking for better ways to accomplish familiar processes and their outcomes. After I purchased some basic wifi-enabled security cameras to monitor the area around my house, one of my older neighbors, Hovhannes, became positively enamored with the technology. This was a man who, despite having several grandchildren, could barely work a smartphone or use the internet. Yet, against all odds, he remained curious about new things he did not understand if he saw the potential for them to improve the quality of his life. Though I had purchased the cameras for the purpose of ensuring the security of my property, he arrived at the possibility of a different use for them all on his own: He wanted to use a camera like mine to monitor his pigs at night from his home.

A nightly requirement of Hovhannes' lifestyle of raising pigs for meat was physically walking from his house every night to his barn outside where they lived and checking on their well-being. Out of context, this sounds like only a minor inconvenience, one that the average Armenian farmer hardly even notices or bothers complaining about compared to the other far more strenuous work they perform most days. But over the course of a lifetime, this nightly chore comes to constitute a significant burden that interrupts recreation and family time. It requires planning around, as one must know in advance when they will be available at home to perform the task. The small inconvenience in the warmer months also becomes much more significant in winter when the weather is less accomodating, and that short walk to the barn might now require Hovhannes to contend with freezing winds and snow. It's the kind of thing I, personally, can't fathom putting up with for very long if there is any other conceivable way of accomplishing the same outcome.

After I helped Hovhannes purchase, install in his barn, and learn to use his own inexpensive security camera, the task that had defined the structure of his nights for years was suddenly and permanently resolved in a far less costly way than what he had been investing into the process previously. Thanks to the use of the superior tools brought to him by modern technology, he wasn't just performing the same process in a more optimized manner (e.g., walking faster to his barn in greater comfort to check on his pigs). He innovated an entirely different method of producing the outcome the task was intended for (i.e., ensuring that they were all present in the barn and safe). Now, all he had to do was check an app on his phone from the comfort of his couch, at any time of day or night, to get access to a live feed of what was going on in his pig barn. He was elated by this positive change in his life, especially as he was entering the sunset years of his life and appreciated the opportunity to spend more of his time with his family and doing the things he enjoyed most. What other repetitive processes of this labor-intensive life might he find ways to obviate if he was more practiced in entrepreneurial thinking and more aware of the full breadth of modern technology available to help him accomplish the goals he set for himself?

Bear in mind that the problem with bureaucratic mentality is not that it enforces rules per se, but that it does so arbitrarily. Rules are not the problem. The creation and implementation of rules are part of the strategy for how we organize our behavior and society as a whole to accomplish our goals. But bureaucracy does not arrive at its rules this way. It sustains itself for the sake of sustaining itself for as long as it can, regardless of the effects its enforcing actions have. Entrepreneurial actors, on the other hand, follow those rules that will best enable them to accomplish their goals. They can only derive these rules through real observation and experimentation, and they must be willing to abandon them when they fail to work or a superior option becomes apparent. When rules are derived arbitrarily and do not actually aid the followers of them in the pursuit of their goals, they are cancers upon them.

CHAPTER 11

ENTREPRENEURIAL PERSECUTION— SOCIAL HINDRANCE OF THE PRODUCTIVE AND AMBITIOUS

MANY MODERN ARMENIANS openly characterize their culture as depressed, victimized, and self-defeating. In fact, I have never been to a country with so many generally intelligent and skilled people who are so deathly reluctant to apply their intelligence and skill in ambitious and innovative ways. **There is some sort of pathological fear of stepping off the beaten and culturally condoned path in both the setting of goals and the devising of strategies to achieve them—a fear that we might call Post-Soviet Self-Defeatism Syndrome.** Only upon receiving unspoken permission from a perceived authority figure does any new idea come to be seen as realistic and worthwhile in Armenia.

There is even lingering nostalgia among the older generations who, on some level, wish they could return to feeling like they are part of a larger collective that will "solve" the essential problems of living for them. If nothing else, the social paradigm of the Soviet Union provided a psychological sense of an in-group to belong to and the illusion of security in life.

But the entrepreneurial mentality relies on no such illusions. In fact, it abhors them because they taint its accurate perception of reality. To the entrepreneur, if life is not working out the way they want it to, it is squarely up to them to innovate ways to improve it. If their role in society is not what they want it to be, they must acquire the knowledge, skills, and tools associated with the role they desire. Furthermore, they must present themselves as the person they wish others to see them as so that they accept this aspect of their identity. There is no bureaucratic mandate to enforce any of this.

Perhaps that is the primary reason why people like my neighbors here won't see what should be obvious opportunities to solve problems and offer such solutions on the market for a profit. They haven't been told by anyone in a higher position of authority what their specialties should be. Even if they already have the requisite knowledge, they don't have the default social identity associations they assume are necessary. The idea of figuring things out on their own through trial and error or self-study just seems way too fraught with risk and investment that carries little promise of ever working out to be worthwhile.

Quite simply, post-Soviet Armenians, as a rule, haven't learned how to believe in themselves and push themselves to become and achieve more according to the natural laws of entrepreneurial interaction. By the necessity of their cultural and economic environment, their focus and contentedness must remain on subsistence-level necessities like rooves over their heads, bread on their plates, and happy families to share these essentials with. It's quaint, and it's admirable to remember what, in our increasingly busy and complex lives, is most important to our happiness.

Yet, there are also severely damaging drawbacks to being conditioned throughout life to be content with very little and accepting yourself as the kind of person who will *always* have very little. Perhaps you will never even try to look for opportunities to produce and acquire more than the baseline standard you've accepted. Such opportunities might remain totally invisible to you even when someone points them out, right in front of your face, and tells you how to take advantage of them. Your mind is not accustomed to processing their existence at all, so even if you can cognize that they exist and how they work, you will not give yourself emotional permission to act on them.

Many Armenians have prescriptively categorized themselves as low-income people. In their minds, that's just the way their lives will go, as though they were born into some sort of medieval caste system in which there is no possibility of upward mobility. So, such people learn to be content with whatever meager amount of opportunity they perceive that life is willing to offer them. This is certainly a virtue on their part, to an extent—to learn to be grateful for whatever they have—but it is built upon a demonstrably untrue premise. Reality is not limited to whatever is most visible to us in the moment of observation.

"Great" communist leaders have always propagandized to their subjects that "the Western way of life" is evil because it capitalizes on the worst of human traits like selfishness and greed at the expense of one's neighbors and society. The fundamental part of human nature that wants more than what it has been given (and, worse, decides independently what actions to take to acquire it) is not the devil on our shoulders that it has been made out to be by those whose place in the collectivized social hierarchy depends upon suppressing it. Strong wants and ambitions, and even the temporary feelings of discontentment that accompany them, are good because they incentivize us to break out of our quasi-comfortable patterns and try new things in the pursuit of higher goals. Conscious discontentment is the true mother of innovation.

The inverse personality pathology—that of the person who can never be content, no matter what they accomplish or accumulate—is no picnic either and not a goal to strive for. In some ways, it is a symptom of the common way of life in the US—or what we might call American Overconfidence Syndrome. Unshakeable faith in one's abilities, even without evidence, is a problem because the world offers us more opportunities and experiences than we can ever pursue in a lifetime. The rate at which they increase is greater even than the rate at which we can become aware of them. So, to be meaningful and rewarding, ambitions must be set at gently increasing intermediary levels we can actually climb to and receive an appropriate level of positive feedback for reaching. And how do we find out what those are in our specific circumstances of knowledge, skills, resources, values, and social settings? Only by trying and, of course, being willing to fail.

As it seems to be with all areas of existence that require skill, ambition, and effort, there is a class of people who seek to knock down others who start to act in entrepreneurial ways not sanctioned by local culture and authority. This, too, is a manifestation of unconscious bureaucratic mentalities. Such meddlers feel impelled to enforce the same rules that were enforced upon them. Even objective evidence that there are alternative methods that may be superior to how they do things is a threat to their sense of identity. The way one arbitrary person happens to have done something must be the only valid way for all people to ever do it. Whatever currently exists must continue to always be what exists. It is a profoundly anti-entrepreneurial way of seeing the world, as an entrepreneur is always on the lookout for innovation and improvement, no matter what must be lost or changed along the way.

In the Soviet Union, many people depended upon black market entrepreneurs to get them the goods they could not adequately acquire through sanctioned State means. Still, they were propagandized to hate and fear individuals who participated in speculation about the value of goods and find advantageous ways to exchange them for personal profit. In modern Armenia, the intelligentsia frequently still think that "entrepreneurship" is not a proper profession for young Armenians to enter. No matter what value they produce or how monetarily successful they are, it does not carry the clout and respect of a high-class job title. Such people are frequently derided and derogated. They are seen as supporting themselves by using their cleverness to spot mischievous opportunities to take advantage of people in need.

Armenians, actually, used to have positive global reputations as talented merchants and entrepreneurs living as minorities within different empires for many centuries. However, the oppressive Soviet experience seems to have stamped out their collective memory of this, including the fact that Armenia was an important trading nexus on the Silk Road.

There are, additionally, well-meaning people from more economically developed parts of the world who, out of a misguided desire to help, do a great deal to gatekeep entrepreneurship from the very people who need it most. They set or support social policies that make it difficult or impossible for the people on the lowest end of the economic spectrum or who lack formal training or accreditation from willfully taking on the risks inherent to making or selling products and services on their own terms. They interrupt the natural process of learning through trial and error how to manage one's own life.

The way such people speak about the poor or underprivileged is akin to the way I would speak about a child or a pet— an unfortunate creature that can only continue to exist under the wing of a benefactor who is willing to sacrifice for the cause of keeping them alive, willing to make choices on their behalf because they lack the intellectual or emotional capacity to make those choices for themselves. While this line of thinking makes sense and is in accordance with the biological nature of things when applied to a toddler or a dog, it's quite a bit more demeaning when applied to an adult human attempting to make choices for themselves.

Even if it *were* true that the majority of the human population of Earth were equivalent to children who cannot manage their own lives without the direct intervention of a benevolent overseer, it seems obvious that the goal should be to prepare such "children" for the trials of growing and learning to take care of themselves. The goal should be to obviate the assumed present need for caretaking, not to perpetuate it indefinitely.

To deny individuals of any status the opportunity to make their own choices and to bear their consequences is to neuter their highest human potential, to clip their wings before they ever even use them. When we treat the majority of the human race like infants incapable of attaining self-reliance, they form cultures and act in accordance with that imposed premise. There is no other sustainable economic path for the individual, the family, the village, the city, the country, or the planet but entrepreneurial self-reliance. All other attempts are, at best, temporary measures at staving off crisis. At worst, they extend and exacerbate the very problems they are meant to resolve.

Sure, this all sounds good in theory or in an ideal world. But to many, it doesn't seem to reflect the way the world actually works. Is it really realistic to expect people who have lived their whole lives not knowing how to systemize their wealth production efforts to start acting entrepreneurially? What about those who have been stuck in conventional career paths all their lives? If everyone were capable of being entrepreneurs, wouldn't they already be on this path and making it work for themselves in their own particular ways? Such questions ignore the cultural influence that still lingers in almost every part of the world, pushing people away from entrepreneurial ideals. The invisible influence is greatly compounded by draconian bureaucratic social policies that actively penalize entrepreneurial efforts, if they don't ban them outright as the Soviet Union did.

Under Soviet rule, you might have had to fear the possibility of being sent to a gulag for forced labor if you were daring enough to start your own business and try your hand at meeting the demands of consumers. But in a modern first-world nation, you might instead only have to pay more money than you've managed to save in order to register your business, followed by heavy monthly fees to keep it operating legally. Or maybe, after you've managed to start turning a meager profit on a shoestring budget, your profits will be taxed heavily by your government claiming to be acting in your best interest. Maybe there are endless amounts of licenses and inspections you will have to put up with. Maybe the State, ostensibly to protect you from yourself and to help the country, will require you to put tens of thousands of dollars you don't have into your fledgling limited liability corporation upfront. Even if the monetary cost associated with these requirements doesn't break your bank account, the sheer inconvenience of having to jump through all these hoops for pencil-pushing bureaucrats with limited operating hours and who might take months to process your paperwork might be all the disincentive you need to prevent getting started as an entrepreneur.

Supporters of these disincentivizing policies will claim that they perform a valuable role by gatekeeping entrepreneurship from people who are not strong or skilled enough to find success with it. "Starting a business is *supposed* to be hard," they will say. Where did these counter-progress and anti-human ideas originate in our culture? Shouldn't our goal be to make it as easy as possible for people to become self-reliant and contribute value to the economy in whatever ways they are able? By cutting them off from the opportunity to do so, we condemn them to always depend on handouts or employment under others who are stronger than them merely to get by.

These kinds of convoluted associations and policies about entrepreneurship make it more difficult for ordinary people to consider themselves entrepreneurs. **They first need to accept that there is no official way to become a bona fide entrepreneur, and holding on to popular ideas about what being one is supposed to look like only keeps ready and qualified people from trying.** Does being an entrepreneur require running a big business with lots of employees? Why would it, exactly? In what way would changing the size of a business or the number of people directly employed guarantee any fundamental change to the value you would be producing for yourself or others or the nature of the means by which you produce it? Every product or service that enters the market, just by virtue of existing and being desired by consumers, requires or creates opportunities for others to also apply the value of their knowledge, skills, and tools in some productive manner.

If your business requires you to ship physical products to far-off customers, it means you either need to employ someone directly to perform that function within your business model, or you need to hire someone who offers a shipping service independently of you for every sale you make. You will choose whichever option you perceive to be more equitable for the situation you are in. But the structure of the business model pertaining to shipping the goods you sell does not have any effect on the demand that is being created and, with it, the opportunity for someone to get paid by meeting that demand. Merely by selling shippable goods, you are already creating jobs for couriers, delivery boys, oil companies and their employees, auto mechanics, box and packing peanut manufacturers, and everyone else who plays an active role in ensuring that your packages get where they belong. Whether they are part of your organization and payroll or you pay another organization separately for their service makes no difference. Whether in-house or outsourced, the value being produced remains the same.

Anti-entrepreneurial attitudes also tend to come from people who are incentivized to maintain the status quo because that is where they have found their wealth and comfort. Licensed taxi drivers fight for legislation to ban private ridesharing apps because they see it as unfair that they have had to suffer and pay so much to the State for the exclusive privilege of charging people money to drive them from point A to point B. People who have followed the rules all their lives are often threatened by those who found a better way to get things done on their own terms. Indeed, I have even been witness to violent altercations in some countries where rioting groups of licensed taxi drivers have physically attacked private drivers picking up or dropping off their paying clients. Who do you think the real menace to society here is?

When all cultural and legal impositions are ignored, entrepreneurship comes naturally to us in its most primitive form. Children are drawn by their exploratory impulses toward minor risk-taking behaviors for the perception of their possible rewards. Games without consequences for error frequently also feature no reward for success, so we quickly grow bored of such low-stake adventures. And while many children are inclined to pursue risk too brazenly and end up suffering the consequences, a mature adult learns in time through these experiences where their own tolerable level of risk lies.

What happens to children when they are cut off from realizing the consequences of their mistakes, or their ability to make mistakes at all is disabled? They never learn the qualities that make it possible to build to a scaled-up level of responsibility and control over the outcomes of their efforts. They rarely become self-reliant adults.

Entrepreneurship is never solely a young person's game, however. Being older and having accumulated known quantities of knowledge, skills, material goods, and interests, in many respects, puts adult entrepreneurs in a superior position compared to young people who might still have to experiment with many paths in business over the course of many years before finding foundations to build their value production upon. Under the conditions granted by greater life experience, it's easier to deduce what the best way to start is because there are many more known assets to work *with* and known liabilities to work *around*. **Entrepreneurship is an entire approach to life that adapts to the natural changes of getting older.**

The longer you have lived, all other things being equal, the more you should know about what you can do and like to do. The more you should know about how the world works and what people might be interested in buying from you. The more capital, tools, resources, and connections you should have to make your efforts more viable.

The young entrepreneur, on the other hand, is still in a state of rapid and rampant life discovery and self-discovery. Their only real advantage is perseverance in the struggle and the ability to move past losses just as quickly as they occur, such that they may hardly ever even notice them. In contrast, the older and more established woman or man is more likely to be accustomed to a certain level of comfort and relative success. When they lose, it hurts, and they are more likely to back off from the fight for fear of no longer having what they have built over their life.

Even the concept of retirement in old age, like many other contemporary ideas about work and finances, is a sorely misguided one that, in its present form, does much to harm and inhibit people's abilities to take control of their own lives. Retirement is built into cultures differently, passed on from olden days when one's productivity was limited to their years of peak physical strength. Past a certain age, a man becomes considered feeble and fairly useless to society, so he and his wife rely on their children, extended families, or State assistance to continue to get by until they die. In the best of circumstances in the West, they will have saved and invested wisely during their productive years so that they can float worry-free on the wealth accumulated in decades past until their time runs out. The modern mythology of retirement isn't too far off from religious promises about working hard and sacrificing everything in *this* life so that you will be rewarded with leisure in the *next* one. All you have to do is make it to 65, and then you'll be living easy off your pension and social security. Finally, you'll be free to enjoy the spoils of your life of suffering.

Contrarily, I find that the idea of becoming too old to be productive but still young enough to live is inherently nonsensical. So is the idea of segregating life into such broad swaths of sacrifice and leisure. To live is to produce wealth, and to produce wealth is to reap its rewards at any stage of life. So long as you can think and act in any capacity, you can be productive. You can do something of value for yourself and others, which, as covered, is your greatest form of security in life. So long as you can do anything of value, you will always have a place in society, and there will always be ways for you to acquire the things you cannot easily do for yourself.

It's unavoidable that our bodies and minds will change as we age, in many ways for the worse. But it is also possible that, for the longest time, they will improve in specific and important ways, enabling us to get better and better at our chosen pursuits and find new ways to combine our disparate knowledge, experiences, and skills into emergent complementary avenues. All other things being equal, the older you get, the more you should be capable of doing, and you don't need the permission of society or an employer to keep doing it after 65. After all, one of the wonders of the advanced economic state of our world is that we can, if we prefer to or are forced to by circumstance, specialize so heavily around our strengths that most of our weaknesses get totally obviated. Even real-world quadriplegics who have lost almost total use of their bodies can go on to produce immense value through the contributions of their minds alone.

Even ignoring the fact that taking control of your earning ability while you are young means that you can strategically save and invest for decades, there's no reason you have to give up earning income at any point before you die. All you have to do is be flexible and adaptable enough to transition the manner in which you earn to match your abilities (and various lifestyle factors) as you get older. If you fall into the cultural trap of basing your whole earning ability around the repetition of a limited series of tasks, you risk losing everything as soon as you are not able to perform those tasks at the level you or your employer have grown accustomed to or that the market demands.

THE NATURAL LAWS AND QUALITIES OF ENTREPRENEURIAL INTERACTION

IT'S NOT HARD to understand why there still exists a palpable amount of nostalgia for Soviet times among the older generations in Armenia. Despite the objectively poor ability of Soviet economic planners to provide the necessities of life for its citizenry efficiently or effectively, many people were happy having such choices made on their behalf by a paternalistic State entity. It eliminated the stress of choice—of setting goals for oneself and devising the optimal strategies to achieve them. **And when people spend their whole lives in avoidance of making meaningful choices about the most important determinants of their lives, the ability to do atrophies and dies.**

By all accounts, the transition in the 1990s from a totally planned economy to one much more determined by the choices of all people participating in it was not a smooth one. When the Soviet Union collapsed, the rules of the game changed quickly for those who had been under its wing. Those who were not given a primer on the rules of the new game struggled to adapt to a world where they were suddenly responsible for managing their own wealth production and consumption. Rapid systemic change always stresses existing structures.

Today, the young people living in Yerevan have a better understanding of what entrepreneurship is and how it works than their parents and grandparents before them did. As a result, they have a radically different model of the best way to interact with the world around them. They exist in a transitionary state between generations and cultures. On the one hand, modern young Armenians were raised by a generation that adapted to live under extremely rigid infrastructure, laws, and capacity for choice. But they have also been exposed to the far opposite from abroad as it has seeped into their now much more open culture.

Armenia, in particular, has been eager to invite its descendants who left the country during the last 100 years from the time of the Ottoman Empire genocide starting in 1915 or during

Soviet rule to return and repatriate here, thereby bringing their foreign influence and ideals with them in this new status quo the country is gradually building. Incidentally, it was only because of my Armenian grandmother who fled to California at the start of World War I that I was initially inspired to learn about Armenia, visit here, acquire citizenship through my family descent, and eventually settle down here out of all the eligible places in the world I have visited.

It is in the best interest of everyone living here, no matter which generation they hail from, to learn the rules of how life works when you are in control of your own destiny. No one can produce intentional outcomes in any domain of life, least of all entrepreneurship, without first aligning their actions to the natural principles inherent to that domain. There is nothing in this world that does not function according to natural and identifiable patterns and principles, even if no one knows what they are.

Yet, so many people seem set against thinking about human interactions with the same empirical perspective they apply to other systems in life. Perhaps they cannot easily see how the language that describes economic interactions applies just as much to natural ecosystems as it does to man-made societies. Perhaps some part of us does not want to accept that there are absolute rules that describe what we do when we interact with each other under the framework of this beautiful mechanism we call civilization.

People often seem to analyze the science of economics through the lens of how they feel it *should* work rather than how it demonstrably *does* work. The mind boggles at the idea of this outlook being applied to other empirical fields of study. If your computer were to stop working, it would be quite foolish (and possibly insane) to expect it to start working again merely due to the inconvenience its failure would cause you and your preference against it. But with even a rudimentary understanding of the principles that govern electronics and modern computing, you might stand a good chance of getting it to work the way you want it to again. Embracing life as a functioning entrepreneur in a real economy is much the same.

Because so many people are unaware of the basic, empirical economic principles that govern human interaction, learning them can actually give you a powerful competitive advantage over others. You may quickly become impressed by what you are capable of accomplishing, even with only very simple skills and tools at your disposal, if you acquire knowledge of the mechanics of marketplaces and mutually beneficial exchange. There is no telling how much more success you might find with your existing endeavors (or how many previously impossible endeavors you might take on) once you begin to analyze their inescapable principles.

The first principles of entrepreneurship are unchanging and at play whenever people make choices. And, just as most of the first principles of physics are pretty intuitive and easy to understand for anyone who has interacted with matter and energy, the first principles of economics are also pretty intuitive for anyone who has ever interacted with people. Despite their sometimes esoteric-sounding labels or descriptions, there is no reason to be intimidated by these principles. You only need to learn to see how they apply in a way that matches your experience of the world.

Economics is not exclusively a scholar's subject; it is awareness of the principled and observable rules of how we as individuals come together to pursue our mutual goals and make our lives better in ways we could not do on our own. It is appreciation of the possibilities created by organized human cooperation and respect for the inviolable boundaries of human psychology, physical scarcity, and exchange. The whole of the progress of human society can be described in economic terms that reveal the hidden mechanics behind what so many people still consider to be unexplainable about our world. There *is* an objective sociological reality at play here, and its rules must be obeyed to be commanded.

Principles make a mind adaptable. Working from first principles, you garner the ability to derive the solutions to complex problems on your own. This is because every complex conclusion is just an arrangement of the simplex principles you will already know. It is the opposite of how most people approach multifaceted problems, which is to treat every new one as something unique and totally set apart in its causality from all other problems previously encountered. Reasoning always from the same inescapable premises, every new problem becomes just a slight variation upon territory already explored. Perhaps you already have the relevant knowledge and experience to solve the new problems you encounter. But without a structure of base principles in mind, no one can see the hidden connections between different situations.

Instead of seeing a business or an entire functioning economy as something vast and beyond your ability to understand or influence, look for opportunities to insert yourself and begin intentionally interacting with the flow of human exchange according to the rules you can be certain are in play. They apply just as much to everyday non-monetary exchanges (which constitute the majority of exchanges but are often less obvious) as they do to massive money movements among buyers, sellers, and investors. To understand the natural laws of economics is to understand the substance of society.

In many ways, living in this developing part of the world feels like navigating a genuine frontier market, a bit like going back in time compared to the West. Because there are so many unnecessary inefficiencies, there are also opportunities to improve upon those inefficiencies. There are known solutions to most of these problems, and there is little to lose by experimenting with other ways of doing things instead of just repeating whatever everyone else has done. But what is lacking is the entrepreneurial curiosity necessary to even begin to wonder if there is a better way to do something than the way one repeatedly suffers through. As the entrepreneurial mindset spreads here, it is easy to predict how many of the daily repeated frustrations of people's lives will dwindle until they disappear entirely. Where there are problems, there is opportunity.

CHAPTER 12

SUPPLY AND DEMAND—THE CONFLICT BETWEEN WHAT IS AND WHAT'S WANTED

TO BEST UNDERSTAND any subject, it should be simplified as far as possible to its base defining elements under which all the downstream details can be categorized. **In the science of economics, all the comprehensive and esoteric details can be understood as derivatives of two things and the relationship formed between them: Market supply and market demand.** But why should this be so? How can we know that these are accurate and adequate premises upon which to build our understanding of how the whole of commerce operates, including our place within it?

The answer to that requires backtracking one step further in fundamental human psychology. The basic unit of societal behavior, including the subset that we think of as buying and selling products and services, is individual choice. Everything large scale about society is, in actuality, an arrangement of individuals feeling and thinking (in that order) and then making choices based upon those feelings and thoughts. That much is a given postulate that cannot be ignored. That is the essence of the "demand" part of the relationship.

"Supply" is our perception of the options available to achieve or acquire what we demand through the choices we make. So, in an ironic way, the common phrasing "supply and demand" is actually logistically backward. It *should* go "demand and supply" because the concept of supply has no meaning until there is an individual's demand to make it relevant.

Look beyond the modern economic jargon and dull market analyses. The whole of global civilization and the entire history of human choices can be understood as billions of individual people across the eras doing their best to get what they want from what they have. When one understands that all commerce is just a scaled-up system of countless individuals making choices about how to achieve their demands through the supply they become aware of, one can feel much more confident about the choices they make about how to participate in commerce as an entrepreneur.

In education, the simplification of seemingly different incidental events under one principled umbrella concept is known as integration. Integration is essential to gaining greater leverage with our knowledge over the countless incidentals of reality. That's how every new situation stops seeming like foreign chaos for which we have no recognizable strategy to deal with and, instead, starts seeming like just an unassuming variation upon a familiar pattern we have encountered countless times before. What we typically call a wise person is one who recognizes the principles behind new situations and, therefore, always seems to have something profound and relevant to say about them.

At the intersection of what human beings want and what they are capable of providing, we will find either conflict or collaboration in pursuit of acquiring more of what we value. The goal of commerce is to make collaboration the preferable choice for meeting our demands. **The willful entrepreneur is someone who seeks to create the opportunity for a peaceful way through this potential crux of conflict.** The alternative when someone wants more than what the world readily provides for them is to use their resources to take it through theft and violence.

Fundamental economic rules like supply and demand can be understood quite easily by anyone who has ever bought or sold anything. No, actually. Scratch that. They can easily be understood even in contexts where no money changes hands, ordinary everyday interactions we seldom think of as economic in nature but function according to the same principles. In fact, you can derive nearly everything by observing your own buying habits and preferences and asking yourself why you make the choices you do under different circumstances.

In my village, the cost of a common bale of hay, something every keeper of cattle has in abundance to feed his herd past the growing season, is the equivalent of about $1 USD if purchased during the summer months and about $3 USD if purchased during the winter months. Why the discrepancy? The answer is clear if you know anything about seasonal climate changes, growing cycles, and the eating habits of cattle. From spring to fall, the type of grass that hay is harvested for grows abundantly in the wild, reaching the peak of its growth in late summer or early fall here. The available supply of this natural resource is the highest at that point that it will be throughout the year. Incidentally, the consumer demand for it is also the lowest due to the fact that the cattle who feed on it are able to roam and eat freely from it. There is no reason for a human being to apply their efforts to harvest or refine the hay grass into a commodity. The cows do that work on their own and are capable of tending to their own needs.

At this point in the growing season, the grass can be considered a "free good"—an unprocessed natural resource with a supply that so greatly exceeds its demand that there is no need to even calculate its price. There is no labor or thought that goes into harvesting and preparing it for consumption. There is no reason even for neighbors to compete with each other to ensure that all their animals eat enough of it to survive. In other words, there is no reason for an entrepreneur to manage and ration it for optimal consumption in the local economy.

Under these conditions, economic calculation does not matter because there is functionally no scarcity. Without economic calculation, there can be no price. Price is the result of the scarcity caused by the conflict between low supply and high demand. It's the same reason that we generally don't have to pay for air or sunlight. In most places where humans have created civilizations, air and light are so abundant and accessible that there would be no profit in trying to systemize their production or distribution. There is no conflict for those who want it over how to get it. It's the same with hay grass in the summer here. There is more of it naturally available than all the cows in all the surrounding villages can consume.

However, even free and abundant resources like air and sunlight have their exceptions. There is still a market for oxygen tanks and tanning beds in specific and exceptional economic situations. Furthermore, technology enables us to concentrate the desired qualities of these commodities in smaller, more convenient consumable packages compared to how they exist in their natural states. You don't need an entire atmosphere of air if your goal is to be able to breathe underwater for a time; you only need a compressed gas of oxygen molecules in an appropriate container. You don't need an entire yellow star if your goal is to synthesize vitamin D or darken your skin; you only need a device that emits the appropriate wavelengths of UV light in the location your body will be located for a predetermined time. In an equivalent manner, we are smart and technologically enabled enough to dry, shrink, and compress high-calorie-density foods into small and convenient forms like food bars, canned goods, or beef jerky that could never exist under natural circumstances, despite how abundant edible substances are throughout the natural world.

Intelligent self-interested people can determine when they might need more of something that is naturally freely available before its natural supply becomes unavailable. Fortunately, the Earth's seasons tend to be remarkably predictable. When winter comes around at the end of every year, the economic situation concerning the feeding of animals changes quickly and drastically. The previously abundant source of food disappears from the land. What remains are only the resources intentionally harvested ahead of time by forward-thinking humans who acted when supply was at its predictable peak in the months prior. Every farmer knows to amass more hay than they need at the time they need it least in preparation for the time they will need it most. Cows are, generally speaking, not very good at this because they can neither predict the future nor delay their own gratification by laboring now for a reward that will only come months later.

Do you see the intuitive entrepreneurial mental mechanisms at work here? Even though the villagers who adhere faithfully to this routine year in and year out might not think of themselves as understanding the science of economics, they are naturally taking advantage of a predictable cycle of the change in the supply and demand of hay by converting it from a free natural resource to a scarce processed commodity in the form of bales of dry hay that will inflate in value when winter comes around. They also know that the cycle of its swinging supply and demand will repeat itself with an astounding level of regularity each year, regardless of whatever else changes in the world, in society, or in their personal lives. That's why they don't work harder than necessary to stockpile an infinite amount of hay before the start of winter. They know they will only need enough to get through a few cold unfertile months before the spring sun will rise again and naturally begin the growing season anew. When this happens, the enormous subjective wintertime value of their hay will deflate again to very little.

In fact, any hay leftover and uneaten when spring comes around again might be of so little value to the farmer that it is more of a burden to store than it is worth to keep at all. Hay bales are large and heavy. They take up a lot of space and are difficult to move by hand. Furthermore, they need to be protected from the rain and humidity because moisture will cause them to rot. Wild pests might want to invade the farmer's property and eat or make a nest in their hay. All these are liabilities that must be accounted for if a farmer is to store large supplies of hay, so they have little incentive to do so except exclusively during those few winter months. Why expend the extra labor now when you know it won't pay off after the winter has passed?

Farmers build their lifestyles around such predictable changes in subjective value over the resources, commodities, and goods that are most pertinent to them. So do you. So does everyone, in fact. This is our natural entrepreneurial perspective coming out to organize how we produce and manage what we consider valuable.

Any commonplace items and commodities can become scarce and uniquely valuable as soon as environmental factors shift. It happens all the time, as nothing is ever static for long. Moderately skilled people can quickly become seen as vital market-leading experts when everyone around them knows less than they do and suddenly depends on them to perform tasks none of them can do on their own. Mediocre quality tools become invaluable if they are the only ones available to work with, as they will still certainly be exponentially more efficient than trying to work by hand. Even a lowly spoon, being a poor and minuscule imitation of a proper shovel, can still eventually dig a prison tunnel.

What is the value of a simple consumption good like a common bottle of water? Like all other things, it depends on who you ask and under what economic conditions you ask them. It depends on how thirsty they are. It depends, most importantly, on how scarce they believe their access to water will be for the foreseeable future, just as the value of a bale of hay depends on the foreseeable availability of natural grasses, as illustrated earlier.

For most of human history, reliable access to water has defined the infrastructure of our societies. The reasons why are pretty obvious. More than any other single resource, we depend on water. There is nothing else we have discovered or invented that can ever act as a functional substitute for it. Food, though marginally less important than water for survival, comes in an incredible variety of forms, and there is no single food that we are dependent on to avoid starvation, especially in the modern age where we can acquire with minimal difficulty staples and exotic foodstuffs from all around the world.

We do rely on air in a similar way to how we rely on water as an irreplaceable resource, but, as mentioned, breathable air is so abundant and freely available almost everywhere on Earth that we hardly ever have to consider access to it as a factor in designing our choices and lifestyles.

We need water not only to biologically survive but also to maintain our comfort and livelihood in countless other ways (including the ability to produce any of the various different foods we also survive on, whether plant- or animal-derived). Take away reliable access to water for any significant length of time and, no matter what else we have going for us, our quality of life quickly crumbles. Take it away for too long, and we quickly die.

Thanks to modern indoor plumbing, however, we usually overlook our supreme dependence on this one-of-a-kind substance. The average cost of tap water in the West is less than a penny a gallon—cheap enough to be disregarded by most people. It is functionally a free good to them. But despite the inexpensive abundance of this vital resource, there are still many situations where the price sharply rises because supply suddenly drops at the same time that demand suddenly rises.

What do you expect to pay for a small bottle of water at a common convenience store? Generally, hundreds of times more per volume than what you'd pay for the same amount of water out of your tap at home. And while the argument could be made that the water in the bottle may be of higher quality than the water that comes out of your tap, what you are primarily paying for is the convenience offered to you through its packaging in a portable, lightweight, resealable plastic bottle in a situation where you do not have easy access to a tap and receptacle to drink from. Hence, most people only buy bottled water in situations where the much cheaper alternative of tap water is not conveniently available.

Now, how much do you suppose you would be willing to pay for that same small bottle of water in a truly inconvenient and desperate situation? Perhaps one where there was no potable water source for many kilometers in any direction? If you were stranded in the desert, dying of dehydration, and believed you had no other options to acquire water? My guess is that you'd pay almost any price for the same water that under other circumstances you'd normally only pay pennies or, at most, dollars for. The physical discomfort of extreme dehydration aside, you'd recognize on some level that all your money and worldly possessions would be pretty worthless to you if you didn't make it out of the desert alive. That ounce of gold you were holding onto, waiting for its value to appreciate so you buy thousands of dollars of fancy stuff with it? You'd gladly exchange it for a single ordinary bottle of water, just so that you could make it back to civilization alive and continue to participate in commerce at all.

Like the bale of hay in the context of different seasons, the important thing to keep in mind here is that the bottle of water itself did not change in quantity or quality; only the environmental factors contributing to its immediate subjective value did. **No one can ever determine the worth of an asset by looking at the asset in isolation.** There is no objectively correct cost for all people under all conditions. They must always take into consideration the person who will be using it, what their intended outcome with it is, and their perception of other options to fulfill the same function.

These evaluations apply just the same to the things they buy as to those they will wish to sell. Those who understand the fluid nature of valuations will be better able to position themselves as buyers in settings where low prices work in their favor because they are not desperate and out of options. They want the opposite that sellers do: Economic situations where the price of what they are offering is as high as the market will allow because the people they are selling to are in positions where they really need something and don't currently have any other way of getting it. These natural variations in marketplace evaluation incentivize buyers and sellers to move their effort, attention, and capital where it is most equitable, which is what leads to market equilibrium. Buyers are rewarded with more abundant options and cheaper prices by planning ahead when times are good. Sellers are rewarded with higher profit margins and quicker sales by going out of their way to offer things that are underrepresented and inordinately needed in specific contexts.

Even a basic understanding of these economic mechanics makes it clear why merely trying to go into business the same way everyone around you already has is setting yourself up for limited success or absolute failure. Things do not necessarily have to cost what you are used to seeing them cost. Products and services do not have to take the forms or exist under the conditions you are used to experiencing. If there is a more advantageous way to make or offer them, any entrepreneur is free to find and implement it for personal gain. That is how innovation works and why progress for all people involved in a market populated by entrepreneurs is inevitable.

CHAPTER 13

FUNGIBILITY AND SCARCITY— WHEN ONE THING IS OR IS NOT LIKE ANOTHER

THE WAYS WE categorize the value of the products of our efforts determine how we organize those efforts. The ways we conceive of the utility of any given thing we must labor or spend money to acquire determine how we spend our labor or our money. We all conceive of the things we own and use in terms of what they do for us and what we must do to acquire them. If we can acquire a functionally similar kind of utility that offers greater benefits (according to what we subjectively want) and requires fewer costs from us (according to how we value what we must give up to get it), we will always choose the cheaper (i.e., less costly) option.

While no two objects or experiences are truly identical, they are often similar enough that we conceive of them as belonging to the same categories. When is one thing like another? When can one object or action be functionally interchanged with another with no noteworthy difference? And when does this stop being true?

The way we group activities or things together in our minds is always changing and often for arbitrary reasons. It is easy now to mass-produce the requirements of modern life out of functionally identical raw materials. Modern machine processing allows us to do this to degrees of specification so fine that the difference between one factory-produced screw or sheet of aluminum and another cannot even be detected by the unaided human eye. The rise of identical interchangeable parts was a major part of what made the Industrial Revolution possible because it streamlined and simplified the production process, optimizing its efficiency. When parts are fungible, we only have to solve one problem many times, not many problems one time each.

Without modern fungibility, simple problems would become complex, inequitable nightmares to solve because every solution would have to be arrived at independently from the start. Imagine having to replace your whole car every time it started to break down. Or imagine having to have replacements parts made from scratch to fit the exact size, shape, and composition requirements of your unique engine instead of being able to reliably swap any component out for one from the same model. Imagine if no one could agree on what electrical outlets were supposed to look like and how many volts our electronic devices should run on. It would be impossible for manufacturers to offer products that they could expect the general public to be able to use under general conditions. Currently, that's only a problem when we bring their devices from one country to another that might use a different outlet design as its standard or when Americans accidentally fry their 110-volt electronics by forgetting to bring a voltage converter to Europe, which uses 220-volt electricity as the standard.

On the other hand, there are things we produce specifically to be irreplaceable, which is likely a relatively recent development in human history. It's a result of the state the modern marketplace has evolved to. Almost every tool or product we have relied on for most of history has been something that we could find or make anew to roughly the same degree of effectiveness on the fly. All production was limited to the tribe- or village-wide scale, and all resources came from the immediate environment. Everyone knew what resources were available, and everyone had roughly the same access to them.

The first instances of irreplaceability probably came from trading with other tribes or villages that had access to different resources or production techniques that enabled them to create products not readily available at home. If we lost or needed more of them for any reason, we couldn't just make more with the local resources or knowledge we had reliable access to. We now had to rely on outside suppliers, and that meant being subject to the scarcity of our limited ability to meet with them and arrange equitable exchanges for the specific items we wanted, assuming they even had a surplus of them beyond their own needs to exchange at all. The first complex supply chains were almost certainly born this way, and with them came the first logistically complex economic calculations to solve.

Today, we have reached a point of economic development such that rareness or even true uniqueness is a selling point unto itself. **Knowing that a limited number of something was made in the past or ever will be made in the future gives us extra incentive to acquire it.** It instigates the "fear of missing out" in us. If we know that there is an unending production run of any given product, virtually guaranteeing that it will be available at any future date that we should decide we want it, we have no sense of urgency behind the drive to purchase it now, when we know for sure that it is available. But if only a limited amount of something will ever be made, the economic calculation and our buying habits change completely. There is now a limited pool from which the supply can only be subtracted. And because the price we are willing to pay for something is partially determined by our perception of the available buying options for any given function we are seeking to fulfill, we might suddenly be willing to pay significantly more for it, even if the objective utility of it has not changed.

Why do we value gold and diamonds so highly? Part of the calculation is their natural beauty and industrial application. But a much bigger factor on the price is our perception of their natural scarcity. There is only so much gold that exists in the earth's crust, and it requires increasingly more advanced surveying and mining techniques to find it and get it out in a useful commodity form. The same is true of diamonds, which are primarily valued in the market as symbols of wealth for the scarcity of their purity and cut. And in the case of diamonds, much of that perception of scarcity is actually an illusion carried out by the companies that own most of the supply. They know that consumers will pay much more for their fancy stones so long as they maintain their narrative value as rare signifiers of luxury.

Collectible items are those that have features that make them difficult or impossible to replicate. Household items that come from a certain historical era, for example, will contain certain qualities that are signature to the time they were made and the functions they were intended for. Over time, their design features become obsolete or go out of style. Who needs a rotary landline telephone in the age of cellular smartphones?

Of course, today, we still maintain the technology to produce rotary landline phones in abundance and to a far higher degree of quality than the ones that were popular in 1950s America. If a manufacturer were so inclined, they could easily find creative ways to implement all the features of a modern smartphone into that retro bulky rotary phone design. But there's a very important reason that almost no one produces rotary phones anymore except as homages to the old-fashioned design: There isn't a strong market demand for them anymore. It's simply not equitable for major phone producers to try to sell rotary phones when the vast majority of modern consumers prefer modern designs for their objective practical advantages and trendier aesthetics.

Nowadays, smartphones represent the peak of objective utility and have near-universal demand. Yet, it is easy to predict that they will be all but forgotten in some decades' time due to the demand for the utility they provide shifting over to some yet-to-be-invented technology that performs the same functions better or obviates their need altogether.

Even though we are still technologically capable of producing outdated products like rotary telephones that are identical in form and function to ones from the vintage era, there is still one quality those old phones have that it would be impossible for any modern manufacturer to replicate: Their history. The scarcity of antique collectibles does not usually derive from the fact that we lack the capacity to make things like them anymore but from the fact that modern reproductions cannot share the same authentic history. That is a form of scarcity that cannot ever be challenged because none of us can change the flow of time or create more of it. The only exception to this would be if a previously undiscovered supply of a scarce collector's item were suddenly discovered in someone's attic and sold off, flooding the availability on the market and temporarily driving the price down. But no new identical items with the same history can ever be produced, so, in the long run, the supply can only go down. And without collectors to value, keep, and maintain these scarce items over the course of many years, there probably wouldn't be any left at all because they would be disposed of as soon as they ceased to be used for their original consumer functions.

Consider what your options would be if you decided to invest some of your wealth into gold coins. Gold itself is fungible. One ounce of gold in a vacuum should be functionally identical to and carry the same monetary value as any other ounce of gold. But actual gold comes in a variety of forms, including coins, bars, ingots, ores, anodes, and jewelry. Each of these forms will carry different market values based on many factors, such as the amount of craftsmanship required to produce them, which is referred to as their premium over the spot price of the metal itself.

Now, imagine you are a manufacturer of gold coins. What measures might you take to maximize the market value of a particular coin you want to produce above its material value as gold? Knowing the mentality of people who collect gold coins as something precious and scarce, you would realize that it was in your best interest to limit the production of your coins to predetermined numbers and advertise this fact to your buyers. Knowing that only 1,000 of a specific coin in a series you produce will ever be available forces the market of potential buyers to compete among itself so that only those willing to pay the highest prices will be able to buy it.

This works out well for the coin collectors who purchase it, too, as they are speculating that the resale value of the limited design will go up over time more than a generic coin of which millions have been produced and continue to be released into circulation in accordance with ongoing demand. The artificially implemented scarcity makes it more attractive to investors. It gives them a reason to favor it over some other generic form of gold, where the value would be practically interchangeable.

The same principle applies no matter what material commodities you might be using to produce something of greater and more specific value. Every entrepreneur who works with tangible materials (even those who work primarily with intangible information-based assets) is tasked with determining how to add scarce and non-fungible value to their base material value as commodities. The author crafts an intangible template for arranging ink and paper in such a specific way that its value is completely different than other arrangements of ink and paper crafted by other authors. The cheesemaker implements a process for turning the common and mostly interchangeable value of milk into specific varieties of cheeses that will satisfy different consumers to different degrees and that cannot easily be substituted for one another. The carpenter turns wood into specific forms as furniture and other crafts. The painter uncommonly arranges common paints on a common canvas. The musician creates a special template for sounds that can be reproduced across ordinary vinyl records, cassette tapes, compact discs, and the ones and zeros of computer hard drives everywhere.

Merely understanding how the perception of scarcity affects buyer evaluation in the marketplace can have a profound effect on how much money you can expect from what you offer. Let's say you own ten of a finite product, something for which you know there is an artificially low supply cap of only a few hundred in total circulation. It could be a signed first edition of a famous book, a limited edition designer purse, an authentic Stradivarius violin, a vintage video game console in working condition, or one of the first action figures of a character from a fantasy space opera still in its original packaging. What are the advantages of offering all ten of them at once for sale? What are the advantages of only offering one at a time and not making the next one available until the first is sold?

If a buyer who has been looking for your rare item but has been unable to find it suddenly learns you have only a single one for sale, they might be inclined to purchase it as quickly as possible at whatever (reasonably) high price you ask for it.

However, if instead, they learn that you have ten for sale, they probably won't feel the same sense of urgency and might even feel they can get it from you for less than you initially ask. They won't worry as much about other buyers quickly snapping up all ten before they have a chance to make up their mind or nego- tiate the price they want. They may even assume that you have several more in reserve that will still be available after these ten have sold. The price and speed of the sale will be influenced by the perception of scarcity.

Of course, there are also advantages to offering all ten at once. If a buyer is looking to buy more than one, then having more than one available upfront gives them that opportunity. It may even be something that is only worth buying to them if they can get the exact number that they need. Having just one might be useless to them until they can get nine more. This is common in things like building materials. It's not going to do you much good to buy only enough paint to cover half or even 90% of the room you want to paint, so you probably wouldn't just buy as much of that rare color as was available if it was still less than the amount you needed. You would be more inclined to pick a color that you knew you could get enough of.

Under ideal economic conditions, entrepreneurs are free to innovate as many new non-fungible variations upon exist- ing categories of goods and services as they can imagine and willingly bear the risk of bringing to market. These conditions are what lead to unending specificity, specialization, and choice for consumers to acquire whatever form of tangible goods and intangible services they perceive will best suit their tastes and needs compared to all other available options. It's the direct op- posite of a command economy that functions most efficiently by cutting variation down to the absolute bare minimum possible. The choices about what will be best to produce and consume are made *for* the consumers instead of *by* them.

If a producer of value has no incentive to improve and adapt to what will best suit their consumer's needs, introducing new variation to their products just means adding unnecessary complexity and expense to their production model, machinery, and specialized labor. When one central authority is controlling everything, that authority will be incentivized to run its factories in a manner streamlined for singular output. Appropriately, whatever the Soviet State produced for its people, like clothing or food, was usually of very poor quality and had very little variation. Its products were only used because there were rarely any other options available. One lackluster pair of standard Soviet shoes was as good as any other. No matter how poorly they held up to damage from use, how little you might like the style, or how uncomfortable they were, you had no other choice but to wear them unless you wanted to wear no shoes at all.

When foreign-made goods from economies that encouraged entrepreneurship found their way onto the Soviet black market, there was a rush of demand to buy them. Often, Soviet citizens didn't even care what the item being sold was or if they had a personal need for it as consumers. They just knew that, whether it was a nicer pair of shoes or a vinyl record of foreign music, it would be of higher quality and different than what they could normally get in the sanctioned Soviet marketplace. That fact made virtually all foreign-made goods universally valuable because, in addition to the utility of their intended functions, they could be used as scarce commodities to exchange with others who one could speculate would inevitably want them. It was one of the best ways people under such tightly controlled conditions for producing and managing their own wealth could actually accumulate it in a tangible form and exert control over it. Predictably, such behavior was shunned and condemned by propaganda that asserted such people were the enemies of Soviet society for being so brash and selfish as to want to acquire better quality goods or protect their wealth from degradation or confiscation.

It is clear that there are situations where an asset being as generic and fungible as possible will be an advantage and situations where the exact opposite is true: Where it will be better to be as distinct as possible. What matters for the marketplace success of the entrepreneur who produces and seeks to exchange these assets always falls back to what their customers find the most subjective value in, which depends on the utility they seek from it.

CHAPTER 14

SPECULATION—AESTHETICS, VANITY, AND THE ANTICIPATION OF DEMAND

HOW DO WE explain why some products that seem to be functionally and materially similar to others in their market can command significantly higher prices, often on superficial differences like color or brand name alone? Like it or not, vanity plays a part in the utility of every kind of product or service ever bought or sold. We rarely buy things purely for their practical functions without at least subconsciously considering how our sense of social identity is affected by our ownership of them and the values they represent.

A handyman, in a social vacuum, buys the hammer, the drill, and the saw that best perform the functions he needs them to in the line of duty according to objective performance metrics. But here, when shopping in the real world full of classes, people, and competing categories of ideals, he compares countless competing narratives and images about what different tools mean about the kind of professional he is, the quality of the work he does, his personality as an individual, and, most importantly, how well he can live up to some intangible ideal he has in his mind about what a handyman is and, therefore, how he ought to be. There's a reason people associated with certain trades tend to wear certain styles of clothing, for example, even when those styles don't necessarily impart any useful function (such as higher visibility, extra insulation, or added bodily protection against hazardous materials) to the work they do. Who told bankers to wear formal suits, doctors to wear white coats, and lumberjacks to wear flannel and jeans to work? Only the standards imposed by collective expectations.

When someone needs a belt for the function of holding up their pants and chooses to spend dozens of times more than the cheapest functional option for something associated with beauty, luxury, or noteworthy social status, it's because they have made a subjective evaluation that the perception of those things is important to them. They know that they can accomplish those goals with the same purchase that accomplishes the goal of holding their pants up. They probably don't consciously recognize the buying process in these terms, but this is why some logos and signature designs are so highly sought after—because their buyers expect the people they socially interact with to also place a high subjective value on them for their aesthetics and clout.

This kind of second-hand evaluation applies to everything in commerce. If you purchase an asset for the sole purpose of profiting by reselling it at a higher price to someone else, you are speculating that other people will perceive it as valuable for their own reasons, even if you personally find no utility for it. The person you sell it to may, in turn, only be buying it to fulfill their own aspirations of passing it on to someone else who values it at an even higher price than what they pay you for it. And maybe this escalation of value will continue organically with few corrections in the opposite direction for years or generations, as is the case with precious metals like gold and silver that have been valued all around the world throughout history and are still seen as good long-term investments today.

But maybe, eventually, this speculative valuation bubble will burst. Maybe, for one reason or another, the pool of people that you previously anticipated would hold something you purchase in high regard will change their minds and lose all of their interest in it. Maybe there weren't actually that many people interested in it to begin with, and the only reason it kept changing hands at all was the ill-informed speculation that there must be lots of people who really want to keep and use this thing for its actual intended function.

This happens all the time and quite rapidly in the fashion world, for example. Imagine paying hundreds of dollars for a trendy handbag because it employs a style that is very popular at the moment and will earn you lots of social clout. Is that a long-term or sustainable investment in utility for you? What happens next month when fashion trends change and the people who previously rewarded you for your buying choices adopt a new standard for vanity? You will be forced into a buying pattern that requires you to stay on top of the trends if you wish to receive the social rewards you are seeking. It's one form of planned obsolescence.

There are complex sociological and psychological explanations for why this happens. Some are natural and unavoidable features of the marketplace; others are direct and intentional interventions by designers and manufacturers to create hype and profit for their new products to generate purchases that otherwise would not happen.

During the time of the Soviet Union, individuals who engaged in what the State considered to be "speculation" were eligible for imprisonment if caught and even the death penalty for the most successful businessmen operating on the black market. It was considered one of the most heinous crimes a Soviet citizen could commit. The Soviet penal code phrased the practice of speculation explicitly as "the purchase and resale of goods or other items for the purpose of profit." You might recognize this as being a core function of *every* business that has *ever* existed and every conscious choice ever made.

Think about how, applied unilaterally, this edict would change all your spending habits, large and small. You are forbidden to purchase anything with the hopes or intentions of it increasing in value. So, immediately, all forms of investing go out the window. Every asset you buy must be done so exclusively to be used and consumed for its intended function in the immediate future. You cannot store large quantities of any type of property you foresee eventually using without catching the attention of the militsiya, who will accuse you of selfishly hoarding the wealth from others who need it more than you, which is also a serious crime. So, accumulating material wealth of any kind becomes essentially impossible. You and everyone else in your economy only purchase exactly as much as you need of something at the time you need it, ensuring that there will not be enough to go around when market conditions change and supply goes down and/or demand goes up.

This is one of the principal contributing reasons that so many varieties of consumption goods were in notoriously short supply throughout Soviet rule. And, ironically, the goods that there *were* more than enough of to go around were things no one wanted because they were not produced in response to actual consumer demand. They were usually the result of Soviet factories following mandates from on high about how many pairs of shoes in a particular size to produce, even if there weren't enough people who actually wore that size to buy them. So, they sat unused, taking up space and degrading through entropy from their already poor mass-produced quality into waste products lacking any utility at all.

There's always a speculative risk and the possibility of reward (i.e., "profit") when you purchase something for any reason other than its immediate practical and objective utility. A hammer will still be capable of hammering just the same even if everyone in your society suddenly decides not to value the act of hammering very highly and no one wants to buy it from you. You can ignore their interpretations and drive as many nails as your heart compels you to all the livelong day. The same will remain true even if it is a non-name-brand hammer and carries little respect among your fellow hammerers. Similarly, any well-made belt lacking a Gucci monogram will still hold your pants up just the same when fashion trends change. Whenever you depend upon the value that other people place on what you purchase to derive value from it yourself, be prepared for the possibility of losing it at any time. You cannot control how other people respond to anything.

Does this revelation imply that all aesthetics are superfluous? That wise spenders, investors, and entrepreneurs should focus entirely on function without form in the assets they accumulate? No. That would be absurd. The real practical utility of aesthetics is the emotional reward they bring to the people who curate them carefully according to their own artistic tastes.

If one piece of furniture in your bedroom is a different color than all the others, it might cause you stress or disquiet every single time you look at it, no matter how functional it remains in every other aspect of its design. It might prevent you from fully relaxing at home because of the visual inconsistency. So, for you personally, it might be worth paying significantly more to get the same model of couch in just the right color that the theme of your room requires. This is a subjective interpretation of aesthetics that does not depend on the passing judgments of other people to matter.

The same is true for what might seem to be overpriced pieces of either conventional or esoteric art. Only you know what kind of emotional value a particular painting, sculpture, or entire collection of pieces will bring into your life. Only you can decide how much money it is worth to you, in the same way you make that choice for everything else you ever buy. The only real danger to be wary of is to catch yourself when you are falling into a pattern of making your aesthetic purchasing choices based on your perception of how *other* people interpret the aesthetic value of something instead of how you do yourself. Just because high society has deemed something to be a great work of art does not mean that you will be in a position to reap the emotional rewards of enjoying it. You have to know your own tastes and values.

Imagine a situation where you purchase a few paintings made by your amateur artist friend for a few hundred dollars. You do this because you genuinely like the paintings. It brings you joy to hang them on your wall and to be able to look at them every day in your home. You don't care if anyone else thinks they are as great as you do. As well, you feel good about supporting your talented friend, who has yet to break out in the art world and find fame or a consistent way to support themselves through their passion. You like them so much that you keep and take care of them all the years that you own your home.

Then imagine that in 30 years' time, your friend has become world famous, and their art is displayed in museums and sold at galleries for millions of dollars. In this situation, it's likely that their earliest works (those they painted before anyone had ever heard of them or knew how valuable their art would become) would be considered substantially more valuable than the low price you originally paid for them 30 years ago.

Perhaps, in this situation, it is only because you were the only one who believed in your artist friend and who was willing to buy and safeguard these paintings at a time when the world ignored them that they even still exist at all. Perhaps they would have been thrown out or damaged due to careless mistreatment in a second-hand thrift shop long ago. Your reward for being the one who made the right call and saw the value that no one else would is the profit you will receive should you choose to sell them at their now greatly inflated market value.

Should your artist friend hold a grudge against you for having purchased their work at such a cheap price when it is now worth so much more? Or should they be grateful that you gave them that financial and motivational support when no one else would, encouraging them to go on to become someone who would produce new work worth millions more? We can only wonder how many amazing works of art, inventions, or ideas the world never got to know about because they never found a receptive audience in their time and were lost to entropy.

A speculative "bubble" is when people buy something purely due to the speculation that it will go up in value, not because it has an actual increase in demand from those who intend to consume it. It's a bit of a temporary self-fulfilling prophecy in the market that then quickly undoes itself when the truth is revealed.

If the demand to move to Los Angeles doubles in a year, all other things being equal, the housing prices should also double. But that's not a bubble because there is actual demand representing the practical utility of the houses. It's a bubble if all the people buying up houses in Los Angeles are only doing so in the hopes of selling them later for profit because they expect that other people will want to move to Los Angeles and that demand never actually gets realized. It's a game of chicken with each real estate owner waiting to see who will lose faith and cash out before the others. That's when a crash can happen, when many speculative buyers suddenly decide to sell because they realize the authentic demand they were waiting for isn't coming. The market gets flooded with supply, and a relatively small pool of buyers suddenly has plenty of options to compete on price with. Rapidly rising supply combined with rapidly falling demand equals crashing prices.

I bought my house here in the village somewhat under the speculation that demand in this area would gradually increase because of the developments being made here and in the surrounding areas. There are a limited number of houses and plots of land available for people who want to live here, so prices should organically rise in time, assuming more and more people actually do want to come live here. Of course, I also wanted the practical utility of living in my village house. If I can derive practical utility and organic investment appreciation from the same asset, so much the better.

What exactly will make my house potentially several times more valuable when I sell it in the future than the price that I purchase it at now? Objectively, it will be in better condition due to the capital and labor I am putting into refurbishments. We can assume that buyers will value the better physical condition the house will be in and be willing to pay more money for it.

But the biggest increase in market valuation will come simply from the fact that I will have had the foresight to purchase something in a state of low demand before the demand sharply rose. Price is always determined by the conflict between how badly people want something (demand) and what they perceive their options to be for getting what they want (supply). If "what someone wants" is merely a house in Armenia with no further qualifiers, then every house on the market in this country contributes to the supply. All of them are functionally identical according to the subjective wants of the buyer, so prices should be relatively low.

But if "what someone wants" is a house specifically in my village, there is a much greater scarcity of options that meet that criteria. So, I will be able to ask a much higher price for my house than I would be able to compared to an identical house located in any other Armenian village selected at random. The objective condition of the house is not changing in this analysis—only the invisible market dynamics of supply and demand, and those dynamics are at play just the same in every type of product or service you could ever buy or sell. Objective and practical utility only matters in market evaluation to the degree that it informs a buyer's subjective evaluation.

Expanding your mind enough to try to picture things from other people's points of view is an essential part of starting to think and act entrepreneurially, and it's one of the most difficult steps for many people who aren't used to thinking this way. Most of my neighbors here only think of the buying process from their own perspective. They project their own buying habits onto the rest of the world. Accordingly, they cannot picture what other people might be willing to spend lots of money on because they rarely ever spend lots of money themselves.

What surprises me most about this variety of tunnel vision about buyer mentalities is that these people do not live in abject poverty without access to modern consumption goods. They also do not live totally cut off from and unaware of standards of living led by the residents of Armenia who live in bigger towns less than an hour away (that they visit regularly) or the capital city of Yerevan just two hours away. They know that there are plenty of people within reach of them who do, in fact, regularly spend relatively large amounts of money on so-called luxuries that they themselves wouldn't necessarily choose to buy.

This massive undervaluing of the products of their labor also has an opposite but equally problematic manifestation. There are many cases where if I attempt to purchase an item already owned (but not necessarily produced) by one of my neighbors, such as an old used piece of furniture, they will set an arbitrarily high price for it. They do this even if it is not an item they are particularly keen to hold onto and would much rather have any amount of cash than it.

In these cases, I am certain that they would not ask for such unrealistically high amounts of money if they were dealing with someone they perceived to be of the same socio-economic class as themselves. But somehow with me, they make the economic calculation that if someone who they perceive has more money than they do wishes to buy anything from them, that person should pay a proportionally higher amount than others at the same level as them would have to. It does not even change the analysis in their minds if I show them that I can easily find the same or a similar fungible good from another seller at a much lower price than what they ask.

Evidently, part of their culture includes believing that the market value of what they own depends upon the relative wealth of the person interested in buying it, ignoring completely other external factors like the other options the prospective buyer has for accomplishing the goal sought by the purchase in the first place. They would rather lose the sale than take the same amount of money that they would gladly take from someone they perceive to be of the same economic class as them. And everyone loses opportunities for win-win exchange and increasing their own wealth because of it.

CHAPTER 15

DIVISION OF LABOR—THE HARMONY OF SPECIALIZATION

NO MATTER HOW knowledgeable and skilled you are, no matter how many tools of production at your disposal, the complex production and exchange of value in the economy cannot occur in social isolation. It is always dependent upon the choices and actions of other people participating in society. This applies to the production process just the same as it does to everything that comes after on the way to actually getting the asset of value to the people who will buy, own, and consume it. To maximize productive output and the value of intentional actions, any entrepreneur needs to make relationship forging and maintenance a normal part of their outlook. No one operates in a vacuum.

A simple way to think about the principle of relationship synergy is like so: What I do is more valuable because of what you do and vice versa. The element of synergy can be so important to the value of what you do that your creative efforts might be lacking any worth at all without the creative efforts of other people to actualize them. So, while I have stressed the importance of taking control over your life and becoming self-reliant through entrepreneurship, part of that means developing the social skills necessary to identify, create, and maintain profitable relationships.

People who follow conventional career paths often become accustomed to having a manager or some other sort of superior to delegate their company's productive tasks among different specialized departments and individuals. Their role is mostly to wait for instructions and follow them in the ways they have been trained to. As such, many long-term residents of the corporate world never have to develop an overhead perspective on the flow of multi-party labor that leads to a finished and valuable product. They probably don't develop the eye to see the relative strengths and weaknesses of different individuals with their own personalities, knowledge skill sets, and experiences who must somehow find a way to arrange those idiosyncrasies in a complementary fashion to create the maximum gain for all involved.

The division of labor principle promises that any group undertaking works best when everyone involved does as much as possible of what they are best at and as little as possible of anything else. These strengths and weaknesses are never identical for different people because no people are truly identical. So, to work effectively with other people, you need to understand well the things you do best. And the people you work with need to understand this about you too. Appropriately, you also need to understand almost equally as well what the people you work with do best relative to you and each other. And you all need to be in agreement on these things, or you will have no rational and easy means by which to determine who should be focusing on what tasks and what the value of everyone's contribution is.

All other things being equal, asking one person to perform

many tasks is less efficient than having many people each dedicate themselves to one task they can specialize in. Even if you are multi-faceted and experienced enough to do a serviceable job at everything required for what you seek to create and offer, the end result will not be as good as it could be if you focused your efforts strictly on what you do best.

Imagine a primitive tribal society slowly realizing the benefits of specializing and dividing its labor among the individuals best suited for different tasks. A hungry person is unhappy and seeks food to make himself momentarily happier, but diminishing returns quickly come into effect. The moment his hunger is satisfied, collecting greater amounts of food (or forcing more down his gullet) will produce less and less pleasure than it did initially.

Likewise, a cold naked man has only so much need for clothing. The moment his skin becomes protected from the elements, the utility and value he gains through additional articles of clothing quickly shrinks. No additional loincloth or cotton tunic will ever be as important to him as his very first one. Now, he must find ways to satisfy his many other shifting needs, not least of which is the hunger for food that befalls him multiple times a day.

Both men could divide their time throughout the day, tending to each need for themselves. In this simplified example, each man might spend half his time hunting food for himself and the other half making clothing for himself. But if they each recognize that the other person shares these needs (and the ability to fill them), they can reach an arrangement where one of them exclusively hunts food, and the other one exclusively makes clothing. They can then barter the products of these activities with each other, and each will have his needs met in a manner that is subjectively better than they were able to when working alone.

This synergistic arrangement works out well for them because, naturally, the person who is better at procuring food and finds the task less displeasurable will be better suited to fill the role of hunter exclusively. They will produce a greater output of food for lesser input. The person who is better at producing clothing and finds that task less displeasurable will be better suited to fill the role of clothing making exclusively. They, too, will produce a greater output of clothing for lesser input. This way, they will begin to optimize their efforts together. They will be producing the maximum possible valuable output for the minimum possible input as required by the laws of nature. This even works out well for each participant if each invests their productive energy on something that they personally have no need for but know that the other person does, so long as they are in a better position to fill it. Suddenly, everyone has a personal incentive to help others get what they want or need instead of focusing exclusively on tending to their own problems.

Now, obviously, modern economies and complex production processes are much more nuanced than just two types of producers filling two types of needs. But the principle remains the same at any scale of operation. It will remain the same even when humanity is colonizing the far reaches of the universe because it is a product of the limitations of the laws of physics and ecology colliding with the nature of the human pursuit of value through our choices. **Some people will always be better suited to perform certain types of tasks by their natural temperaments and the specific arrangement of knowledge, skills, and tools they acquire through the act of living.** As well, the environments we have access to will always feature their own specific arrangements of resources that each of us can access and derive utility and value from. It does no good for the hunter to try to hunt food where only wild cotton is abundant and the clothing maker to try to harvest fibers where only wild game is abundant.

Additionally, the better our techniques and technology become, the greater the levels of specialization and differentiation we can apply to the tasks related to production. What was once one task can be divided into many different micro-tasks if it is more pleasurable and efficient to produce the intended outcome that way. The specialized task of "producing clothing" can be subdivided into the even more specialized tasks of farming cotton, harvesting cotton, ginning cotton, spinning cotton, weaving cotton, dyeing cotton, sewing cotton, and so forth. Each can be performed by a different specialist if, for some reason, they are measurably better at any of these specific tasks or enjoy them more. Or one person can still do all of them but broken up into stages of batched work. Or they can do a few of them at a time and find someone else to do the rest. It's up to them to work out the optimal arrangement according to who is available and what they are willing and able to do. The more complex and multi-faceted types of work you can arrange and organize together for a common goal, the more nuanced and potentially valuable products you can create.

In almost any complex endeavor you take on by yourself, there are going to be tasks that need to be done, someway or somehow, that you end up enjoying more than others. And there are going to be some aspects of the process you, frankly, don't like at all. Most of us have been so conditioned to repetitively perform tasks we hate, both in work and the many other areas of life, that we accept them as inevitable. Work is suffering. Life is suffering. Or so the narrative goes.

But why have we accepted that it is necessary to structure our lives like this? Presumably, it is because most of us cannot see any alternative. We look around, and this is all we ever see: Necessary inconveniences and struggles. But this is part of the beauty of humanity's natural diversity of strengths and preferences. For everything you are naturally bad at, there is someone naturally good at it. For everything you naturally find distasteful, there is someone who loves it (or at least finds it significantly more tolerable than you do).

When you have developed a knowledge base and skillset to a reasonable degree of competency, you can get into the habit of applying them on your own to produce profitable products and services that other people will happily pay money for. Until you reach this point, it makes sense that the primary focus should be on education and training—the increase of useful knowledge and skills to apply in the market.

But where does the budding entrepreneur go from there? Do they just keep digging ever deeper into what they know so that they can become elite in a specialized field of knowledge and ability? Perhaps, if that suits their capabilities, their ambitions, and the conditions of the market. There will probably always be a place for the top rocket scientists and brain surgeons, at least so long as there are rockets and brains in the world.

Or would it be wiser to branch out from where they begin and acquire new types of knowledge and skills to enable synergy between different disciplines? Do they even have the time and other resources necessary to devote themselves to many different fields? Are they naturally gifted in enough different areas that learning them will be an efficient pursuit? They might be. But in many cases, it will make much more equitable sense to spend their time forging relationships with people who can do the things they can't and whose values and goals align with theirs.

And once they have those powerful, mutually beneficial relationships, they start to recognize the importance of nurturing and maintaining them. The way they treat the people they end up working with and for becomes essential to their success. If they lose the respect of the people who matter to their entrepreneurial success, they will not be able to rely on their knowledge, skills, and tangible assets when they need them to complete the tasks that generate their value and income. Furthermore, if they treat anyone extremely poorly, it will eventually end up negatively affecting their reputation (which constitutes their personal or professional brand), making it much more difficult in the future for potential customers and associates to trust them and engage in win-win interactions.

CHAPTER 16

ARBITRAGE—EVERYONE IS A MIDDLEMAN

EVERYTHING IS ONLY worth whatever people are willing to give up to acquire it. It doesn't matter why some people value one particular asset over another and why there might be a big difference between the monetary price from one seller versus the price from another. **You can still profit by recognizing that these facts are true, even if you don't share the same subjective evaluation of the asset in question.**

If, for example, you see a desirable consumer product or commodity like a particular child's toy or bulk rolls of toilet paper being sold for a lower price than what you think the market ought to be willing to pay, you can take advantage of the perceived value difference, even if you have no personal need for additional toilet paper or children's toys at that moment. Maybe the product in question is not being advertised very well to its target market, and you only found out about it because of some specialty or niche knowledge you happen to hold. If you are willing to take on the risk that you might be wrong, there is nothing stopping you (possible interventionist laws aside that penalize such behavior) from buying a substantial supply of the undervalued asset and attempting to resell it at whatever higher price the market shows it is willing to offer.

The profits from arbitrage can come right away if there is a large discrepancy between the price sellers are willing to sell at and the price buyers are willing to buy at. Or they can come over time as the going rate of something appreciates due to long-term market factors. In this situation, your reward will come from your ability to judge the relative value of something on the market in the near-term future better than the general market itself can. If everyone could predict the future price of goods and commodities as well you (and they had capital available to take advantage of their predictions), other people would be buying the toilet paper with you now at the lowest foreseeable price. The fact that you know enough to act before they do and buy more than you personally plan to use so you can resell it later when there is less available in the market supply actually helps ensure that there will still be some available when there would otherwise be none, just at a naturally inflated price to reflect the increased demand and reduced supply.

Everyone only buying as much of everything as they will immediately use (as was commonly practiced in the Soviet Union where hoarding and speculation were punishable offenses) ensures that supply becomes less reliable as market factors change—and they are always, in some ways, changing. Some people having more than enough of a given asset keeps the supply alive when natural shortages emerge due to decreased production or increased demand. The people who have too much become incentivized to release some of their pre-obtained supply back into circulation, where they will make a monetary profit instead of just sitting on it for ages until they happen to finally use it all.

Does taking advantage of arbitrage to make money like this still seem somehow cheap, unfair, or without merit? It might be hard to see how this actually serves a valuable role in the overarching marketplace. Arbitrage helps move assets from places of low subjective value to where they will be more highly valued, and everyone profits along the way. You can think of the money you make in this situation—the difference between what you have to pay to obtain an asset and what you are able to receive for the asset (factoring in any additional transactional costs and taxes)—as a sort of finder's fee for your service. The buyer you sell to is ultimately giving you a tip because you knew what to look for and were willing to go through the trouble of finding and bringing it to them when they otherwise would not have had the option.

This is one of the many reasons why I advocate that new entrepreneurs get involved in businesses they understand from the perspective of both production and consumption. How can you know, for example, what the appropriate market price for something you want to work with should be if you aren't used to participating in its market as a consumer? How do you know what is scarce and valuable to some buyers versus what is common and universally ignored? Guesswork doesn't cut it, unless you are looking to gamble. You need experience and evidence for whatever purchases you want to take calculated risks on.

Years ago, I stumbled onto the opportunity to turn a simple silver coin collecting hobby into a thriving resale business simply by paying attention to what kinds of coins were hard to find and in demand by certain kinds of collectors. If I could spot one I was reasonably sure was being offered at an undervalued price, I risked my own money purchasing and sometimes waiting for months to find a buyer willing to pay the higher price I set it at based on market evidence that such buyers existed and would eventually seek to buy it.

I showed a friend in the village, Arpineh, how I was able to flip these coins for a decent profit by seeking out inefficiencies in the marketplace that turn into opportunities to buy them cheap. In one case, a local seller of a limited mintage Armenian-themed silver coin was selling it in their shop for the equivalent of $50 USD. However, I knew from prior market research online that there were buyers willing to pay at least three times that price for it. Yet, it had sat unsold for months in this small shop because the manager of the shop was failing to expose it to the very people who would value it highly enough to pay even its current low price for it. So, nobody benefited; the seller did not receive the money he wanted, and his potential customer did not receive the coin they would want.

Recognizing the opportunity at hand, I promptly purchased this Armenian silver coin and began the work of marketing it online to a totally different base of potential buyers. Merely by taking some nice pictures, including relevant keywords in its description, and listing it for sale in some highly visible places, I found a buyer for it at $150 within days of posting it for sale. That was a $100 profit for what equated to several minutes of my time and a $50 risk. That's 100 additional dollars that the original seller could have snagged for himself had he known to make a few easy changes to his sales approach.

My friend Arpineh was not impressed by this feat, however. In fact, she claimed that what I was doing was unethical. "If the real value of the coin is $150, it was wrong of you to only give that man $50 for it and make so much money off him," she scolded.

I understood where she was coming from with this line of reasoning. On the surface, it seems like I am taking advantage of this man's ignorance regarding the market value of his coin and/or his poor sales process. But I wanted to unpack this subject with her because I knew there was an important philosophical concept at its core.

"Which part of the process I participated in was unethical?" I asked. "Two mutually consensual and beneficial transactions took place. First, I exchanged $50 for the coin with the original seller. Was that ethical?" No response from Arpineh. "Second, I exchanged the coin to someone new for $150. Was that ethical?"

"I suppose that... it's unethical that you didn't let the original seller know the true value of the coin and give him the chance to decide for himself, fully informed, how he'd like to proceed with the transaction," she responded.

"What an interesting concept," I said. "The *true* value of the coin. What determines the true value of it? I know its true weight was one ounce. I know its true diameter was 39 millimeters. I know its true molecular composition was 99.9% pure silver. I know these things because they can be objectively measured and demonstrated as such. But how can I measure its true *market value* in the same way? Did I know its value would be $150 when I bought it for $50? I had no guarantee that I would be able to sell it at that price. I listed it at $150 because I made a guess that that's the price I would be able to find a buyer at without having to wait a longer amount of time than would be worth it to me. That's what its value was for me. The guy I bought it from listed it at $50 because, apparently, that's what he thought he could sell it for. We know that that's what its value was to him because that's what he was willing to exchange it for. But what if I had listed it at $250 and sold it at that price? Would that make $250 the *real* price of the coin? What if the person I sold it to for $150 went ahead and resold it for $250 after buying it from me? Would that be unethical? Would he have been defrauding me in some way because he did not inform me that the 'real' price was $250 when he bought it from me for $150?"

"Maybe..."

"What about this? Would you think it was okay for me to sell it for only $51 after buying it for $50? Would only profiting

$1 have made the whole series of exchanges fair and ethical for everyone?"

"Well, that would've been more reasonable. Since the difference would have been only a dollar, the buyer wouldn't have any grounds to object to it," Arpineh continued.

"But if I had only profited $1, it wouldn't have been worth the trouble of spending hours researching these opportunities, risking my $50 investment by buying it, and then going through the trouble of reselling it. Do you think I would spend my free time searching shops for esoteric silver coins if I was only going to make $1 from it? I was only incentivized to find and buy his coin by the opportunity of making a decent profit from the work I had to put into it, not to mention the years I have had to spend learning about this stuff."

"Ok, that makes sense from your perspective. But it still seems like you took advantage of this man."

"Do you think it would have been better for the original seller if I had not purchased his coin at the price he was asking and for him to make no money? After all, the only reason I purchased it was due to the speculation that I could resell it at a higher price and make a profit. I never actually intended to keep the coin for my own use. If I had not been trying to 'take advantage of him,' as you put it, I would not have bought it from him."

"Well, no. Obviously, he wanted you to buy it. But I still think you should have been honest with him when buying it," Arpineh replied.

"In what way was I dishonest with anyone? The original seller made the claim that he had a specific coin in a specific condition and that he would exchange it to me for $50. The only claim I made was to my buyer that I had the same coin and would exchange it to him for $150. Does the fact that I only recently acquired the coin for $100 less than what I charged change the nature of what I promised my buyer or the value of the money the original seller asked for?"

"It just seems like common sense that acquiring an item for a certain price and altering it in absolutely no way doesn't magically make its value suddenly triple," she insisted.

"You're absolutely right. Objectively, I did not do anything to alter the functionality of the coin at all. It was in essentially the same condition I received it in when I sold it for three times the price. It's not like an old car I bought cheap, spent hours of my time fixing up, and then sold for a profit due to the objectively superior condition it was in. What I did was find a way to move this ambiguously valuable collectible, which has functionality as a commodity metal, a piece of art, and a long-term investment, to a position in the market where it would be *subjectively* valued higher than where it had been previously."

I saw she still wasn't buying it.

"Thank of it this way," I continued. "Would it have made a difference if a collector of obscure Armenian silver coins had hired me and paid me an hourly wage to research and find coins to add to their collection? Let's say they agreed to pay me $20 an hour for my services, and it took me five hours to find this particular coin being sold at $50. In that situation, they would end up paying me $100 for my service and $50 to the seller of the coin, a total of $150, which they would have considered a worthwhile price to own this coin that they otherwise would never have even known about let alone have had the opportunity to purchase. Does this economic breakdown change anything about the fairness, ethics, or value of what I did? The end result is the same. I was compensated $100 to find a coin for $50 that someone somewhere was willing to pay $150 for, a coin that they otherwise would not have been able to buy or may have had to spend even more than $150 for with another seller. In the end, all three people involved in this economic interaction got what they were seeking. The original seller got his $50, the end buyer got the coin he wanted at a price he considered fair, and I got paid to facilitate the transaction. By taking the entrepreneurial initiative to find this opportunity before someone else who might have hired me to perform labor for them, I shouldered the entire burden of success or failure. The risk was all mine to manage. My monetary reward was the result of that risk working out in my favor. But there have been plenty of times where I have been wrong about what coins I could resell at a profit. Sometimes, I end up having to hold onto them for months, or I just barely break even when I finally do end up selling them. It wouldn't be fair or moral to force me to shoulder the losses of being wrong but not allow me to reap the rewards of being right. Right?"

Arpineh was starting to come around to my perspective. What she said next revealed to me that what she had been focusing on was only the end outcome, not the transactional processes that had to occur along the way to make that outcome possible. "It may seem naive of me, but all of what you're describing could've been easily achieved by telling the original seller that he was not selling his coin in the best way possible and that he could be charging more money for it. Couldn't it have?"

"Yes, I certainly could have done that. And the result of the coin being sold for $150 instead of $50 would have been achieved all the same. But what would *my* incentive have been for finding this undervalued and poorly represented coin in the first place? What would have been *my* compensation for informing this man of what he should be doing to make more money? How many poorly listed items do you think people are trying to sell right now around the world? How many items struggle to get sold or don't receive as much money as they could under ideal circumstances? Why aren't you telling me to go reach out to all those sellers too and help them improve *their* business models?"

Her response was a bit more tepid now. "Well, you don't have time to go around finding every problem and helping everyone. I see your point."

"Right. Imagine a sales consulting firm that ran around offering advice to everyone and never charged money for their valuable insight. Such a consulting firm would quickly go out of business, and its employees would have to find another way of sustaining themselves. Imagine I had approached this shopkeeper as a stranger and made him the offer that I could tell him how to sell his coin faster and at a higher price, but only if he paid me $100 for my few sentences of wisdom. Do you think he would have agreed to that offer? There would be too much risk involved for him. He doesn't know who I am. He doesn't know anything about the quality of the advice I might offer him or why he should believe me. So the probable outcome is that he would decline my offer and just keep trying the same non-working sales methods he was used to. And he would probably have to wait a very long time to sell his coin, even at just $50. By doing what I did, buying his coin at the price he was asking when no one else would, I took the burden of that risk away from him by placing it on myself. I had a high degree of confidence in the validity of my ideas about how to sell it better and get it in the hands of someone who would value it more, so I acted on them. I tested my hypothesis. I put my money where my mind was, so to speak. I created an opportunity that did not exist before because I was willing to take the risk of being wrong in order to profit a decent amount from my knowledge and skill."

What was the important premise my friend Arpineh was missing from her economic paradigm? **For a marketplace to function, everyone participating in it needs to be incentivized to do the valuable actions they perform.** In other words, they need to get something they want from the successful implementation of their choices. Arbitrage is how entrepreneurs are rewarded for fixing inefficiencies in the market, for moving things toward a more ideal state of exchange. The ideal state is the one where both sides of an exchange, the seller and the buyer, get as close as possible to the outcome they want. That is where market equilibrium rests. The buyer gets the item they want at a price they consider low enough to be reasonable, and the seller gets rid of the item they don't want at a price they consider high enough to be reasonable.

But because of various factors, including legal intervention in the marketplace that threatens fines or imprisonment to people who buy or sell above or below certain prices (or at all), lack of knowledge from both buyers and sellers about the items they are exchanging, and just generally poor buying and selling practices, the market is always in an unoptimized state. There are always people seeking to buy things at prices lower than what are available (if what they want to buy is for sale at all), and there are always people seeking to sell things at prices higher than what buyers are willing to pay (if there are any buyers at all). Recognizing these inefficiencies and taking the risk of correcting them improves the satisfaction and efficiency of all parties involved and rewards the entrepreneur for being bold enough to take the initiative that no one else would.

Arpineh was making a valid point, however, just not the one she thought she was. Under what circumstances would I have had a social or ethical obligation to inform the original seller of the coin that he could raise his price and sell it quickly by following my advice instead of taking advantage of the opportunity for profit myself? The answer seems clear to me: If the seller were a friend with whom I had an established relationship and expectation of that kind of reciprocal courtesy. We all make agreements with the people in our lives, and most of them are unspoken yet faithfully adhered to. So, we consider it fair when the people we associate with continue to treat us in the manners we have grown accustomed to, and we reciprocate the same to them.

SECTION V:

ENTREPRENEURSHIP APPLIED

IN REALITY

I'M OFTEN ACCUSED by my Armenian acquaintances of portraying the entrepreneurial process as too simple, perhaps even too good to be true. It couldn't possibly be this easy, could it? Do these principles really apply just the same to the poorest and least privileged people on Earth as they do to the wealthiest and most powerful? To Westerners and Easterners alike? To first-world and third-world nations all the same? To our past cave-dwelling ancestors and our future space-faring descendants equally?

If these principles are natural and universal, why do people in the real world not usually act in accordance with them? Why aren't more people independently employed or financially free and comfortable? Surely, there must be more to the process than what I've outlined here as the optimal path to economic sustainability and self-reliance.

Conversations with incredulous listeners go something like this:

"Alright, Gregory. If it's really as easy as you keep saying it is, how do I make money?"

"I keep telling you. Just give somebody something they want."

"Ok… but what if they don't have enough money to pay me for it?"

"Simple. Give somebody with enough money to pay you something they want."

"Fine. But just giving one person with money something they want isn't going to be enough to support me."

"Of course not. So, just give lots of people with money something that they want."

"Ugh, ok. But I can't just do anything. I don't know how to do most things. Or I don't have the capital and other resources I need to do most things."

"Oh, that's easy then. Give people something you are in a position to give them. Or, alternatively, read a book about something you want to learn how to do. Then do that. Maybe you'll get some capital from doing that and can then do other more expensive things that require it."

"But what if I hate it?"

"Then give them something you will enjoy giving them."

"But I don't even know what kind of work I enjoy doing."

"Well, I guess it's time for you to start exploring different things you might enjoy doing more than what you are used to getting paid to do at the job you also hate."

"And how can I possibly compete with other people already doing something like what I might want to do?

"Do something other people aren't already doing. Or something you think you can do a little better. Besides, don't you think the best way to get better at something is to start doing it and learn from your mistakes?"

"And then what? I just keep doing that thing until I die?"

"If you want to, but a better outcome would probably be to figure out how to scale that thing and other things related to it so that over time you are doing more and more stuff with less and less effort. Who knows what your professional life will end up looking like in the long run? But it has to start with something, and just showing up every day at the same job you already know you don't want to do forever isn't going to improve your level of satisfaction in life or help you make more money. If you persist, though, and build off of what turns out to work, it stands to reason that over time you will have more and more options for making money that require less and less from you. And your ability to think and act entrepreneurially will organically improve through experience. Or would you rather not and just stick to the non-entrepreneurial path you are on? Something tells me you wouldn't be talking to me if you were satisfied with your professional life right now."

By that point in the conversation, they already know every relevant bit of economic theory they need to understand logically how and why the mechanisms of entrepreneurship work. They can analyze clearly the entrepreneurial actions of other people and see why they were successful or not. But still, they more often than not hesitate to begin aligning their own choices with what they know is true, and it gets harder the older they get and the more accustomed to thinking bureaucratically and following orders that they become. That's why it's vitally important to introduce the virtues and benefits of entrepreneurial thinking to people everywhere as young as possible, before non- or anti-entrepreneurial cultures have much of a chance to take hold, crippling capable thinkers for life.

Proper entrepreneurial education, though vital, isn't enough. Confidence, being an emotional concept, cannot be transferred to someone by merely saying the right words that give them information they may have been lacking before. It is developed through repetitive successful action, like muscle memory. In that sense, we might categorize confidence as a skill.

Like any skill, confidence is developed and applied through targeted bodily actions, and that includes the balance of neurochemicals that determines our present state of feeling. Children, teenagers, and young adults who have not already endured decades of life unconsciously training themselves to feel and act unconfidently will have a much easier time adopting the actions associated with confidence. They will have less "muscle memory" to undo, so to speak. And, like any other skill, its practice must begin at the level one is adequately prepared to attempt, not any of the infinite and more complex levels beyond it.

That is why you have seen me advocating the idea of starting small in entrepreneurship, at a level where risks will be minimal and the new things one must learn to do well are easy enough to adjust to. That is the best way for someone who has grown accustomed to living a non-entrepreneurial life to begin to think like an entrepreneur and see the unending possibilities for opportunity that exist all around. The musician who understands their instrument and the variety of possibilities for creation with it hears music all around them. The entrepreneur who recognizes the rules of the game and the potential for applying their knowledge and skills to reality quickly realizes that they will never run out of opportunities to generate wealth at a profit.

Does it make sense, in any complex endeavor, to begin only with the ideal outcome in mind and overlook any opportunities that do not seem to immediately grant it? There are always intermediary steps between what makes sense for us to do now and what we think we would eventually like to be able to do. But cultural inhibitions often prevent us from seeing and considering those intermediary steps and instead only focusing on the successful outcomes that survive the trials of development.

How, for instance, does someone learning to play the piano determine which song, out of all the infinitude ever written for piano, to learn to play first? Do they begin with the most complicated and well-known piece by the most famous and talented composer that they can think of? The type of classical masterpiece that will impress everyone who hears them play it? Or would they be better off beginning with a simple yet effective piece that will give them the opportunity to improve their skills and increase their awareness of what is possible for them to do with a piano, even if that first song never sounds all that great and does not conform to what they would like to one day be able to play under ideal circumstances?

Familiarity breeds blindspots and bias. Like the apartment owner who fails to see how his present liability of an empty and unkempt apartment could actually, with a relatively small amount of work, become a thriving asset for them, people who fail to think entrepreneurially because they are used to being told exactly what to do with their impressive knowledge and skills must somehow muster the ambition to break out of their holding patterns. What they know and can do is so familiar to them after a time that they forget that not everyone automatically holds the same qualities and perspective. They don't even consider that there are plenty of people who want and need what they know and can do and would therefore happily pay them to provide these things. They cannot see the market value of their knowledge and skills outside the limited professional or lifestyle environment in which they have grown accustomed to applying them.

It is ironic that people at opposite ends of the professional spectrum can suffer from the same disease of a stilted and non-entrepreneurial mentality. The person who has never had ample opportunity to be productively employed will likely view money as a scarce and unobtainable thing that it is not their lot in life to be blessed with. Appropriately, they will not look for opportunities to generate it. They probably do not even see that they have skills that can be monetized because they never use those skills to make money.

At the other extreme, the person who has consistently made money but only through manufactured roles created by an entrepreneurial employer knows that they have valuable skills. Still, they have come to rely on a convoluted social hierarchy to participate with their skills in the economy as they understand it. That's why there is such panic when they lose their jobs. They only see the monetizability of their skills within a corporate framework where they will be made to follow orders and perform a narrow range of tasks that complement the similarly narrow ranges of tasks performed by their coworkers. They do not see the skills themselves as the source of the wealth they generate—only the mandates passed down from above about how to apply them.

CHAPTER 17

MARKET VIABILITY—DETERMINING WHAT'S IN DEMAND AND EQUITABLE

THE MAJOR OBSTACLE facing would-be entrepreneurs is not that there aren't enough viable options for starting a business. The problem is the one caused by the burden of unimaginably vast choice. In all but the most destitute and controlled of market conditions, there are more businesses that could turn a profit than any human mind will ever be able to fully consider. The question then becomes one of how a prospective entrepreneur chooses which path, out of the infinite, is best to pursue first. **The burden is not *lack* of choice but having too many choices and no reasonable methodology for selecting which among them is most viable.**

However, the skill of choosing, just like any other skill, atrophies without regular use. As Soviet workers were never allowed much choice about the types of value they would produce or their strategies for producing it, the burden of choice remains too great for many of their descendants to take on. For generations, someone somewhere in a position of social power determined for all workers what value to produce, based upon what they perceived the nation needed and who was best to provide it, all according to unilaterally applied but usually arbitrary and nonsensical metrics of success. Compared to the unending responsibility of having to decide for yourself exactly how you will be principally productive in society by going into a business of your own choosing, the burden of choice was practically non-existent for the Soviet individual.

Proponents of the Soviet Union would boast about its "100% employment rate." It was a point of national pride that just about everyone who lived there had a part to play in the economy. No matter who you were or what your skills were, someone in a position of power was guaranteed to be able to find something for you to do. But because the focus was merely on having *something* to do, they overlooked the importance of making choices about the *right thing* to do. Determining and taking the risk of choosing the right thing is the burden of the entrepreneur.

What did it look like to have the economy shaped by the goal of everyone merely having something to do? Well, consider that despite everyone being employed, the Soviet economy still failed to produce enough food and the other necessities of life for everyone. How is that possible? Shouldn't more people working equate to more wealth being produced? Only if you mistake input for output. Remember that the goal of efficiency is the *maximum* possible output for the *minimum* possible input. Employment is a measure of input. Bragging about maximum employment is bragging about maximum input, which is, by definition, part of the equation for *inefficiency*. What would have been an impressive claim is that you are producing the most bread possible with the *least* amount of labor (i.e., employment) and other costs required to do it. Paying people to dig holes and then paying them to fill them back up again will keep everyone plenty busy, but it will not produce any real wealth for the money spent and labor expended.

In some cases, an attempt to measure output was made, by it was defined by arbitrary and inappropriate metrics. Output is wealth that has utility that the people consuming it will find valuable. Often, utility was measured in isolation without reference to if it was actually what people wanted or needed. A shoe production factory might have been considered successful by Soviet standards if it could produce the maximum possible number of shoes, especially compared to other factories that produced fewer pairs. But this isolated metric was worthless because it ignored other important variables like the quality and durability of the finished product, the size requirements of the people who would be wearing them, or even individual stylistic preferences. You might be able to make twice as many children's shoes with the same amount of material you could use to make adult's shoes, but that does not equate to twice as much value if you do not have twice as much demand for shoes from children as adults.

None of the people directly involved with the production or distribution of shoes dealt with the positive consequences of making the *right* choices or the negative consequences of making the *wrong* ones. But making choices is a natural and necessary human ability, as is dealing with the consequences of those choices, whether they be positive or negative, in accordance with the reality of their effects. When entire generations of people have had their biggest life choices stripped away from them, it's understandable that the culture created and perpetuated by them would continue to discourage the re-emergence of that lost ability.

Most of the Soviet citizenry lacked even the perspective to know that the near-total absence of personal choice was unusual in the world and so harmful to them. In addition to incoming media from the outside world being censored, travel within and outside the nation was strictly controlled, as was incoming news and media. It was forbidden to visit other countries and experience other ways of life unless given special permission for strictly predetermined purposes and durations. So, the average Soviet worker had no idea how the rest of the world operated outside the mandates they followed and accepted as necessary and normal.

Try, as an exercise, to assess what it is possible and viable to invent in light of everything extraordinary that has already been invented by countless people before you. You may get discouraged at the apparent challenge of having to come up with something that the millions of human inventors before you did not. But the number of things that *can* possibly be invented will always be infinitely larger than the number of things that *have* been invented. As well, the portion of that infinite possible space that we can reasonably foresee grows exponentially with each new invention we are exposed to. Once we know that it is possible to arrange matter according to its natural laws in a new way that produces a specific desirable outcome, we also begin to become aware of ways we could improve upon that outcome or apply that outcome as a tool to produce newer outcomes still.

It is extremely unlikely that anyone could think of how to invent the flying car if their level of locomotion technology had peaked at horse-drawn carriages. But once the personal internal combustion automobile has been invented and become a ubiquitous piece of technology of which everyone in a culture is aware, it becomes possible (perhaps inevitable) to foresee the next desirable leap in the relevant technology. Likewise, we can all be sure that once flying cars are universally available for human consumers seeking superior locomotion, someone forward-thinking inventor will conceive of the next leap forward after that. Only futurists and science fiction writers seem to have the skill set necessary to look several leaps down the road from where they are at any given time, though their predictions remain in the realm of fantasy far more often than they make their way into our reality as real technology and inventions. While it is relatively easy to predict what is broadly physically possible for humans to do based on known principles, it is much harder to predict what exactly we will end up doing and what specific form it will take. With each new generation of radical change in the way we do things, it becomes exponentially more difficult to predict what will reasonably come next.

The same principle of exponential emerging possibilities that applies to physical technology also applies to marketplace entrepreneurship. With each new improvement that someone somewhere makes to how we produce and distribute the products and services that people want, countless new improvements also become foreseeable. The proactive entrepreneur is the one who operates at the edge of their present state of marketplace norms and recognizes an opportunity to move them forward in at least one regard, profiting along the way by improving things for everyone who participates in commerce with them.

But infinite possibilities do not guarantee that anyone has what they need in order to pursue all or even a few of them effectively. Everything we ever do requires the consumption of resources like time, effort, and calories and incurs entropic wear upon our bodies and other physical assets. In business, what we do also frequently requires spending or investing money because, as discussed, money tends to be the most efficient and effective means to facilitate the exchange of goods and services. Perhaps if we are lucky, our fledgling little business babies will survive their rough first years and slowly start to turn a small profit to reward us for all that time and money we had to sink into them. But that is still time and money that we could have chosen to sink into some other entrepreneurial idea instead that might have returned a bigger profit in a shorter time. We can't do everything. Even in success, there are opportunity costs.

For the new entrepreneur who does not already have a lot of their own money saved up or easy access to a low-interest loan to use to get their business going, there is little reason to begin their journey with a business that requires a large upfront investment of resources. It is more prudent to assess the businesses they are considering getting involved in through the filter of the minimum amount of risk required before they will be able to produce some meaningful level of market results. Then, whichever ideas prove through experimentation to have the highest market viability are the ones the budding entrepreneur can continue to focus on and invest more resources into while disregarding all the rest.

How does one reasonably determine the appropriate level of risk and commitment to take on for an entrepreneurial idea? There is no universal, easy answer. Everyone's experience is different. Everyone's tangible and intangible assets are different. Everyone's liabilities are different. Everyone's goals are different. The same question could be asked about how one is supposed to reasonably determine how much time, effort, and other resources are appropriate to invest into a romantic interest, knowing full well that there are billions of other options available on Earth and that their analysis of how well things will go could be quite inaccurate.

What *does* make sense in every situation, whether in courtship or entrepreneurship, is to incrementally increase investment and risk according to real evidence from actual experience about what is working. Those who attend every first date with marriage preparations already in mind and money already spent on wedding venues are almost certainly setting themselves up for disappointment and loss. They are not look-

ing at the actual chemistry and potential of the relationship before making big choices and submitting themselves to big liability. They are not even considering the wants and opinions of the
other half of the equation—the target of their affection whose
choices will also play a role in the outcome. It is the same if an
entrepreneur were to assume from the get-go that the interesting idea they have for how to make a profit is necessarily going to become a massive multi-year operation that returns back
to them many times over the life savings they feel impelled to
throw into it and hope for the best. It is foolhardy to assume
every new business must be an all-or-nothing adventure without even considering your role in it or what the market actually
proves to want from you.

Consider the classic case of the hopeful start-up entrepreneur who takes out huge bank loans to pursue their big entrepreneurial dream. This is exactly the situation my talented and
ambitious entrepreneur friend Ashot fell into here in Armenia
by projecting his ambitions further than he could reasonably
confirm their market viability. He used borrowed funds to fi-
nance the construction of an impressive three-story structure
that was intended to function simultaneously as guest accommodations, a coworking space, a restaurant, and an art school.
He did this because he had a beautiful vision that he was willing to risk everything to accomplish.

But the tragic side effect of choosing this path of heavy upfront investment was that Ashot, the entrepreneur behind this
massive project, was chronically worried about the level of debt
he had gone into, even as his beautiful building approached a
state of completion and he was getting ready to open his doors
to paying customers of many types. Now he had a big problem
to solve. Because he had chosen a business model that required
such a large investment of capital long in advance of any business activity occurring (capital he had to borrow and pay inter-

est on), the pressure to start making money had built up during the several months his venue was being constructed and during which he had no income.

This long-time pressure was worsened by the fact that though his mind was bright and his ambition was great, Ashot had no prior experience running this type of business (or rather, any of the individual sub-businesses that would constitute the total vision for his venue). He was planning to learn how to best brand, monetize, and manage his business as he went along. This would have been a great strategy had he been in a position to take things at a leisurely pace and had he not been obligated to meet any specific performance metrics on a rushed schedule. But because he needed to start turning a profit as quickly as possible after the building was complete, he lacked the freedom he needed to be leisurely and experimental in his approach. He needed money *now*, by any means that he could get it.

It is wise to avoid the front-loading of responsibility and risk in a new business venture unless one is experienced enough with what they are doing for it to not become an emotional and logistical burden that affects the quality of life and the performance of the business. The amount of risk assumed should correlate with the amount of expertise available so that the entrepreneur can attempt to accurately predict an equitable future instead of just leaving it up to chance that their big dreams might work out. I am absolutely a fan of flying by the seat of my pants and attempting to figure things out one obstacle at a time as they arise—but this approach only works when there is a certain amount of lifestyle freedom that allows for it and when there isn't a lot riding on the line.

The first-time entrepreneur does well to learn to ignore the cultural conception that starting a business requires big upfront risks or the adage that you necessarily need to spend money to make money. It makes more sense, when feasible, to look for what small things they can do that just might return a profit right away or in the very near-term future. With small risks, the entrepreneur can spread themselves out much further and double down on whatever pays off most quickly.

Do you recall the case of my village neighbor, Artur, who was reluctant to try his hand at making and selling furniture on his own, despite having the necessary skill for it in abundance? The hardest step was convincing him to build something specifically for the purpose of selling for a profit. I told him to look around the room and pick any simple piece of furniture he knew he could make. We settled on a small table as his first product for no other reason than that it would be easy (and therefore not require risking many hours of his time), it would use few raw materials (and therefore not require risking much of his money), and its demand was general enough that it would not be a stretch to find someone somewhere who needed one.

Yet, despite the fact that this man had built many tables and similar pieces of furniture in his life for personal and family use, it was a nightmare trying to get him to see that it would be possible to sell the table he would build at a respectable price on the open market the table. Every part of the process was comfortable and acceptable in Artur's mind except the part that required him to find someone—*anyone*—who would be willing to pay a price for his creation that exceeded the cost of his materials and compensated him adequately for his time. This poor, talented, Soviet-born man had spent so many decades being indoctrinated both explicitly and unconsciously by his culture to believe that he had no place participating in the selling end of commerce that it took hours of lecturing and encouraging from me to even get him to agree to try it. He believed in himself so little that he could not accept that anyone would ever pay for a table he built, even though he was perfectly aware that everyone needed tables in their homes and bought them all the time from many sources.

What would have been a better use of Artur's time? Sitting and arguing with me for hours about whether or not it would be possible for him to make and sell a table? Or using that same time to just make the damn table and find out the answer directly through his own experimentation with trying to sell it?

Of course, it's generally a good idea to try to project and reason your way through a plan before you ever put it into motion. But that's only true so long as the plan is one that would require more risk to actualize than it would to contemplate. If figuring out how to read a map to your destination takes more time than just driving around the neighborhood for a few minutes and finding it, it's not an equitable use of time to read the map anymore. Maps, which are simplified symbolic representations of reality, only make sense to employ as tools when the reality they represent is sufficiently more complex than their representations and using them to derive accurate knowledge is easy. But the first steps of entrepreneurship frequently do not have to be complex or risky. The cultural expectation that participating in business must be complex, risky, difficult, or available only to people of a certain social stature is what prevents ordinary people from seeing the obvious: That entrepreneurship is as simple as we can figure out how to make it.

If you can learn how to sell one thing one time successfully, you can scale up from there according to patterns that are shown by growing evidence to be predictably equitable. That might mean, after selling one table, that you take the larger risk of producing a variety of different kinds in a similar style and seeing if you can sell all of them too. Then more. It might mean experimenting with one table in many different styles, then making more of whichever one sells the best. Unless you are entering a business that absolutely requires large, upfront, long-term risks before there can be profit and proof of concept, there is no reason not to approach life as an entrepreneur this way.

What, if you had to, could you do to apply your existing skills and knowledge in some way to produce something of value and sell it for an amount that made your investment of resources worthwhile according to your own evaluation? Or to somehow transform something someone else produced and add substantial value to it? Or could you even just take advantage of your expertise in some area through arbitrage by moving something desirable from a position of low subjective value to a higher one and profiting from the difference? The options are everywhere and endless once you've trained your entrepreneurial mind to spot them. Even if what you end up doing is far from the ideal job that would give you everything you've ever wanted from your professional life, if it is new, you should be learning something from it. Entrepreneurship is not a vocation; it is a way of seeing the world.

CHAPTER 18

ASSET UNIQUENESS—PRODUCING SOMETHING WORTH PAYING ATTENTION TO

ANY PERSON WHO contributes to the creation of value exchange plays a vital role in the progression of society. The entrepreneur either improves upon an existing source of value or innovates a new one. Anyone who attempts to go into business without accomplishing one of these feats will quickly realize that they cannot justify their existence in the economy (unless they manage to misrepresent what they offer, but then they are acting criminally instead of entrepreneurially). Whatever is produced must be different than what existed before. The new entrepreneur cannot effectively fill the exact same space as entrepreneurs before them.

What natural limitations make it so it must be this way? Why can't unlimited amounts of people just keep adopting the same profitable business models and do exactly what they see others already doing?

Answer: Human demands are never met or stable. People make partially informed choices about what to do with their time and material resources, including money, based on what they perceive will best fulfill their passions or resolve their present discomforts.

Every choice involves the pursuit of a subjective positive or the avoidance of a subjective negative. **If these positives and negatives could ever be totally understood, predicted, and made to be static and unchanging, it would be easy to arrange the global economy in such a way that they would be forever optimally met.** The only changes would come from advances in technology that would enable us to produce and consume the same things over and over, only faster and better, in perpetual pursuit of the same dopamine high. Such a static economy would be a central planner's utopian dream finally realized, one where everyone conformed perfectly to mandates about how all forms of value must be produced and consumed for the good of society.

This fairy tale version of society is how many people in modern positions of power over the masses still see the world. They believe that the flaw is in mankind for not conforming to their prescriptions for optimal living, and the people who diverge the furthest from universal mandates are the first to face harsh punishments or removal for the crime of ruining the illusion of a perfect society for everyone else.

The entrepreneur, by nature, must do the very opposite of the bureaucrat to survive and gain a market advantage. They must look beyond what choices people happen to be making with the opportunities they are aware of, the restrictions imposed on them, and the habits they have fallen into. The entrepreneur must iterate, innovate, and improve in some meaningful way and demonstrate the subjective value of their actions to those they wish to help. And to do that, they need to understand the dynamics of the products or services they work with and why people choose to buy them at all.

Every product or service in the world becomes easier to conceptualize when you strip it down to its core defining categorical elements. Everything then becomes a variation upon its categorical role—its Platonic ideal that exists only in a theoretical plane of perfect implementation. When is a table no longer a table? When it ceases to serve the agreed-upon functions that are essential to what table consumers collectively consider a table to be.

Stripped to its core defining elements, the concept of a table is a flat elevated surface upon which to place objects for more optimal storage or use than if the flat elevated surface were not available. This mechanistic description robs a good piece of furniture of its narrative and aesthetic appeal, but it is functionally accurate. These qualities apply to every table that has ever existed. The moment they cease to apply, the object is no longer functionally a table.

To see how true this is, all you have to do is look at an unfurnished home or apartment. Then, imagine the order in which you would acquire each piece of furniture as you encountered an organic need for it (as opposed to buying an array of pieces merely because you had some preconceived notion of what was necessary or appropriate to put in each room).

If you moved into a dwelling that lacked all manner of tables, you'd quickly realize that it's quite inconvenient to have to eat every meal standing up or sitting on the floor. You'd want to be seated upright with your food close to your face in front of you, in a position that would make it easy for you to manipulate it with your arms and hands. If you try to do this with a non-flat raised surface, you will grow frustrated with how your food slopes or rolls instead of staying in one place. You may break a few dishes that drop to the floor. If you want to work from a computer or place a lamp beside your bed, similar issues will arise if you lack tables for them. So, the conclusion should quickly become clear that a table of some kind would have great utility and be tremendously valuable to you. You will quickly enter the initial state of demand that organically motivates someone to purchase a table.

From the original realization that a flat elevated surface would offer you some valuable utility and the subsequent desire to acquire one, you would then be faced with an enormous burden of choice about the variety of aesthetic and functional options available to you.

The factors that go into determining the ideal table for you to acquire are practically endless. In what room of your house will your table go? You'll want it to be of a color and material that goes well with the existing décor. How big is the space you plan to put the table in? What shape should it be—square, rectangular, round, or something else? What type of activities do you plan to use it for? A computer desk will have different design choices than a dining table, patio table, coffee table, or end table. You could spend hours sorting through all the available varieties of tables at your local furniture superstore, not to mention the countless more options you might find shopping around online or in small artisan shops. Then you have to narrow all those details down even further to a buying choice that matches the price range that you would consider an equitable exchange of currency for the value you foresee deriving from your table purchase.

The point of this pedantic illustration is to demonstrate how what seems at first to be one basic, functionally fungible product and a simplex buying choice can actually take on an endless amount of non-fungible forms, limited only to the variety of ways that people can think to use them (or that a salesman or marketer can inspire them to).

So if an entrepreneur decided to go into the table manufacturing business, they would never be competing with the whole category of products that contains "all tables everywhere." They would be competing only with the subcategory of tables that would realistically be used by table consumers to fulfill the same specific arrangement of utility as the tables they wish to sell. Poker table manufacturers are not realistically going to be competing with dining table manufacturers because people buy them to fill completely different needs. Every product is competing with whatever other products fulfill a similar need, so it stands to reason that every entrepreneur should seek to make the needs their products and services fill as unique as possible within their subcategory of function, so long as they still appeal to some predictable demographic of buyers. It does no good to be special if no one wants your particular manner of specialness.

This competitive analysis applies not just to objects you might sell but also to any type of service you could derive from your knowledge and abilities. A service is merely value delivered through an action instead of an object. Buyers seeking service providers will apply the same categorical view of the specific value they are seeking to the service and its providers that they do to static things they can hold in their hands or keep in their houses.

The difference between a product and a service is ultimately only cognitive. It's about whatever way is most convenient to conceive of and categorize a form of value. Anything commonly bought as a product could instead be sold as a service and vice versa. The existence of "productized services" demonstrates this. If you hire someone to clean your house, you might pay them for the amount of time they spend working at the task, either the number of hours or a solid day of labor. However, the value you receive from this service does not derive directly from the time spent on it but rather the end product of a clean house. The cleaner could just as easily choose to sell the end product of clean house for a fixed price, and the value you receive would be just the same. However, arranging payment terms that way might be less convenient for them to factor in their own costs and investment of resources.

The inverse applies to any physical object you might purchase. It might be most convenient for both buyer and seller to conceive of common household knickknacks as the fungible physical form they take on at the moment of exchange. Still, there is no law of economics preventing manufacturers from charging based on the time and materials they put into the labor of creating them. How an entrepreneur arranges their offerings of products and/or services should be shaped by how their market of buyers will find it most convenient to think of them, compare them to similar offerings, and determine whether they are equitable purchases.

Whatever is offered to others, it's strategically important to figure out in what ways it will be non-fungible with other available offerings so that it will not easily be subverted or replaced by them. Further still, if all a seller's offerings are functionally identical in the eyes of their customers, they are essentially competing with themselves. There is no real reason for someone to buy more than one of their offerings if the first will accomplish the same thing as all the others they might also have bought. And if what other sellers offer appears to be the same, buyers will probably just patronize whomever happens to be selling at the lowest price or whomever is most convenient to buy from, which may come down to something as arbitrary as whomever they happen to see first.

Upon surface examination, it's easy to understand why many people in developing economies intuitively overlook the importance of marketplace differentiation or uniqueness.

Imagine that you are in a position where you have saved up a meager amount of money from hard labor with which to try running your own business for the first time in your life. Out of all the infinite possibilities, what kind of business are you going to go with? How are you going to run it? Are you going to innovate an unprecedented but potentially wildly successful new product and business model? Unlikely.

Almost certainly, you are going to do what you see that other people in your situation have done and found at least a minor amount of success with. To minimize your perception of risk, you will copy them as closely as you can for fear of doing something wrong and failing. You will want a cookie-cutter copy-and-paste generic business model that is practically guaranteed to turn a small profit. You will want this because your priority at this early stage of basic financial security will be to avoid losing what small amount of capital you have, not to take on big risks chasing fantastical untested ideas. This is how your culture will have trained you to interact with reality, and not just in regard to business.

In cities across certain parts of the world, it is common to see endless rows of identical shops selling roughly the same items in much the same manner. No one taught these fledgling business owners how to think independently or the advantages of doing things differently than the competition. They probably don't even conceive of the other identical shops along their street as competition, as they don't think systemically enough to realize that every customer has a finite amount of money to spend and will make a limited number of purchases to satisfy the needs associated with the items being sold. These shop owners may make enough money to stay in business (for now), but their potential for success is capped at a very low level—the same level shared by all their indistinguishable competitors offering the same types of products in similar venues.

There is, too, an opposite danger associated with the far extreme of differentiation from what is normal in one's familiar marketplace. **If the entrepreneur makes it their explicit goal to do something totally unlike anything anyone around them has ever done before, it might be difficult to find any customers at all.** Why though? Aren't new things exciting and interesting? To a degree, yes. Novel things incite our curiosity and grab our attention. But what we often overlook is that the excitement response tends to happen within a narrow window of novelty in our perception. We get excited about things that are just a little bit different or noticeably better than what we are used to and already know we want.

A different kind of response is generated when we encounter something that is so new that we aren't sure that we should want it or even what to do with it: Confusion, indifference, or even fear, all of which are things you definitely don't want someone who is in a position to give you money to be experiencing. People make buying choices when they think they will be getting something greater in return than what they must give up to get it, and that analysis requires clarity and familiarity. If a product, service, or business model is *too* new, people may not even recognize it enough for the value it offers to consciously want it.

Remember the fallacy of assuming that what *is* happening is what *must be* happening. No one should just accept that the way other entrepreneurs are doing things is the only or best way they could be done. Perhaps a company that produces a spectacular physical product is, for unrelated reasons, terrible at customer service, communication, organization, and other aspects of consumer interface and interaction. All other things being equal, would most people prefer to buy from a provider or a store where it is easy to find what they are looking for, where transactions happen quickly, and where there is someone available to communicate clearly and address any concerns they might have? Of course. So, if even just these qualities unrelated to actual products and services are a weakness among the competition, the fledgling entrepreneur can make it a point to focus on doing notably better here.

Entrepreneurs should always learn from and, to a degree, imitate other entrepreneurs—but only when it is advantageous to do so. There are countless offerings in the world that perform their intended functions reasonably well for most people's needs but fail to fill the more specific needs of specific types of people. There are infinitely more products that have not been brought to market yet than those that already have been because human needs are infinitely refined and expansive. Consumers choose the solution that appears to fit their needs the best out of all available options. Under economic conditions that favor and encourage entrepreneurship, there is nothing to prevent the forward-thinking entrepreneur from refining a popular and general solution into something that accomplishes a much more specialized result and, therefore, appeals better to some category of people.

Learning to see what viable new variations there might be on what you can offer takes some getting used to if you have been working within a particular area for a while. What if you have been a dancer all your life, never really participating in any other professional area? What if it is your sole passion and source of income? How many specialized variations are there upon the categorical skillset of dance and everything tangentially related to it? What if the worst should happen, and you break your leg and can never dance again? Is the lifetime of knowledge and skill related to dance you've built up suddenly worthless?

First things first. Knowing what we do about minimizing the risk of wealth loss, was it wise to structure the entirety of your value-producing pursuits in such a way that they were wholly dependent upon a fragile variable you could not sufficiently control, such as the health and functioning of your legs? Even if you have known since you were a young child that dancing is your biggest passion and that you have far more natural talent here than in any other domain, you placed yourself in an extremely risky and limited position by not at least allowing for other possibilities for wealth generation to develop in your life. The same tragic story applies any time someone stakes their ability to engage productively with society on something specific, attuned, and fragile.

These situations are why insurance companies have emerged in the market to help people with fragile sources of great value minimize the monetary loss in the event of their sudden disrepair or destruction. They offer to take on the risk themselves in exchange for a service fee that the insuree finds equitable.

Like any other skill set, the ability to make a living as a dancer depends upon how the consumers participating in the dance market subjectively value its products. If no one values dancing, they aren't going to willingly pay you to dance.

It's tempting to look at the most skilled, most famous, and most successful outliers in any professional domain and seek to structure a professional path after theirs, but the outliers can never be seen as indicators of the general industry related to their skills. The fact that the world's best ballerinas will probably always have opportunities to make a living through professional performances is not a good indicator that everyone in the world who has some talent and passion for dance will also be able to make a living. Likewise, the existence of a handful of rich and famous Hollywood actors means nothing about the career prospects of every aspiring star who moves to Los Angeles dreaming of fame and fortune.

No wealth-producing knowledge or skill is completely safe from loss. Injuries that affect expertise or ability can happen to anyone. The promising young football star hurts his throwing arm, ironically throwing his career away. The piano virtuoso develops carpal tunnel syndrome or rheumatoid arthritis and cannot ever play the same again without severe pain. These stories are tragic not only due to the fact that they represent the loss of a rare variety of proficiency at a valuable task but also due to the loss of that talented individual's social *identity*. Who are they now without their signature ability to perform what they love so much and now that their celebrated social position might be permanently gone?

When an impassioned dancer permanently injures their leg, a sudden loss of physical control has robbed them of the application of their most valuable intangible asset: Their skill as a dancer. Remember that skill is always the result of applying knowledge through the motor skills of the body. But unless their brain has also been damaged, they will retain all their *knowledge* of dance. The damage to their leg only means they will have lost the relevant motor control (i.e., the *skill*) associated with dancing. As well, the lifelong professional dancer has certainly accumulated countless valuable *relationships* with people who are in a position to work synergistically with them to bolster the valuable effects of their efforts. As much of an adjustment as it may be, all is not lost in the domain of the value they can produce related to dance. Such an unfortunate person just needs to learn to think creatively and entrepreneurially about what other ways they might apply what they know and can do in a psychologically rewarding and financially profitable way, no matter how unconventional it may seem.

The very concept of a profession is often the result of social paradigms about how we are supposed or allowed to embody our identities as individuals in society. John, the barber. Samvel, the carpenter. Sheila, the dancer. Andrea, the guesthouse manager. These are useful constructs to the extent that they make it easy for the rest of society to categorize us and derive value from our knowledge, skills, tools, and other resources. A categorical label helps the rest of the world know how to perceive and interact with us. But it also encourages us to rely exclusively on one source or form of proper productive output, and that makes our wealth-producing activities liable to greater risk than necessary. Such a convenient social framework makes it harder to think creatively about all the ways our assets could be better applied for wealth generation.

"Better" can mean a lot of different things in the context of the marketplace. Better can be cheaper. Better can be a new variety. Better can be more attractive packaging and a compelling story about a product's origin and creation. Better can merely be a wider level of advertising and distribution. Whatever it is, it has to be something that some equitable sector of the market of cheese buyers views as favorable and unique compared to the other options they are already aware of. Whatever gives your product or service that quality is what entrepreneurs refer to as a unique selling proposition (USP), and that is what will form the basis of your product's public identity, which in turn leads to your brand identity as an entrepreneur or business entity.

The alternative to improving in a specific way upon something people already spend their money on is to offer something they don't yet *know* they would like to spend their money on. There is never only one way to fill any given needs of an individual, no matter how accustomed they are to relying on some particular form of value consumption. There are also always new needs to uncover once consumers become aware of the possibility of adding a new type of benefit to their lives.

Most of the technology that defines the modern way of life would have been unimaginable generations ago. This isn't just because people back then did not know how to create the machines that give us access to the internet or that allow us to fly around the world. It is because all but the most forward-thinking scientists and philosophers could not have even contemplated a need for such things. Not only could the typical Middle-Age peasant not fathom the mechanics required to construct and mass-produce a machine capable of sustained flight, but they would probably never even dare to imagine that such technology would be desirable for them and the whole of the human race in the first place. Likewise, what use would the peasant have for internet access? No matter how much objective utility we see in it now, it would be incompatible with their paradigm and lifestyle.

The same applies to all cutting-edge technology that seems extravagant or unnecessary to us in the present day. We cannot say for sure what the technological norms of the generations to come will be, but we can say for sure that it will be entrepreneurs who bring civilization-altering benefits like space travel, virtual reality, and life extension to everyday consumers. And each entrepreneur who undertakes such a task will have to be well-suited to the new types of value they choose to produce and/or manage for the rest of us.

All other things being equal, creating something new is more difficult than improving something old because it requires a greater level of change to the existing inertia and habitual human behavior. It is relatively easy to take an existing impulse in someone and redirect it in a slightly different and more desirable direction. Little direct education is needed. Usually, mere demonstration is enough. But *instigating* a new type of desire in someone that they previously had no space in their mind for requires them to be much more open to new ideas and willing to change the habitual structure of their life. In either case, it is the sales and marketing process that creates the necessary change and allows for new products and services to take hold in society.

CHAPTER 19

MARKETING AND SALES—BUILDING AWARENESS AND MOTIVATION FOR NEW ACTION

THE MARKET CAN only approach equilibrium when buyers and sellers alike have ample accurate information about their options for attaining the goals they seek. Indeed, they cannot even set optimal goals, let alone strategize about how to achieve them, unless they first know enough about what the hell is going on. In other words, people have to know something of value exists before they can consciously demand it. That cognition is a necessary aspect of the "supply" part of the "supply and demand" relationship. It's not just about what is possible for you to buy. It's about what you are aware of and can conceive of strategizing to acquire and use. And even once someone knows of the existence of an asset, they have to be convinced of its value according to their changing and subjective standards. These processes are commonly called marketing and sales, respectively, and they play a more vital role in how we go about attaining our goals than most people ever realize.

The forms that marketing takes are not limited to how we typically think of pop-up ads on cheap websites and smarmy salesmen at used car dealerships. They are present in every new idea or object we come to accept as working parts of our paradigms or integrate into our strategies for getting what we want out of life. Everyone enthusiastically participates in marketing whenever they talk about something they value to someone else they think will be interested in hearing about it. Every social media post shared or "like" given is the active and willing participation in the process of marketing whatever is shared or liked. Marketing applies to buyers too. When someone makes it publicly known that they are in the market for a house of a certain type, in a certain location, within a certain price range, they are marketing the opportunity for sellers of such a house to do business with them.

The lifeblood of all economic relationships is clear and accurate communication from which expectations can be set and filled. It is impossible to derive the benefits of synergy from and for every party participating in a collaborative system without the ability to share opportunities and expectations. New opportunities cannot ever be acted upon until the appropriate people become aware of them. Needs cannot be met unless they are communicated effectively to the people capable of meeting them. As we will see, frequently, it is not a physical lack of ability or capacity that leaves demand unfulfilled but only inadequate awareness and strategizing caused by poor marketing.

Both sales and marketing often get bad press, though, because of unscrupulous sellers who intentionally mislead the market about either the problems people have or the nature of the solutions that they offer. The more obscure the domain the seller operates in, the less the general market of buyers will know about what value they actually need from it. In the West, certain types of professionals such as mechanics can even be categorically seen as suspicious parties by customers who don't know enough about cars to assess whether the prices they charge are competitive, the work they do is adequate, or even if any work has been done at all. Because of the knowledge imbalance between them, it is too easy for the seller to create a false demand in the buyer and profit monetarily without providing adequate value. For similar reasons, some people view even the entire concept of marketing through a dubious lens, assuming that every claim and attempt made to incentivize a purchase must be motivated by a desire to take advantage of buyers who do not actually need what is offered.

Yet, for every misleading advertisement that ever tricks someone into buying something on false grounds, there are a thousand more that make us aware of options for wealth accumulation that we were unaware of or help us make better choices about how we will invest our limited capital toward the achievement of our goals. Marketing in every form is an important part of making the economy function as efficiently as possible because it is the best way to communicate truths on a broad and massive scale. There is not enough time to have a personal conversation with every potential buyer about every opportunity for wealth exchange that could ever happen. Simple images and messages maybe be all that are needed to incite curiosity about opportunities and instigate the first steps of acting on them. A failure to communicate immense value effectively all but guarantees that form of value will fail on the market, no matter how objectively useful it might be.

Before I arrived here, there were a lot of things I took for granted about life in the village, things I would have just expected to be available and on offer by default here that were, in fact, starkly lacking. The house I purchased was quite old and in a state of disrepair initially, so I needed to hire at least a few experienced handymen and construction workers to help clean it up and modernize it. The grocery stores in town were far away and inconvenient to shop from, so I needed the means to purchase common food staples from people who grew or raised them locally. I didn't have a car yet, so I needed some reliable options for whom I could hire to drive me into town until I could procure one. And, most importantly, I needed someone to speak the local Armenian language with me and teach me the basic grammar and vocabulary so that I could begin to communicate effectively on my own with my neighbors. So I began spreading the word that I was looking to hire people for all of the above, fully expecting that it would not take long until locals from the surrounding villages showed up at my door or called me eager for the work.

To my frustration, months went by with virtually zero interest being shown by anyone in the village or surrounding areas in taking me up on the jobs I offered. It didn't compute in my head. I knew there had to be many people looking for work. In fact, I interacted with them frequently. I knew that many of them had the skills and experience to do the kinds of work I needed, as I regularly saw them performing these tasks on their own property. What was missing was a sense of urgency and motivation to spread awareness of this obvious match between what I wanted (demand) and what they could provide (supply). As well, there was the inverse economic relationship to consider. What I could provide was money, and it was something in great demand by almost everyone in the village. So why wasn't anyone jumping at the new opportunities I presented? Why couldn't we forge quick and easy mutually profitable economic relationships?

The answer, I eventually realized, was multifaceted but in every way related to outdated expectations and poor communication. For starters, there was no primary channel through which to make these needs and opportunities known to the people who would be best suited for them. So, the few people who ended up hearing about the work I needed performed had no convenient way to get the necessary details or investigate things for themselves to see if they were still available or appropriate for them. All they heard was that there was an American now living in the area who needed some vague work done on his house. They did not know who I was, where exactly my house was located, what kind of work I needed, the amount I would pay, how long the job would last, if there were other people already interested in the job, if I would be providing the necessary tools and materials, or how serious I was about the offer at all. Of course, I had clear and definite answers to all these questions, but there was no efficient and effective way for me to communicate them on a large scale to all the people wondering.

As a result, the job opportunity went unfulfilled for more than six months until a curious neighbor, who I happened to be talking to for unrelated reasons, brought the subject up out of the blue and asked if I happened to still need some work done on my house. I told him that yes, indeed, almost no work had been performed for the six months I had been publicly seeking workers. As soon as he learned the details of the job, he seemed surprised, just about as surprised as I was, that people weren't jumping at the opportunity I had been offering. He came by my house the following day, we worked out the terms of the job over the course of a single conversation, and he got to work right away at a rate significantly higher than what he had been making previously by alternate means to support himself. He happily remained in my employ for more than two years following that conversation, and he told me regularly how grateful he was for the opportunity, at one point even candidly admitting that it was the first time in his life he felt like he could comfortably provide financially for his family.

Consider the enormous and important change in the economic arrangement that occurred immediately after communication was cleared up. For six months, I had been in a position of needing ample important work done on my home with no foreseeable way to get it done. For six months, this man (and countless others like him in the surrounding villages) were unemployed and without comfortable means to provide for their families, despite their abundance of relevant skills and experience. The solution to this imbalance, this symptom of marketplace inefficiency, was incredibly simple and easy to enact. So why did it take six months? Why might it have taken much longer if not for the fortunate coincidence that enabled that critical conversation that instigated everything to occur?

Similar situations exist on larger scales with more disastrous consequences all around the world. **Are people the world over principally unemployed because there is literally not enough demand for any type of value that they could fulfill with their intelligence, creativity, tools, and labor?** Or is there, for some reason, a misalignment between what is perceived to be wanted and what is perceived to be available? In many cases, there are legitimate natural obstacles that prevent providers from meeting the needs of those who desire what they are capable of providing, obstacles like the cost of transporting people and goods long distances to where they would be applied most equitably. However, better technology and marketplace organization inevitably lessen the costs and inconveniences caused by these obstacles. Thus, the disincentive to act on opportunities diminishes.

In other cases, the marketplace obstacles are arbitrary and artificial. Social and legal restrictions are put in place by human institutions that prevent people from applying their knowledge, labor, and products where they would be most equitable—restrictions that disincentivize or outright prevent travel, transportation, and commerce. Some of these imposed restrictions we've accepted as normal for so long that we hardly notice how arbitrary and unnecessary they are, such as state and international borders, tariffs and embargoes on specific types of labor and products, restrictions on the professions that individuals can enter, mandatory hiring caps or quotas, and taxes that make certain kinds of value inequitable to produce according to the whims of the individuals in power to extort profits from the entrepreneurially inclined. And just like the Soviet authorities of bygone generations, every individual or institution that wields power to limit how we provide value to each other claims that they do so "for our own good," as it were.

Extrapolate and try to imagine how different things might be for the members of my village if there were even a rudimentary communication channel in place that everyone had economic incentive to participate in. Imagine what an optimally efficient system for matching market demands with market provisions would look for everyone, even on such a small societal scale as a village or area of neighboring villages. Everyone here owns a cell phone (of either the "smart" or "dumb" variety), most own computers, and there are centralized locations where information like job opportunities and people looking to buy certain local products could be listed on a public physical medium like a bulletin board. With this information accessible and constantly updated, how much more convenient would it be for each individual to get access to the requirements of comfortable living that they do not produce for themselves? How much easier would it be for each individual to apply their lifetime of acquired knowledge and skills to produce income for themselves by producing something of value for others?

It is primarily the collective ignorance of causality here and in other places like here that prevents anyone from implementing these obviously beneficial systems and channels to improve the collective communication ability and transfer of goods and services to where they will most be valued. It is also partially a tragic sort of self-fulfilling prophecy. **Perhaps people are so used to opportunities being scarce and unreliable that they have stopped looking for them.** What would be the point in setting up an elaborate communication network if they could assume ahead of time that nothing noteworthy would come from it? People have a self-inhibiting way of denying even what is happening right in front of their eyes so long as they are predisposed not to notice it or to categorize it as something other than what it is.

When we think of marketing in the conventional business sense, we usually limit it to meaning just trying to make as many people as possible aware of the fact that we have a new product or service available and we would like to convince them to consider spending their money on it. But the principles of marketing apply just the same to better ways of thinking and doing things that already exist but that have yet failed to spread as far as they deserve to.

Under communist control, there was little reason to try to make people aware of better options and convince them to take them because they had so little personal freedom to make such choices about the quality of their own lives anyway. It is a completely different story when dealing with individuals who are masters of their own destinies. Marketing and the spread of valuable ideas about what it is possible for us to choose to do in the pursuit of what we value are vital to the functioning and improvement of a free society.

However, even once new customers have been made aware of a new product or service that promises to offer superior subjective value, entrepreneurs cannot count on their customers quickly being convinced of the accuracy of the claim. To find marketplace success with a better idea means forging economic relationships with the people poised to gain the most from its adoption. It means building the appropriate images in their heads that incentivize them to make choices that they previously couldn't have realized would benefit them. It is in stark contrast to the Soviet authoritarian methodology of forcing people to act under threat of violence, even if the authority in place truly believes their mandates are in the best interests of the masses who, in their eyes, are too stupid to see so. The entrepreneur does not make people buy their products or get interested in their ideas "for their own good," as it were. They provide them with the inspiration and information they need to make that choice on their own.

What entrepreneurs call a "target audience" for a product or service is not delineated merely by the grouping of people who happen to have the needs they seek to solve but also those who are in a position to realize that the exchange would be equitable for them, and so they actively seek it out. If potential buyers do not realize this on their own, they can only be educated into accepting it as true. This process is a far greater investment of resources than merely placing the right product in front of people who already know what they need and what they are willing to give up to acquire it, but it is necessary for all but the most eager buyers.

Sales, in some way or form, exists in every business. That's because sales is the process of convincing people to spend their money on something they may not even realize they will find valuable, and no one knows everything they will find valuable or what forms of value exist as options for them to acquire. No one's wants are static, and neither is what the market can provide at any given moment. Both supply and demand are in a state of perpetual flux. So, whatever is produced must somehow be positioned to the people who are intended to be its buyers in such a way that they come to the natural conclusion that it is what they wish to buy, even if it means first making them aware of a wish they might have previously ignored or assumed there was no equitable means to acquire.

Sales requires learning how to look at what you produce through the eyes of someone else. But not just anyone else: The people who are intended to buy what you are trying to sell because they will find it valuable. Convincing someone that it's a good idea to buy something is both an intellectual and emotional process. People need to know that what they are considering buying will perform the function intended. Overpromises without proof of the ability to deliver garner mistrust for brands and individuals. Alternatively, positive reputations build trust that whatever one is offering will deliver the value it is supposed to. There are risks involved with any purchase. If a seller can't directly demonstrate that what they are trying to sell delivers what it is intended to, they will have to be prepared to verbally address any number of insecurities related to the risks of the purchase.

Imagine that you are someone with a reputation for solving a specific type of problem particularly well. People regularly come to you looking for help with the difficult situations they believe you are uniquely suited to alleviate. Understandably though, the people who know you only via reputation will want some personal assurances that the help they will be paying you for is the most viable fit for what they happen to need. Perhaps they feel, rightly or wrongly, that no one else has needs quite like theirs, so they are not confident in how appropriate your help will be despite your impressive experience. Perhaps they have a long history of being disappointed with the quality of similar solutions they have procured in the past. In these situations, a long sales conversation may be necessary to organically persuade such prospects to move forward with buying from you.

What kind of conversation is the right one to have with this anxious prospect? You might think the ideal choice is to recite a memorized script of attractive selling points. But that's not really a conversation because it does not involve two-way interaction. What if, in your haste to get the pre-decided pitch across, you make too many assumptions about what the buyer is actually looking for and what the source of their hesitation about moving forward is? What if instead of addressing what they are directly telling you they need help with, you go on and on about something you presume they should care about more than what they are clearly showing you they do? The probability is that they are going to be so preoccupied with what they already know is important to them that they are going to ignore anything you say that doesn't immediately address it.

Just as every purchase you make carries the risk of turning out not to be equitable *for* you, the same applies to everyone who might ever make a purchase *from* you. Clarity in communication about what utility the individual buyer is expecting to receive and the subjective value they ascribe to that utility helps reduce the risk of buyer's remorse. Everyone is happier when expectations match as closely as possible to the reality of the situation. Another way to remove this risk is to guarantee that your work or your product will deliver some specific metric of performance or satisfaction, including the opportunity to get a refund, repair, or replacement if it does not. Or, if you are performing a service, this might include offering revisions to the work performed at no additional charge until the predetermined level of quality has been achieved.

Remember that the goal of an ethical sales process is to persuade through demonstration and reasonable argumentation that a choice will turn out to be equitable for someone according to their subjective values and assessment. Anything that does not fall under this umbrella is coercion, bullying, or manipulation. Sellers who rely on these underhanded tactics to make money likely do not have much confidence in the actual value represented by their offerings.

CHAPTER 20

PRICING—FINDING AGREEMENT
BETWEEN BUYERS AND SELLERS

ALL OF US have been in the position of complaining that the price of something we wanted to buy was too high. Likewise, we may often find that the price at which people are willing to buy something from us is what we consider to be too low. How do we arrive at these conclusions about what amount of money is correct in each situation? Where do our ideas about what things should cost come from? Like everything else essential in economics, the answers can always be derived by a proper understanding of the axioms of supply and demand.

Lacking analysis, the question of the right price for any given good or service on the market seems like it might have a million valid answers. Perhaps, the inexperienced entrepreneur would do best to pick a reasonable-sounding number at random and hope for the best. Perhaps they should just charge one penny less than their most direct competition. Are these methods of determining a price any better or worse than any other? Or is there a more optimal way to derive pricing based upon our knowledge of the natural principles that govern exchange and interaction?

The Soviet Union fixed its in-store prices for consumption goods each year based on the State Planning Committee's arbitrary impressions of what various goods *should* cost. Predictably, goods priced lower than the equilibrium of actual market supply and demand sold out quickly, leading to ongoing shortages. People bought large quantities of them because they recognized good deals and wanted to ensure they had enough for their foreseeable future needs. Besides, with rapidly inflating currency, they knew that the longer they held onto their money, the less it would ultimately be worth, so they had incentive to spend it as quickly as possible. Meanwhile, goods priced higher than the market equilibrium sat unsold throughout the year, despite the fact that there were plenty of people who could use them. They weren't willing to pay the artificially high prices the State determined for them. So, the unused goods ended up offering no value to anyone and became nothing but waste products.

To make matters worse, because production models and quotas were typically predetermined on a yearly basis, there was nothing anyone working in the factories that produced these consumption goods could do to address the state of chronic shortage or waste. Obviously, the market would have benefited from increasing production of the cheap scarce goods and decreasing production of the expensive surplus goods, but there was no causal connection between the market of buyers and the market of producers. So long as the central economic planners maintained the power to dictate and enforce their ideas of what the Soviet economy ought to look like, no communication took place among producers and consumers, and the market could never hope to approach a state of optimal function or equilibrium.

No matter how strongly we might feel about it, there is no "right" or "wrong" price for any good or service you could

ever attempt to sell to or buy from anyone. There is only what someone somewhere is willing to sell it for and what someone else is willing to pay for it, both of which are influenced by how much the prospective seller and buyer perceive fungible or categorically similar items tend to be sold and bought for.

If you had no pre-existing knowledge of how much a particular type of asset was usually sold for, the amount you would be willing to pay for it might be significantly higher or lower than what you normally pay for it, even though the asset itself would still provide the same utility. This is because two important things would change in your perception of the value of the asset. First, you would not be able to compare the buying opportunity in front of you to other buying opportunities you knew you could count on being available if you were to decline this one. Second, you would lose the perspective of what other consumers of that asset were demonstrably willing to pay for it and similarly fungible ones. You would be left to evaluate solely by your own subjective value metrics what price you would be willing to pay to acquire something and come away having gained more than you lost.

Pricing rules apply equally to loaves of bread, bales of hay, life-saving medicines, metal ingots, subscriptions to online streaming services, teachers' salaries, and the newest cryptocurrencies. There are no exceptions to the natural principle, so long as no one is ever forced to act against their best interests. If the product or service is being offered at a price that people consider to be an equitable exchange for it, the exchange will occur. If not, it will not.

Economic exchanges of all kinds continue to happen so long as there are assets people need available at prices they consider subjectively worthwhile and the inverse for people who have things they are willing to get rid of. As soon as prices rise above or below this mutually equitable range wherein both parties feel they are subjectively benefiting from the exchange, economic activity ceases. It remains absent until at least one of the determining factors changes. Either those who want something come to want it more (thus justifying a *higher* price than they were previously willing to pay) or those who have something come to want money more (thus justifying a *lower* price than they were previously willing to receive). All human marketplaces the world over and throughout history can be summarized and understood this way.

Ignoring this logically necessary relationship by pretending that there are certain prices that buyers and sellers of certain products and services *should* be willing to buy and sell at does not alter reality. It does not suddenly make equitable for individuals that which is actually inequitable for them. In fact, it prevents what exchanges would have happened at the real mutually agreeable prices that have been subverted. The inevitable result is that fewer people get less of the stuff they consider valuable and fewer producers are able to offer their value to others. And thus, money itself ceases to serve its objective function, and shortages and waste abound, just as they did in the USSR.

If the object or action being sold is one that people buy and sell regularly, the entrepreneur should expect that there will be an established "going rate," "fair price," or "market value" for it. Other things being equal, there is no reason for a seller to sell at a price less than what they know someone else is willing to pay, and there is no reason for a buyer to buy at a price greater than what they know someone else is willing to sell for. Thus, market equilibrium is quickly achieved for goods and services that are commonplace and interchangeable enough that both sides of the market know roughly what to expect from each other. Marketplace communication channels help everyone participating become aware of price trends and adjust their buying and selling behavior accordingly.

If gasoline is being sold for a few cents cheaper per gallon at the station down the street, gas buyers might justify inconveniencing themselves slightly more to fill up their tanks there instead of at the one they usually go to. Though the consumer price of gas changes on a daily basis, these changes are clearly and quickly communicated through large signs promoting the day's price outside each station. So, not only are gas consumers immediately informed about where the best deals are, but gas providers who might be trying to compete with each other on price also know what the others in their domain are charging. This incentivizes them to offer competitive prices to consumers (assuming there are no other factors about the quality of their gas or the experience of getting it from them that would justify paying more) instead of choosing an arbitrarily high price and hoping consumers just mindlessly accept it. Similarly, when in-store shoppers can look up the online price of expensive items in mere moments with their smartphones, it encourages vendors to compete with these prices.

But, just like everything else going on in the market, the price arrived at by market equilibrium is never totally stable. The conditions affecting how difficult it is to produce and bring something to market (i.e., supply) and those affecting how much people want or need it (i.e., demand) are never stable. Despite the best efforts of central planners who seek to commandeer the wants and productive actions of the populace to suit their visions for what human society ought to look like, external manipulation cannot last or create the desired effect. Natural economic principle always takes over in the end. You cannot command the market to want something more or less than it does or to be better or worse at providing it than it is— any more than you can command the seas to part for you in violation of the natural laws that govern them. You can only seek to understand these laws and align your choices with them to the greatest degree your mind and body will allow.

For the same reason, no one can remove or change a major variable of the marketplace and assume that everything else will remain the same or conform the way they want to their tailoring. No one can eliminate a species from an ecosystem and expect that everything once affected by that species shall remain the same as before. Nature and economy abhor vacuums and rush to fill them whenever they appear because that is what serves the interests of the individual processes and organisms that constitute the whole. Everything that exists is opportunistic. **Whatever can exist is what continues to exist.** Whatever cannot ceases to.

The equivalent fallacy committed by the individual entrepreneur is to assume that they can set whatever arbitrarily high price they want for the goods and services they sell. They arrogantly assume that buyers will simply pay without further analysis. Just the same, buyers cannot demand arbitrarily low prices for the goods and services they wish to purchase and expect that sellers acquiesce to their evaluation. The best anyone can do is make an offer to buy or sell at a certain price and wait to see if economic conditions are such that the corresponding seller or buyer will respond favorably and if an agreement of mutual benefit can be made.

More developed parts of the world are most likely to benefit from stable supply chains and predictable levels of demand than places where major destabilizing events (of natural, industrial, or political origin) are more common. **But no place is immune to changing trends or economic black swan events that rattle even the most qualified predictions about the monetary value of things, and no local economy is an island.** For that reason, it is wise to buy more of something when economic conditions seem to favor buyers and sell more of it when economic conditions favor sellers until equilibrium returns. This is especially true with commodities and consumption goods that retain their value for a long time and are easy to store and transfer, for reasons outlined earlier.

Part of understanding the subjective and changing nature of the value of all things is respecting the fact that anything that exists on the market can gain or lose subjective value at any time for physical or psychological reasons. And just as quickly as it gained or lost it, it can lose or gain it back to where it was before. How these sporadic changes will affect you depends on when you choose to buy or sell something that is subject to them.

Supply and demand are the only all-powerful gods of the marketplace, no matter the business you are in or the asset you are dealing with. And both sides of this equation are always shifting. Maybe the supply starts to run low because of physical or logistical issues like unseasonably bad weather that blocks access to a natural resource. On the flip side, maybe a once-rare asset suddenly becomes much more available due to a discovery of a large natural deposit or the innovation of methods that make accessing or processing it exponentially easier. Remember the story of our old friend aluminum, who was once scarcer and more expensive than gold and is now so cheap and abundant that we regularly throw it away without a second thought.

The demand can also change, often for psychological reasons. Maybe a superior product emerges in the marketplace that makes the old one irrelevant, causing almost everyone who was previously demanding it to lose interest. Maybe the country that produces the primary supply of an asset suddenly decides to impose massive tariffs on its exportation, artificially raising prices and creating a disincentive to purchase it. Maybe a celebrity starts talking about something previously overlooked by the general public on social media, and an overnight trend of hype begins to build around it.

Collectors are people who buy rare, vintage, or noteworthy assets that they believe the value of will organically rise over time as the already limited supply naturally diminishes (because some amount of what currently exists will invariably get lost or damaged, reducing the circulating supply) and demand naturally increases (as the number of people who wants this rare and noteworthy thing goes up over time as more people become aware of it). If they are right in their predictions and willing to wait long enough to be proven true, they stand to receive massive profits from their investments and foresight.

Often what seems to be a loss is not yet actually realized as a loss. And conversely, what appears to be a gain cannot yet be confirmed as such. The game is still in play and the conclusion in flux until the relevant moving pieces have settled and we make meaningful choices based upon their positions. But we humans, as emotional creatures, tend to react drastically and immediately to whatever the situation appears to be in any moment. Without practice, it is difficult to distance ourselves enough from momentary appearances to focus on the bigger picture of what is happening and where things are likely going next. The entrepreneur must plan within the predictable future, however. It does no good to end up being right long after you are dead or long after the opportunity to act on marketplace changes has passed.

Where the question of pricing becomes most difficult to derive an answer is in areas that are not so ubiquitous in a market that people don't know what kind of pricing to expect or when a change in quality or function is significant enough that what is being sold cannot be appropriately compared to categorical equivalents. When buyers do not know what utility and value they will be receiving from something that appears totally new and are not aware of what other options they have for acquiring that utility and value, there is a much larger range of prices they might be willing to pay for it. Some might only buy it at a very low price because they perceive they are taking a higher-than-normal level of risk by exchanging their money for something they are not fully accustomed to. Others might be willing to pay a very high price for the same good or service because they perceive that it does something for them nothing else on the market can and that they have no other options for acquiring it at a cheaper price.

Meanwhile, the provider of such unprecedented value needs to perform their own calculations about their cost of production, the effort required to find appropriate buyers, and what amount of profit will make the entire operation economically worthwhile. Selling a few items with a huge profit margin is not quite the same as selling many items with a low profit margin because the work required will not be the same. Maybe they only have a few items to sell and can reasonably predict that there are a few buyers somewhere out there in the market willing to pay a very high price to acquire them. How long is the seller willing to wait to find those few buyers? How many other resources are they willing to put into the process, and will the profit received when/if sold still be worthwhile for them? Maybe it will be a more optimal choice to set a low but still profitable price and watch the items fly off the shelf in the hands of eager buyers, assuming they have the inventory and manpower to manage so many transactions. But then again, there will be some buyers who perceive the item to be of lower quality if it is sold at a lower price and might actually be less inclined to purchase it than if they saw it listed at a higher one. There is no one perfect answer here. Every price arrived at will carry some advantages and disadvantages to the entrepreneur. They must select their own priorities carefully and figure out how much experimentation they are willing to do to create a business model that works for them.

Does all this over-analysis seem intimidating? Many people in non-entrepreneurial cultures believe that they cannot go into business on their own because they do not consider themselves to be capable of performing the math and accounting that goes into ensuring that a production model is optimally profitable.

I heard this argument made repeatedly by the members of my humble Armenian construction crew. One of them repeated his go-to excuse for why he could not manage his own business model any time the subject of entrepreneurship was brought up: He did not think he was smart enough to perform the necessary accounting. He had never received any official business training or education, so he assumed himself unqualified. The

irony, of course, was that he constantly had to measure and calculate the sizes of rooms, the square or cubic meterage of various building materials required, and the cost of such things as
they varied from store to store. These were all done with the
basic arithmetic he learned decades before during his Soviet el-
ementary education. But he had never been told that the math-
ematical operations he was perfectly adequate at performing
for the purpose of calculating construction requirements were
the same as what would be required to handle the finances and
accounting of almost any simple business model. This is yet another imaginary barrier to entrepreneurship and making choices to improve one's life implanted in cultures by unconscious
collective fallacies.

**The universal function of buying and selling in the econ-
omy is to move the wealth encapsulated by goods and services to where it will be most subjectively valued by its owners.** Whenever a seller willingly sells something, it is because
they have made the subjective evaluation that the amount of
money they will receive in return is worth more than what they
lose in the sale. The willing buyer, meanwhile, has made the inverse subjective evaluation; they would rather have what they
are receiving than the money they are losing to receive it. The
exchange cannot happen without the consent of both parties
and, therefore, their mutual profit. The function of a monetary
price as denoted in absolute numeric terms of a common unit of
measurement such as dollars, Bitcoin, or grams of gold grants
both buyer and seller the ability to set their own terms to the
exchange and reach some kind of agreement that serves them
both without either party sacrificing more value than they need to.

CHAPTER 21

BRAND IDENTITY—UPHOLDING THE SYMBOL OF A PROMISE OR IDEAL

THERE'S YET ANOTHER major overlooked consequence of living in the aftermath of a culture like Armenia, where there was little to no trust in the long-term future of any endeavor, and survival depended upon focusing on whatever one could gain in the immediate future. Many people have become skilled at procuring short-term gains; often though, through the very same choices, they sabotage their prospects for long-term repeated gains. Under unsustainable communist rule, there was no reason to build up a personal brand or professional reputation because the State assigned your work and your salary for you, and its whims were beyond your influence or reasoning.

When we embrace entrepreneurship and the willful production of value as a total paradigm, it becomes obvious that choices that might benefit us in the short term often end up harming us (and others) to a much greater degree over time. As well, our short-sighted choices or narrow focus might just externalize costs and liabilities that we don't want to be responsible for, leaving other people in the unfair position of having to pick up the slack of our errors when they never willfully entered such a position. What is best for us five minutes from now might not be best for us five years from now. The scale of perspective we are capable of adopting and assessing the merit of our choices through is a byproduct of the level of responsibility and control we have established over our lives. Eventually, we grow quite happy to endure short-term sacrifices that we can predict will become great sources of value to us over time.

People, you may have noticed, do not choose whom to give their money to randomly or haphazardly. There are principles and patterns to their choices. **Of the many businesses and individuals you spend money with, the majority are repeat sources of goods and services for you.** You probably do not go out looking for a new place to buy the various stuff you need every time you shop. Your default response is to return to sources of value you have had positive experiences with before and from which you know what to expect. At the very least, if you don't have firsthand personal experience of good suppliers for the products and services you seek, you will listen to popular opinion and personal suggestions from other people like you. There is no reason, in most cases, to go somewhere unknown and risk having a bad experience when you already have positive associations with known value providers. Those associations form a major aspect of their brand identities.

When you do choose to explore and experiment with new providers, it's probably when you need something you can't get from the providers you already know, when you are looking for a better price, when you've had bad experiences that disincentivize you returning, or when you are just curious about exploring new or unknown opportunities. But the bulk of your money is spent with known entities because, in your perception, familiarity minimizes risk.

Think of how you formed the positive associations you hold with the people and institutions you habitually give your money to. You are far more likely to spend money more than once with people if they communicate well with you, set your expectations appropriately, and go out of their way to fulfill those expectations smoothly so that you incur the least possible losses to your time, money, mental well-being, and other resources. These are the fundamentals of a working relationship of any kind. It is on the foundation of repeated positive association that entrepreneurs are able to expand beyond one simple and easy provision of value to many logically related ones and scale up their efforts to a point where less and less is required of them to produce ever greater value. A memorable and remarkable brand identity facilitates this function for existing and prospective customers alike.

A brand reputation or identity is more than a logo, a color scheme, a typeface, a catchy slogan, or an earworm jingle. These superficial elements are merely the artistic representation in tangible space of the intangible promise made by the brand. The brand itself is a collective association of the value generated by a person or entity consisting of multiple people working in synergy for a common harmonious goal. When there is a need for order of a specific variety, it is your conscious and unconscious knowledge of the brand identities of relevant value providers that tells you who to buy from or hire. It is the same when people want to buy from or hire you for the value you promise. The better that brand reputations capture an accurate picture of what someone offers, the greater confidence all buyers can take in the economic exchanges they make to address the problems of living.

Across whatever tangible forms it takes, a brand is a representation of what someone who produces or manages wealth and value stands for. It is a symbol of quality, a promise of a standard that can be expected for those who choose to associate with it. That promise is upheld under direct threat of loss of market reputation and untold future opportunities. Without effective brand identities, it becomes functionally impossible for people participating in a complex economy to remember and retain meaningful associations regarding the productive roles of one another. The more complex, specific, or meaningful the value one intends to put out into the world, the more important the function of brand identity becomes for them.

Brands bring logically associated sources of value together under the same umbrella concept. Everyone can be a solver of some problem or some class of interconnected problems. But whenever we solve one problem, we also open the door to higher-level problems that are feasible to solve now that the old one is no longer an issue that demands active attention. Human wants are unending, after all. There is no permanent state of perfect satisfaction, as such a state would obviate the need to make choices at all.

Many of the problems we solve also come with accompanying problems that must also be solved concurrently with the initial problem. In such situations, upselling and cross-selling beyond an initial purchase of encapsulated value become advantageous for buyer and seller alike. It is more efficient for everyone if more value can be conveyed in a smaller number of interactions from a smaller number of sources. So, entrepreneurs providing value in related fields naturally come to see the mutual benefit of forming alliances with one another based upon their respective brand identities for reliably solving certain types of complementary problems. Reputations influence business-to-business relationships just the same as they influence business-to-consumer ones, so brand identity plays a vital role among entrepreneurs who associate with one another to deliver greater value than they could on their own. This is, once more, the principle of market synergy in action, and it is one of the leading causes of exponentially increased wealth production and consumption in modern entrepreneurial societies.

There are no forms of value that exist in isolation from all others, and we cannot possibly provide all the forms of value connected to the primary ones we cater to. A television requires electricity to turn on and movies or shows to be watched on it. Tiles for your new kitchen floor require delivery, grout, adhesive, and the service of a tradesman who knows how to lay them. Piano lessons require a piano, music to play, and a place to give them. It's obvious that a carpenter is nothing without their tools, but it is equally true that the value of their work depends on countless other marketplace factors such as the ability to display and promote their creations to the people who will decide to pay money for them. The person who has embraced the entrepreneurial mentality will not just see the individual role or craft they know how to contribute value to society with. They will focus on the systems their role depends on and the part they play in those systems too.

With an overhead view of the creation and exchange of valuable things, it will become easier to spot opportunities to produce products or services that disproportionately benefit an existing system. Whatever currently exists might be lacking a crucial component that would make it many times better at helping people. As well, it will become second nature to rope complementary but disconnected products and services together into the same model to optimize their value, possibly by uniting them all under one brand heading or merely arranging them in proximity to each other so that the presence of any one improves all the others, and the others all improve the one. The entrepreneur both optimizes existing systems by adding new components to them and forges new systems where disparate component parts lack proper management. That is why I have said that an entrepreneur is someone who produces *or* manages the value of wealth. It is enough to work better with what already exists to optimize its valuable output without necessarily having to create something new. **Wherever there is dysfunction, disharmony, unmet needs, and unnecessary stress induced by the mismanaging of needless problems and inefficiencies, there is work for entrepreneurs to straighten things out and be duly rewarded with monetary profits and a sense of genuine contribution to the world.**

So, when you look around you and see problems that need straightening out, it should become apparent where your knowledge, skills, and tangible assets will be most equitably applied in the tactical improvement of your situation. And it should just as quickly become apparent what obstacles are still in the way of the further effecting of your value upon the dysfunction you seek to resolve. Are things doomed and destined to remain at their present state of inadequacy forever? Is the obstacle you perceive just the preordained state of civilization and an inescapable part of the human condition that we must contend with? Or are there steps you can take to begin contracting with others whose assets are needed in conjunction with yours to implement the harmony and solutions your knowledge and experience tell you is possible?

Consider that everything we universally consider backward and unnecessarily problematic about past states of society were once considered part and parcel to human life on this planet. One by one, we have educated ourselves enough and invented superior forms of technology that all but eliminated persistent problems once considered to be inevitable, even among the wealthiest and most powerful people of any given era. Diseases have cures. Ample food and shelter can be produced in countless new entrepreneurial ways. There is no limit to the amount of variety of productive roles to play in society;

therefore, there is no limit to the number and variety of ways for entrepreneurial people to support themselves and increase their personal wealth.

There are already countless forms of wealth in society that are not being applied where they would be most subjectively valuable, and it is often only because no entrepreneurial thinkers are addressing these situations to see what pieces ought to move where for the greatest positive impact. For that type of vision, the thinker has to know the nature of each piece and the value they are capable of providing, how well they will fit into the new system, and how to make them function with the other relevant pieces.

That is where the social phenomenon of brand identification becomes especially vital to the economic improvement of our world. Without an identity to latch onto, it becomes impossible to efficiently calculate how to apply existing assets to create maximum wealth generation for everyone by forming agreements with the people who own and hold control over those assets. It spares us the trouble of having to form personal connections and build up trust from nothing with each new provider we might want to risk a mutually beneficial exchange with. It also means that we do not have to rely on a central omnipotent authority to manage the economy and make these choices for us through force. Positive brand identity means that we can be reasonably sure that we will get what we pay for, even when we have no personal experience to base this confidence upon. We borrow the confidence of others who have dealt with what the brand symbolizes before us.

Without the ability to form reliable secondhand associations like this, there would be a permanent natural cap on how far and wide we could scale our value-producing actions as individuals. There would be a limit to how much our vision could actually reach out to help others who stand to benefit from it.

Just as printed books made it possible to spread knowledge on a scale unknown by live educators and telephones and computers enabled us to maintain relationships with people all around the world, properly implemented branding does the same for those who wish to be known for the value they offer and values they stand for. The wealth rewards of our productive actions scale with how efficiently and effectively we apply them for others.

It's not enough to secure one good sale from a new customer and add their money to the coffer. The transaction does not end with the direct exchange of goods for currency. The buyer must step away from the encounter feeling good about the transaction, looking forward to doing business again if an appropriate need arises, and willingly suggesting that others do the same. That's how confidence in your earning ability comes. It is not about incidental chance and good fortune. It's about building a reliable system upon the most secure assets of your existence.

CONCLUSION

THE ECONOMY RUNS ON CHOICE

HOPE FOR A brighter future lives in the curious and open-minded, which is a group not exclusively but primarily composed of the young in any given culture. Curiosity drives the desire to accumulate more accurate knowledge and improve outdated cultural paradigms. Without it, people are prone to unconsciously copying the habits and values of others. One person's trauma, limitations, or false ideas quickly become another's, and nothing ever really changes on the individual or societal level.

The beautiful thing about understanding problems as principles is that it becomes simple to see how their solutions apply on all levels of complexity. What is good for the individual seeking economic control and determination over their life is good for the whole of a society seeking to do the same. Freedom and its benefits are available and appropriate for everyone, regardless of their cultural and economic past or the outdated obstacles they may still be needlessly struggling with in the present.

There has only ever been one way to help people produce and manage greater wealth and achieve economic self-control. There will only ever continue to be one way. It is to educate them with greater knowledge about how reality works. It is to aid them in developing physical skills that derive from that greater knowledge. It is to enable them to acquire more and better tools that give them bigger leverage and efficiency over how they apply that knowledge and skill in the pursuit of greater wealth and satisfaction. And it is to inspire them to adopt this entrepreneurial paradigm and take those crucial first steps away from their limitations.

Education even solves the problem of social tyranny. No person who feels confident in their ability to make meaningful choices about resolving their problems will hand these choices over to someone else claiming, on arbitrary grounds, to be better equipped to make them. **The more that everyday people learn to take control over the uncertainties inherent to life, the**

less they will feel that they need to depend upon inhumane and ineffectual social authorities to play that role for them. The Soviet Union and other oppressive bodies like it are the result of the large-scale abdication of personal responsibility and attempts at circumnavigating the consequences of personal choice. There are analogs to the USSR in all parts of the world — even back home in the so-called land of the free. Totalitarian agents can only maintain power over the masses they subjugate by promoting the illusion that their restricting hold is needed. Without abdication, there would be no power for them to wield.

The key, then, to helping individuals and societies reach a state of sustainable economic self-determination lies in unlocking the belief that it is within their power to take control of their own lives. It requires upgrading the way they think about how they interact productively with the world, particularly over the portion of it they can claim as their domain. Ownership denotes responsibility and control. Control is choice about how something is used. It is earned by applying our creative and transformative actions to reality to make something useful and valuable emerge from it. Without ownership and accountability, there is no incentive to create and improve. Gradually, the world becomes a better place where people are better equipped to pursue their values due to that incentive being applied without prejudice to all of society.

None of us can ever escape being led by the pursuit of our values. Choice always follows values, and action conforms to choice. We can embrace the responsibility that comes with consciously striving to get what we want out of life. We can work to improve ourselves enough to be worthy of it—or we can refuse to consider the burdens of existence and, instead, deal with the consequences of abdication to others. But what we can never do is escape the facts that we want what we want and that there are immutable rules to the game of acquiring it.

In spite of what could be interpreted as great evidence to the contrary, I remain optimistic about the long-term economic future of Armenia and humanity. This is because I know that people do not have to think of themselves as entrepreneurs or even explicitly understand the principles of entrepreneurship as outlined here to apply and take advantage of them. The label and cultural identity do not matter. What matters is only how well every person is able to align their behavior with the principles that will lead to the outcomes they desire.

In any domain of education, it is always a minority of people that understands the nuances of the subject on a complex level. But still, countless others will be in positions to benefit from that knowledge because of the minority that understands and actively works to enact it. If you have read and understood this message and are ready to implement that understanding in your life, you are part of the progressive force that gradually moves human culture toward a point where self-determination is embraced at face value as obviously desirable by nearly everyone.

However, the spread of economic freedom is almost guaranteed to be slow and require the passing of generations. We have seen how even now, 30 years after communism officially ended for those 15 republics once claimed by the USSR, the destructive and limiting effects of its ideology linger across Armenia and other cultures. Even though no one under 30 years of age today was alive to experience communist rule directly, almost all of them remain heavily indoctrinated and influenced by what their parents and grandparents were conditioned to believe.

The problem will primarily only lessen with the coming of each new generation. Superior knowledge of reality makes its way into culture as the benefits of knowing become clear to self-interested individuals, followed eventually by society as a whole. Culture cannot avoid changing. The future belongs to those who are curious now and can position themselves to b ahead of the ideological curve. Those who understand and apply these principles ahead of time will gain leverage over reality and see substantial improvements to their material quality of life, which, in turn, makes improvement in all other areas of life far easier. They will even indirectly be benefiting those people who are not ready to learn.

There is no telling what ways we might eventually uncover to offer new solutions to the problems of living. But since we are curious and educated enough now to understand the economic principles at play, there is no reason to accept the suboptimal ways that wealth production, management, and distribution occur at the time of the culture we are born into. If we can envision a better way that does not conflict with reality's principles, we can certainly achieve it. The single most impactful choice we can make now is to spread the relevant knowledge and inspiration that will eventually lead to all other downstream entrepreneurial progress.

ЗНАНИЕ
РАЗОРВЕТ ЦЕПИ РАБСТВА·

99

Knowledge will
break the chains of
slavery.

_____

A CASE STUDY IN INFLUENCING THE OPENING OF A STORE IN KALAVAN VILLAGE

RELEASING *EVERYONE IS AN ENTREPRENEUR* was both a cathartic exercise and something of a social experiment for me. It served as a way to see if I could make real progress in the economic paradigm of a part of the world I was now connected to and that, in my perspective, desperately needed it. But over three years of living here, I came to see that my words had to be paired with actions if I expected meaningful results in the paradigms of those around me. So, at last, I took action that directly led to major systemic changes, and it was so simple and easy to initiate the process that I've been kicking myself ever since for not thinking of it sooner.

Nearly every time I would make the hour trip into the nearest major town, Dilijan, a particular neighbor called Shavarsh would ask me to purchase a pack of his favorite brand of cigarettes. The first few times, I didn't mind doing this small favor for him. But it began to happen so often that I usually ended up being too busy running other errands in town that I was unable to procure his cigarettes for him. And because I was the only appointed source of cigarette acquisition in these cases, he depended on me to feed his nicotine addiction. I was the only link available to complete the micro-supply chain between the village and town. My failure in this task meant he would have to go an unknown amount of time without the cigarettes he craved. Lacking a car of his own, he had no other reliable means by which to acquire them except to ask others sporadically going into town if they too might be able to do this favor for him.

After enough iterations of this inconvenient set of circumstances, I asked Shavarsh plainly why he only ever asked me to buy one or two packs of the cigarettes he wanted at a time. Since he knew with a high degree of certainty that he would want more of them in the near- and long-term future, and since cigarettes have a shelf life of at least a few years, he could easily secure a personal supply for himself by purchasing many packs at one time and just consuming them as needed. Why not just buy 10 or 20 packs on one trip into town for the convenience of having them available for consumption whenever he would need them and the security of knowing he wouldn't run out any time soon without a reliable supply chain that would allow him to acquire more? His answer was as predictable as his demand for the cigarettes: He never had enough money to invest in speculation about his future cigarette consumption. As a result, he was locked into an inefficient, unnecessary, and repetitive struggle to manage the supply that the fulfillment of his demand required at great inconvenience to himself and the neighbors he depended on to close the gap in the cigarette supply chain.

I recognized that this was the entrepreneurial teaching opportunity I had been waiting for. The next time I went into town, I spent a few extra minutes of my time finding Shavarsh's favorite brand of cigarettes at the lowest offered price. Then, despite the fact that I had no personal demand to consume them, I purchased ten packs and brought the supply of cigarettes home with me. When I saw Shavarsh, I informed him that I was now the proud owner of ten packs of his favorite brand of cigarettes. The next time he wanted to purchase one, he would no longer need to depend on someone in the village going out of their way to help him on an inconvenient schedule. He could simply purchase one of mine that I had already gone out of my way to acquire before his demand for cigarettes presented itself. And for the convenience I'd be providing him (and to compensate me for the risk of spending my own money upfront), I'd only charge him 20% above the price I had paid for the cigarettes in town. I even showed him the receipt from my purchase, so he knew that I was upfront about the price.

At once, I could see that my offer offended Shavarsh's social and economic paradigm. It was a reaction quite similar to the one I had seen from local parents when I made the mistake of paying money to my young neighbors for working for me at their request. It was a clear indicator that I had committed yet another egregious cultural faux pas. Why should he pay me extra for something I already had in abundance? He knew that I didn't smoke and had no personal use for the cigarettes I had acquired. I should be happy to share them with him, or at least give them to him for the same price I had paid. Right?

In Shavarsh's economic paradigm, when someone has too much of something, they automatically seek to give it to anyone who doesn't have enough and requests it from them. He could not see the new role I was trying to play in the local village economy by stockpiling a non-perishable supply of a commonly demanded good when I went into town (where supply is abundant), ensuring that it would be available and convenient when people needed it in the village (where supply is scarce). The economic dynamics of what I was doing with his favorite brand of cigarettes were no different than every farmer in the village stockpiling hay in the summer (when it is naturally abundant), so there would be more than enough of it in the winter (when it is naturally scarce). Because of my deliberate speculative actions concerning the local demand for cigarettes, the number of options for acquiring them in the village rose from zero to one. A fundamental economic improvement occurred for everyone who cared about acquiring maximum benefits from cigarettes for the minimum possible costs.

As expected, Shavarsh initially rebuked my offer to sell him cigarettes at an inflated price and at substantially greater convenience compared to his other options for acquiring them. Yet, within a few weeks, economic conditions were such that he was able to make the independent choice that buying a pack of cigarettes from me was now equitable. The perceived gains were now greater than the perceived costs. The irregular supply from town he had been depending on had failed to come through for him, and he was at last left with no other choice but to buy a pack from me.

The day I sold my first pack of cigarettes, I congratulated Shavarsh for seeing the economic advantage of buying from me locally instead of relying on complex and inefficient supply chains over which he had little control. Though I'm sure at the time he didn't understand why I saw the purchase as so important, it eventually led to related conversations about what other goods were most commonly acquired in town and brought to the village in an unreliable and inefficient manner. Any time that we could identify an economic exchange that was more difficult or costly than it needed to be, it would be possible for us to simplify and make it more convenient for everyone living here and (more importantly) tourists who would come to stay long-term seeking easy access to their favorite consumable goods and resources.

It took weeks to sell my first pack of cigarettes in Kalavan village. But once enough people became aware through word-of-mouth that I was offering this service as a reliable means of acquiring cigarettes conveniently for what amounted to a surcharge of the equivalent of only about 25 cents USD, I had regular customers start showing up at my house to get their nicotine fix whenever they couldn't rely on an alternate means of buying cigarettes. It became something of a spectacle among those neighbors I had told about the social and economic experiment I was performing in their backyard. Some kept an active count of how many packs I had so far sold so far. None had believed my entrepreneurial venture would be successful at the start.

When the day came that I sold out of the original ten-pack I bought in town (garnering a total profit of $2.50 for me), I could already see there had been a subtle but important change in my neighbors' mentality. They realized just as clearly as I did that if I could sell cigarettes at a profit ten times consecutively, how many more times might I be able to continue doing it? Furthermore, might there also exist the market possibility of doing it with other cheap and ordinary consumer goods that the residents of Kalavan were accustomed to acquiring inconveniently from in town? With this one act, I accomplished more in educating my neighbors about their ongoing economic inefficiencies than the past three years of begging, arguing, and lecturing had been able to. I showed them the superior reality they were ignorant of and missing out on instead of merely verbally insisting that it existed and that they could be part of it any time they wanted to.

The importance of this experiment for me was not the joy of providing cigarettes to consumers who valued them or even the meager profit I was making by doing so. Frankly, the amount of money I made from it was not worth the time and effort of taking the money in the first place from my buyers. What mattered to me was being able to demonstrate to my Kalavanian village neighbors that economic improvements can be implemented anywhere, even among small groups of low-income people with generations of contradicting cultural programming. Self-interest wins out in the end, so long as entrepreneurial actors can effectively market new opportunities to provide more of what people want in a subjectively better manner than before. And all the while, the knowledge sat in the back of my mind that if I had attempted even such a simple and clearly mutually beneficial act like offering a better way to acquire cigarettes just 30 years ago while Armenia was still under communist Soviet control, I'd be branded a speculator and harshly punished for my economic "crime" of interfering with the State's "fair" control of cigarette supply and distribution.

By going out of my way to acquire a single product (Shavarsh's preferred brand of cigarettes) before he otherwise would have bought them in a market where it is quite inconvenient to buy them, I was taking the first vital step toward the development of a fully-fledged store full of goods that would benefit everyone economically connected to Kalavan village who demanded such goods.

I began this experiment as a speculative cigarette entrepreneur because I was in a unique position to recognize the long-term benefits and economic changes that the presence of a humble convenience store could bring to the economically inefficient village I lived in. The economic purpose of any store is two-fold: To simplify the exchange process of the goods it sells and to ensure their consistent supply by acquiring them in advance of their demand being realized. By employing the division of labor principle and economies of scale, a store owner spares their customers the trouble of each having to go out of their way to accumulate the various goods they wish to consume on their own. The economic losses of such inefficiency of exchange became especially harmful to people who live in remote and underdeveloped communities, such as here in Kalavan village. A functioning store is one of the first, most simple, and most impactful economic improvements that such communities can make to the quality of life for all residents. And once the store owner establishes wholesale supply chains, they will almost certainly be able to offer their wares at prices similar to those people are used to paying in town instead of at the inflated price I had to charge in order to make a profit.

Still, my ambition of getting my neighbors involved in starting and running a small store here was met with great resistance and objection.

"Kalavan village is too small. Because not many people live here, there wouldn't be enough business to sustain a store."

This objection assumes that a store has to be operating at a certain size to be more economically efficient than the alternatives. The reality is that a locally stored and more inexpensively acquired supply of goods produces economic leverage at any scale. It doesn't necessarily have to look like the bustling shops that people are used to seeing in town. It doesn't even need to have its own dedicated building. The physical assets managed by the store owner just need to be protected from theft and deterioration, and it needs to be convenient for customers to acquire what they need when they need it. Money is already being saved by buying most goods in bulk at cheaper whole-sale rates than most people in the village pay at retail prices for individual items in combination with the transportation costs and labor associated with frequent trips into town.

"People in Kalavan already buy everything they need by driving an hour into town at regular intervals. Therefore, they wouldn't buy anything from the store if it existed."

The reason the residents of Kalavan village drive an hour out of their way to do their shopping is that doing so is currently the best option they have for getting what they need. By improving the arrangement of the local economy to make a different supply model more objectively efficient and sub-jectively favorable to them, you can change their recurring behavior to actions that accomplish more of what they want through less effort and other costs. Though at first, many people might stick to the economically inefficient actions they are used to just out of habit, it is easy to foresee that there will eventually come times when they realize they can just grab that bottle of cooking oil, roll of toilet paper, or pack of ciga-rettes they need from the supply that has been pre-acquired by the entrepreneurial shopowner who foresaw the recurring need for such things (just as Shavarsh eventually did with the first pack he bought from me). Even if the economics require the shop owner to charge a little more than what people are used to paying in town, the extra convenience and reduced transportation costs will still make this a more equitable exchange for them.

"Perishable goods will spoil quickly, leading to losses for the entrepreneurial shop owner."

Entropy is a form of risk that applies to all physical assets. Everything degrades with time. Everything has a viable shelf life, after which the intended value will no longer be available to consumers. What we call "perishable" goods are those with a shelf life so short that we have to be extra conscious of the rapid loss of their utility and value. We must go out of our way to manage the storage, exchange, and consumption of these goods based on their fragile condition. All entrepreneurial efforts involve predicting the future in some form, but that's much easier to do when one has a longer window of time for their predictions to be proven accurate.

In the context of opening a store in Kalavan, perishable goods like fresh milk, eggs, meat, and vegetables represent a disproportionately large entrepreneurial risk because of the additional storage and time frame constraints. It's one thing to spend money on inventory without a short-term looming time pressure to sell it or risk losing your investment. At the very least, you can always personally consume those things if absolutely no one wants to buy them from you over the several years that their value might remain viable following your acquisition of them. But the strategy for ensuring a profit (or at least avoiding a loss) is different when the entrepreneur has only days or weeks to extract value from their speculative assets. This would be fine if the villagers here could predict with reasonable certainty what the recurring demand for such things would be and, therefore, how many chicken eggs or kilos of pork to stock the store with.

The uncertainty regarding the predictable consumption of perishable goods in Kalavan comes entirely from the fact that the people here are not yet accustomed to purchasing such goods from a local store. It is likely that even after the store opens, they will continue to produce things for themselves, barter directly with each other, or buy fresh goods in town when the opportunity allows for it. But by taking a minimal risk and at least offering the option of buying fresh fruit, meats, vegetables, and so forth, the entrepreneurial shop owner can begin to gauge what the predictable recurring demand for each category of perishable goods will be. They can even adjust their inventory based on changing economic factors that affect demand, such as the changing seasons of the year, tourists coming to visit for extended stays, or even the population of the village increasing as more people learn of its brand reputation and decide to move here.

These objections are symptoms of a larger, systemic mentality problem—one which we could say broadly applies to most residents of developing nations far more than it does to those who are fortunate enough to be born in societies where individual freedom is the norm. The systemic problem is the failure to think long-term and make choices that will affect us positively into the distant future instead of just the immediate one. That is the risk that everyone here seems so intimidated by. The "live for today" mentality is criminally limiting to the health, wealth, happiness, and fulfillment of present and future generations. We can only create sustainable and effective economic solutions for them by gradually encouraging them to fix this fundamentally flawed ideology.

You may be wondering why I never just took the initiative to start a store in Kalavan village on my own and prove what I have been preaching all along to a consistently incredulous audience. Even though I was certain I was right about the superior economic reality that would be created by the profitable implementation of a store here, I also knew that I was not qualified to undertake this process all on my own. The reason I needed to enlighten my neighbors about these simple economic truths was that I would need their help in implementing them. The division of labor principle would be paramount to the success of this endeavor.

Though I knew I was the person in Kalavan with the most entrepreneurial knowledge and experience and that I had the most capital to work with, there were several key aspects for which I was utterly unqualified. Indeed, out of the more than 100 people who live here and the hundreds more in the surrounding villages, I knew the least about the buying habits of the locals who would comprise the target market of customers for such a store. Even if I learned what people habitually bought (and, therefore, what the predictable market demand would be), I knew little about the supply options to source those items from at the best market prices. I was lacking reliable knowledge of both supply and demand, and the language and culture barrier in Armenia made it more inefficient for me to try to acquire all this knowledge than anyone else in the village who might try. The time and labor investments required from me would be far greater than from anyone else, and the results I produced would be of much lower value. High input and low output is the definition of inefficiency. And if I attempted the trial-and-error approach of guessing at how best to offer the Kalavanian people what they wanted, I would certainly waste time and money that would not have to be wasted by someone who did not have the same entrepreneurial disadvantages as me. In doing so, I might even create a negative brand identity for myself and my store.

That was why I depended upon the knowledge and labor of my neighbors, who already had the relevant knowledge, skills, and relationships I was lacking. But what I had that they lacked was the entrepreneurial perspective and experience to see the unrealized value of their intangible assets. It would require the work of an entrepreneur to arrange the economic environment to actualize that hidden value.

Shortly after publishing *Everyone Is an Entrepreneur* in English, the book was translated into Armenian and published locally here in both languages. I gave copies to my neighbors here in the village, not expecting much to come from the gesture but feeling inclined to make it anyway so that at least I could say I tried. But to my surprise, one neighbor actually took it upon himself to study the text in full, ask me questions about each chapter, and begin altering the inertia of his life and actions onto a more entrepreneurial trajectory.

This neighbor took it upon himself to invest the proceeds from the sale of a parcel of land into startup costs and inventory for opening a small store here out of a small, unoccupied building in disrepair located in the center of the village. With the money he had leftover, he even purchased a selection of power tools appropriate to his skills as a handyman, even though he had no perfect and immediate plan to make a guaranteed income with these tools. I saw that he was ready to take his earning capacity into his own hands, to diversify his wealth into a variety of strategies that he could rely on to always be earning an income of some kind, even if he could not perfectly control it.

Previously, he had expressed to me that he could never justify such expenses because they represented too much risk. But this concern initiated a realization in him that he was exposing himself to risk no matter what course of action he took. If he continued with his daily lifestyle of hard manual labor for meager wages into his old age, he was risking the health and safety of his body and the enormous time required of him to maintain his livelihood. If he did nothing, he risked running headfirst into increasing unfulfilled demands as he consumed most of the wealth he had already generated and lost the rest to entropy. And if he invested what monetary capital he had accumulated into a simple business venture that was not guaranteed to be profitable, he risked losing that too. What he could never do was live a life without risk. He could only choose what kind of risk he was willing to take on and cultivate circumstances that would make it more likely to work out in his favor.

My neighbor, upon reading the book, insisted that he had already understood most of the economic lessons the book talks about. I am sure most Westerners feel a similar way. Indeed, the book stresses many times that most of the principles of entrepreneurship come naturally and intuitively to us. Yet, Armenians and Americans alike frequently fail to act on and implement their understanding as best as possible. There is a barrier between how they know things ought to work "in theory" and how they make their choices and perform their actions "in reality." The goal of the optimized entrepreneurial actor should be to adjust their actions as much as possible to match what they know is true, or else they are perpetuating a false reality where things are condemned to function less effectively than they could. That is the world we live in: One where the overwhelming majority of the human population toils needlessly to meet their basic material demands instead of living in relative abundance and luxury, dedicating the bulk of their time to what they most care about. The pivotal change in my neighbor came finally not from radically different intellectual concepts about how to interact with reality better but rather the emotional confidence to begin doing so, part of which culminated from witnessing my profitable experiment with selling cigarettes here at a micro-level. Understanding without equivalent action means little.

The lesson to be learned here for people like me whose ambition is to positively impact developing economies toward entrepreneurship and self-determination is that demonstration does more to overcome cultural inertia than compelling arguments and theories. It is actually only a tiny sub-section of humanity that learns primarily through definitions and structured discourse. It is ironic and humbling for a non-fiction writer and educator, such as myself—whose primary medium of expression is the written word—to admit this and face the reality he is dealing with.

I am, as of yet, unsure how else I will be able to influence the economic improvement of Kalavan and Armenia for the good of everyone. The opening of a store was just the first, most obvious step toward eliminating unnecessary loss from the universal experience of buying and selling common goods here. Everyone here is richer because of it, even if they lack the understanding to see how it benefits them merely by providing a superior option than they had before. Whatever other changes that this brave new venture for my newly appointed shopkeeper neighbor is able to inspire, they will likely come about by mimicking his visible actions as a relatable example to follow. If the other villagers see someone they know, respect, and relate to taking new entrepreneurial risks with confidence, perhaps they will begin to believe that they can too.

Somehow and someway, people who stagnate at the lowest end of society's economic spectrum must begin to make different choices that lead to better actions and outcomes. That is the only sustainable path away from poverty and toward self-reliant wealth. If it can be done here, in some anonymous village in a country that most people only know by association with the Kardashians, why can't it be done everywhere? Most of the overwhelming obstacles are man-made. They can be overcome or rescinded by the actions of men too.

At times, I have lamented that perhaps I have spent the last three years slamming my head against a barrier that will never budge, no matter my intentions or determination. I felt I had become like Sisyphus, exerting ever more effort without hope of seeing the results actualized as tangible change in the world around me. I have stuck to this path not out of hypocrisy and a stubborn insistence against adapting myself to the reality I am dealing with but rather for lack of knowledge of a better strategy for effecting the lofty goals I seek.

Sometimes though, we must remain open to the possibility that progress is happening slowly, so slowly that it might remain invisible to us until a moment of critical mass from gradual accumulation makes it apparent. The cracks in the concrete are showing. We are, indeed, tearing down the wall that halts human progress. And progress becomes exponentially easier after the first major signs of radical change. It may take less time and effort to go from one to 100 than it did to go from zero to one, which is a beautiful meta-demonstration of the efficiency of economies of scale. My hope is at least that some of my direct learning experience here can save others wasted time and that they can move on to more effective strategies and direct demonstration in their noble efforts to improve the economic paradigms of those around them. What begins as a store could demonstrate to the rest of the village the potential for implementing additional entrepreneurial systems here, like restaurants, transport to and from the village, and a variety of professional services they have been equipped to provide all along but too unsure of themselves to take on the associated risks. Time will tell, and I am genuinely eager to play my part watching over Kalavan's gradual entrepreneurial development. In fact, I will do my part to document the economic progress of this burgeoning little social experiment via a new blog at www.kalavan.net. Follow along with me if you'd like.

At the time of this writing, if you look up Kalavan, Armenia online, the results will show you several media puff pieces that promote the undeveloped village as a hub for ecotourism,[1] scientific advancement,[2] and economic self-determination.[3] The narrative sounds terrific, but it is based almost entirely on words spoken to journalists and promises made by bureaucrats who have no entrepreneurial incentive to see them through to success and market equitability. The inaccurate media portrayal makes visitors all the more disappointed when the façade falls and the truth becomes apparent. But it does not have to be this way. The people here have the power within them to build a genuine brand identity and reputation based on the real strengths they have and ideals they seek to live up to. They and the world will be permanently wealthier because of it.

Gregory Diehl
June 2022
Kalavan, Armenia

---

1   https://hetq.am/en/article/78358
2   https://armenianweekly.com/2018/12/12/kalavan-once-an-ob-scure-village-in-armenia-now-gaining-international-fame/
3   https://jam-news.net/kalavan-and-the-art-of-living/

_____

DIEHL'S PRINCIPLED GLOSSARY
OF ENTREPRENEURIAL TERMS

Action

Action is the physical processes of the body that follow as the immediate consequence of the psychological process of choice. It is what we consciously do when we are aware that we want something (i.e., a goal) and how we can attempt to acquire it (i.e., a strategy). Anything the body does that is not the result of choice is an unconscious and automatic process and is, therefore, not action in an economic sense. Action is how we attempt to manifest our choices in reality.

Appreciation & Depreciation

Appreciation is when an asset (either tangible or intangible) increases in subjective value. The increase can come from added objective utility that people value, such as improvements to the condition of a car or house, or merely an increase in the preferences of buyers for that asset (i.e., its demand). All other things being equal, the monetary price of an asset increases in direct correlation with its value appreciation.

Depreciation is any decrease in the subjective value of an asset. In the long run, all assets lose their value with the passage of time due to the unavoidable physical property of entropy that gradually destroys their objective utility. But through the targeted human actions of management and maintenance, we can temporarily increase and preserve the utility and value of nature's various resources and the various forms we produce them into.

Arbitrage

Arbitrage is the difference in subjective evaluation among various buyers and sellers for a given asset. The difference can be caused by natural barriers to commerce (such as a distance one is unable or unwilling to traverse to acquire an asset), artificial barriers to commerce (such as laws preventing someone from acquiring something without the risk of legal consequences), or simple lack of knowledge about utility and availability. Entrepreneurs who take advantage of arbitrage by buying at a low price in one setting and selling at a higher price in another increase the efficiency of the marketplace by closing gaps in pricing and help assets move to owners who value them most.

Asset & Liability

An asset is any form of wealth that provides subjective value for its owner. A handsome face and charming demeanor are social assets if they increase the effectiveness of social interactions. Knowing how something useful works is an intellectual asset that helps us achieve our goals. A tractor is a farming asset that multiplies the production of food for the farmer. Commodities and currencies are financial assets that help us conduct exchanges with others.

A liability is any form of wealth that, if mismanaged, will lead to a decrease in value. Ultimately, any wealth can be a liability because nothing is immune to loss or degradation through accident or entropy. A chronic debilitating health condition is a biological liability because it can lead to a decrease in the utility of our bodies. A house built upon an insecure foundation is a real estate liability (and a safety liability to anyone living there) because it can lead to a decrease in the house's utility as a shelter or speculative asset. An embittered ex-spouse with a vendetta is a social liability because it can lead to a decrease in our ability to function socially.

Brand Identity

The brand identity of an entrepreneur or business entity consists of the collective expectations in the minds of their consumers. If branding efforts are successful, consumer expectations should match the promises and ideals of the entrepreneur. These promises and ideals can come to be displayed through symbolic representations such as logos, typefaces, color schemes, slogans, jingles, mission statements, advertisements, mascots (human, animal, or animated), and even writing or speaking styles.

Bureaucracy

A bureaucracy is collective arrangement of arbitrary policy enforcers. It operates outside natural market constraints like supply and demand through the use of violence to force human behavior to happen a certain way. As a result, bureaucratic actors have no natural incentive to improve the efficiency and effectiveness of their policies. They devolve into mindless labyrinthian constructs of senseless and outdated rules that continue to be followed for the sake of being followed. Anyone who cannot tell you why they do what they do or believe what they believe is thinking bureaucratically. A bureaucratic actor is antithetical to an entrepreneurial actor.

Business

A business is a strategic arrangement of knowledge, skill, and capital that exists for the purpose of producing goods and/or services that encapsulate a form of valuable utility. Entrepreneurs are the people responsible for producing and managing these systems for optimal efficiency and effectiveness, therefore optimizing the profit generated. Any business is necessarily shaped by the market forces of supply and demand, and its success depends upon its ability to work within these and other natural constraints.

Capital

Capital is any asset that is applied as an investment in combination with labor for the purpose of producing more wealth. Money invested in a business to help it turn a profit is monetary capital. A piano used to produce the valuable service called a piano lesson is a capital good or tool of production. Information studied and used to create or innovate better ways to do something is knowledge capital. Because capital is always an intermediary step in the attainment of a larger goal, only people with long-term perspectives will seek to acquire capital goods over consumption goods that satisfy their goals immediately.

Choice

Choice is the ability to consciously assess reality, project into the future, determine subjectively satisfying states, set them as goals, and align our actions with strategies for their attainment. Choice is the product of self-awareness regarding our psychological processes combined with knowledge about how reality works. Through the mechanism of choice, we are locked into an ongoing series of assessments about how to improve our satisfaction by acquiring various forms of wealth, which can be said to be owned by us when we retain control via choice about how they are used. With choice also comes responsibility about its outcome. Whenever the agency afforded by choice is impeded by violence, natural obstacles, or false knowledge, our pursuit of satisfaction suffers.

Consumer

A consumer is someone who seeks assets for the attainment of satisfaction (i.e., what they value). This is in contrast to a speculator, who acquires assets for the purpose of redistributing them to consumers or other speculators who value them more than they do. Art consumers might purchase paintings and sculptures to derive value by looking at them in their homes (or pay to do the same in art museums). Automobile consumers might purchase cars to derive value from driving them (or else hire other people with cars to drive them for the same effect).

Consumption Good

A consumption good is any asset used to attain immediate satisfaction (as opposed to delayed satisfaction with capital goods). What is typically thought of a capital good can be used as a consumption good (and vice versa). You can derive immediate satisfaction in the form of a feeling of security and aesthetic appreciation from owning high-quality tools. You can also use the same tools for delayed satisfaction by making and selling furniture with them. The computer you use primarily for immediate satisfaction in the form of entertainment can also be used for delayed satisfaction by finding a job with it or writing articles you will sell for a profit.

Commodity

A commodity is a natural resource that has been transformed into a fungible and useful form. The form commodities take derive from their general intended uses as components of capital or consumption goods. A bar of refined copper is useful for smelting into various industrial products. A bale of hay is useful as a component of feed for various pasture animals. A barrel of oil is useful as a component of various oil-based energy and consumption goods. A plank of wood, with minor cuts and modifications to it, is useful in countless varied construction projects. And so forth.

Cost

Cost is any subjectively negative requirement of acquiring a subjectively positive goal. It is the input portion of the input/output equation. Costs are most easy to calculate in numerical monetary terms when buying something, but they also exist as the time, effort, opportunity, and discomfort involved in the strategy behind the choice to pursue a goal. There is no action that does not incur some cost, as they all require the loss of at least some time and energy that could have been used for something else. From an entrepreneurial perspective, your customer's costs are everything required of them to obtain and consume (i.e., derive the value of) your products.

Culture

Culture is the sum total of unconscious socially inherited beliefs about how reality works and how to evaluate it. It is in contrast to education because culture requires no study, experimentation, or even acknowledgment of the habits and information being bestowed. The impressions of culture on the mind can be either accurate or inaccurate to reality, and they can be helpful or detrimental to one's goals and the attainment of their values. But they are always arbitrary, and, if adhered to tightly, they act as obstacles to education, the attainment of real knowledge, and the positive evolution of one's paradigm.

Curiosity

Curiosity is the inherent human demand for more knowledge (and everything that follows) than we currently have. It is naturally strongest when we are children and tends to diminish with age and repeated exposure to a similar range of experiences and static paradigms. Only a curious person will ever consider that something they believe about reality could be wrong or incomplete. Therefore, curiosity is a prerequisite to education and the growth of paradigms. Similarly, new and superior forms of entrepreneurial value can only be marketed and sold to people who are curious about how to improve their lives and achieving their goals better, so curiosity is vital to entrepreneurs and the economy.

Currency

Currency is any asset used as a medium to facilitate the equitable exchange of other assets. A currency has to be fungible enough that one unit of it is roughly identical to another. It has to be divisible into units small enough to accommodate specific economic calculations. It has to be transferable enough that buyers and sellers can easily give and receive it during transactions. Its supply has to be scarce enough that the economic value each unit holds is predictable. Most importantly, whoever is receiving the currency in exchange for other assets must believe that other people they wish to buy things from will accept it. A currency's utility derives from our perception of other people's perception of it, so it is wholly speculative. Legal money is currency that is produced and enforced by the State.

Economy

The economy is the collective arrangement of all production, consumption, and exchange occurring across human civilization. It is the intangible structure through which individuals work together, even unconsciously, to achieve their own and each other's goals better than they could alone. The economy's order emerges and adapts spontaneously toward its optimal state of equilibrium (i.e., meeting the maximum amount of its participants' goals for the minimum costs) through the choices of its participants toward subjective satisfaction. When artificial barriers divide the one integral economy into smaller sub-economies, they hinder its ability to reach equilibrium. The same occurs when participants are given false information to build their strategies for goal achievement upon. Though it is often oversimplified and depicted exclusively in monetary terms, the economy actually describes all historical progress from our primitive beginnings to our modern state of scientific and material opulence.

Education

Education is the act of increasing one's explicit knowledge (i.e., their accurate working understanding of how reality works) through study, experimentation, and/or practice. All knowledge has potential utility and value, even if it is not immediately obvious how it could be applied. A curious person pursues knowledge of reality for the sake of the knowledge itself, even without a specific plan for scientific, technological, or entrepreneurial application.

Effectiveness

Effectiveness is the measure of how well an action achieves the intended goal behind it. It is a chosen output as seen in isolation from all other variables. Central planners who choose the wrong outputs to measure are subject to erroneously assuming that an action is effective (e.g., measuring the total number of shoes produced as opposed to the number of shoes produced that match the style, size, and quality demands of the market of shoe consumers).

Efficiency

Efficiency is the ratio of output to input (i.e., the gains to the losses) involved in any chosen action. It is easy for people to fall into the trap of only measuring one side of this equation and ignoring the other. They might see that there has been a big increase in production and assume things are getting better because of it, all the while overlooking a disproportionately greater amount of input. They might see that a lot more effort is going into a process and falsely assume that means a proportionately greater amount of output must be coming from it.

Entrepreneur

An entrepreneur is someone who produces or manages value through their choices according to the principles of reality. As every choice is made with the intention of achieving a subjectively valuable goal, entrepreneurial principles apply to everyone who is self-aware. The opposite of entrepreneurship is bureaucratism, which is characterized by ignoring reality's principles and enforcing arbitrary actions with violence, regardless of their failure to achieve the intended goal.

Entropy

Entropy is the tendency of all tangible assets to fall into disrepair and disorder, which means a loss of their objective utility and possibly depreciation of their subjective value too. Many physical assets are so cheap to produce or are consumed in such a short timeframe that the effects of entropy are hardly noticed or do not matter to their owners. Maintenance is the ongoing effort applied to counteract the effects of entropy upon assets. Since all intangible forms of wealth have tangible components (such as the knowledge contained in a brain or a book), they too are indirectly affected by entropy.

Equilibrium

Equilibrium describes the optimal functioning state of the economy wherein the maximum amount of its participants' demands are being met for the minimum required costs. It is when everyone is getting as much as they can while giving up only as much as they have to. It is the goal all entrepreneurs should be seeking, but it is never a static state, as supply and demand are always changing. Without violent interference or misrepresentation, the economy naturally tends toward equilibrium as a consequence of all participants individually choosing the goals and strategies that best satisfy them. However, when accurate information is scarce, or people are prevented from acting in their own interests by outside forces, equilibrium becomes harder to reach or maintain.

Equitability

Equitability is the measure of how profitable any choice is according to the subjective evaluations of the chooser when all gains and losses are accounted for. If two people have mutually exclusive values, they cannot interact with each other in a mutually equitable way, which is one in which they both evaluate that they are gaining more from the interaction than they are losing from it. The need to measure equitability is a consequence of values being specific to individuals and the ability to pursue them, likewise, being unequal.

Exchange & Theft

Economic exchange is the willful transfer of ownership (i.e., control) of assets that have been produced or previously acquired through exchange. The more advanced the economy becomes, the more its participants benefit from the harmony of specialization that comes from having access to the value produced by other people's knowledge, skills, and capital. Accordingly, more and more of our wealth comes to us through ownership exchange, and less and less comes through our own direct production. It grows ever more advantageous for us to get what we need from other people who can produce it more equitably than we can on our own.

The non-willful transfer of ownership is theft. It is the usurping of control over someone else's assets. Most visibly, theft means the physical removal of something tangible without the owner's choice. It can also include using an asset without their knowledge, lying to them about how the asset will be used, or breaking any pre-existing agreements about its use. Theft, even in seemingly innocuous forms, is always harmful to the economy because it robs its people of their incentive for production and makes it more profitable for thieves to reduce the amount of wealth instead of increasing it. Theft reduces win-win economic exchange to a zero-sum game where there must always be a loser.

Free Good

A free good is any asset for which supply so greatly exceeds demand that it is no longer necessary to set its acquisition as a goal and strategize how to acquire or manage it. However, as supply only refers to assets that are readily available to be consumed without labor, the concept of a free good does not apply to natural resources that, though they may exist in abundance, must be harvested into commodities before they can be exchanged or consumed. Hay in summer is a free good in regards to its utility as cattle feed because the cattle naturally do all the work required to consume it. Air in most places is a free good because we do not have to consciously strategize about breathing it (until we go swimming).

Fungibility

Fungibility is a measure of the degree to which one thing can be compared to others that share similar utility or from which people derive similar value. Fungibility is not determined exclusively by the objective physical form of an asset and others like it but by how the consumers of those assets interpret their functions. Even money, something designed to be functionally fungible for the purpose of facilitating commerce as a medium of exchange, is not totally fungible. One $10 bill is not exactly the same in utility or evaluation as ten $1 bills. Likewise, a crisp new bill is not exactly the same as a ratty old and worn bill of the same denomination, as they cannot be used exactly the same in some instances.

Gain & Loss

Gain is anything subjectively positive (i.e., satisfaction) that results from a choice, even if they were not consciously anticipated as part of a strategy. Gains, once their required costs and realized losses are taken into account, become profits, which are a measure of how equitable a choice is. The anticipation of an equitable gain compared to anticipated costs is the reason we set goals, and what we consider to be a gain will depend upon our subjective evaluation and priorities at the time of analysis and choice.

Loss is the subjective negative (i.e., dissatisfaction) incurred when the risk associated with any choice is realized. Getting mugged on your way to the movie theater might result in the loss of your wallet or physical and mental health. Money spent on a marketing campaign that doesn't produce any sales is a loss. The difference between what is considered a cost or a loss is whether we perceive that what is sacrificed was necessary to the attainment of the goal and was thus included as part of a strategy.

Gambling

Gambling is any attempt at increasing wealth for which the primary factor of success is chance or luck. It is, by definition, a situation in which we have little knowledge or control of the outcome. Running a business is akin to gambling if we do it without any knowledge of the relevant factors to its success or an attempt to apply our knowledge and skills in strategies that will turn the odds of success in our favor. Some element of luck or chance is present in every endeavor, of course, because no one can know everything. But strategy allows the entrepreneur to minimize the chances of things going wrong (i.e., risk).

Goal

A goal is the conscious conception of an attainable state of future value. It requires strategic planning that takes into account the costs of disutility that will be encountered in the act of acquiring it, and those costs must be considered to be an equitable exchange. One who does not take action toward their goals either does not consider the perceived costs equitable or does not understand them well enough to perform the necessary calculations.

Harvesting

Harvesting is the act of acquiring ownership (i.e., control) of natural resources and transforming them through productive actions into assets that can be managed and exchanged in the economy. We determine what resources are worth harvesting by our knowledge of what we can do with them and the technology that makes harvesting efficient enough to be equitable. We cannot strategize and apply resources most equitably for producers and consumers in the economy until they are harvested.

Investment

An investment is the willing sacrifice of a small amount of wealth for the strategic purpose of acquiring a larger delayed amount. Therefore, in the most direct sense, every consensual sale or purchase is an investment for both seller and buyer, as each party is giving up something to gain something they value more. Every intentional act of physical labor is, likewise, an attempt to gain something valued greater than the energy, comfort, and time (i.e., the costs) lost in the process.

Knowledge

Knowledge is the primordial form of wealth. It is the intangible product of education (i.e., an increase in one's accurate understanding of how reality works). Knowledge is applied as skills through the targeted applications of the body upon reality to change it to a more subjectively valuable state according to the actor. Knowledge leads to the creation of tools and technology that amplify the efficiency and effectiveness of the choices people make to pursue their goals.

Labor

Labor is the momentarily dissatisfying act of applying our bodily skills to reality (often through leveraging capital goods to increase our efficiency and effectiveness) to accomplish our goals and achieve a delayed state of satisfaction. Any application of skill that results in immediate satisfaction is not labor in an economic sense; it is recreation. The willingness to perform labor is a product of our ability to predict the future value of our presently unsatisfying choices and invest the resources of our time, energy, and material assets into acquiring that value in a manner that turns out to be equitable once its gains are realized.

Leverage

Leverage is the means by which we increase the efficiency of any choice in the pursuit of a goal. It is what enables relatively small amounts of input to generate larger and larger amounts of output. It is achieved through superior understanding of how to act upon reality (i.e., knowledge and skill) and the technology that enables more precise, predictable, and impactful choices.

Maintenance

Maintenance is any choice made to prevent the losses associated with consumption and entropy of an asset. Taking care of your health is maintenance to prevent losses to the utility of the body. A carpenter sharpening their saw is maintenance of their capital good and the production of wealth it would lead to. A pianist practicing their scales is maintenance of the skill required to perform their craft and produce the value associated with the music they play, which naturally degrades with non-use.

Management

Management is the process of optimizing the value of a given asset for a chosen goal by overseeing the conditions under which it exists and operates. It can include seemingly passive goals, such as the avoidance of accidental damage or loss of function to entropy. When management is applied to people and the products of their labor, its function is to ensure that the knowledge and skills of those under its domain are working efficiently and synergistically. Management even makes it possible to arrange the labor of individuals as part of strategies to accomplish goals that none of them are even aware of or would be very efficient and choosing and pursuing on their own. Its function is a consequence of the optimizing nature of the division of labor wherein everyone does as much as possible of what they are best at and as little as possible of anything else.

Marketing

Marketing is the act of increasing awareness of opportunities to acquire value. Whenever an entrepreneur introduces a new or superior asset to the marketplace for a price, they face the burden of making buyers who consider the price equitable aware of the opportunity to buy the asset. Assets that differ greatly from those that buyers are already aware of will have a greater marketing burden to overcome in order to achieve sales.

Material Value

Material value is the sum total of objective utility any physical asset has when deconstructed to its base commodity components. Money and books are both composed primarily of ink and paper, but they take on many unique emergent layers of utility when those material components are arranged in specific ways. If we were to remove their specificity and return them to their generic states as raw commodities, they would only again be worth what else they could be turned into through specific arrangements, which would require the application of knowledge and skill.

Ownership

Ownership is a claim of agency and control over the consumption of any asset. It is choice about what happens to a given portion of reality. It derives from producing the asset out of a raw state of nature or contracting with the person who produced it for control over it. One who owns something can choose to use it themselves, let others use it on terms they set, do nothing with it, or transfer ownership and agency to someone else. The use of any asset outside the terms set by the owner is a form of theft. With ownership comes the responsibility of maintenance in order to optimize assets and prevent loss to them from entropy.

Paradigm

A person's paradigm is the totality of their understanding of cause and effect principles concerning reality. Every pursuit of a goal occurs according to a strategy devised by our paradigms, which are frequently inaccurate and incomplete in areas that are vital to our success. When we habitually make choices that are inefficient, ineffective, or even counterproductive to our goals, it is because our paradigms are faulty and we cannot strategize effectively.

Price

Monetary price is a set amount of units of a currency offered in the attempt at reaching a mutually equitable exchange between the buyer and seller of a given asset. A price offer can be set by either the prospective seller in the hopes of finding a buyer or the prospective buyer in the hopes of finding a seller. When everything is functioning optimally in a marketplace and both sides of the exchange have ample access to information and assets, price quickly reaches an optimal compromise between supply and demand. When information and opportunities are artificially constrained, however, prices are subject to massive arbitrage and sudden changes.

Production & Consumption

Production is the transformation of natural resources into valuable assets or assets into new, more valuable arrangements. Intangible production can also consist of the arrangement of thoughts into valuable new forms. Lacking any pre-existing conditions of ownership, production denotes ownership and control over the product. Everything that is consumed must first be produced by strategic and chosen actions.

Consumption, in an economic sense, does not require the destruction or deconstruction of a produced asset or the removal of its valuable qualities. It is the act of using an asset to derive its value. Some assets can be consumed repeatedly without any significant loss in quality or depreciation in value. Some actually appreciate in value through consumption, such as if a well-crafted violin is played by many famous virtuosos. Others, like foods, can only be consumed once because their material destruction is a necessary part of deriving their value through ingestion.

Profit

Profit is what remains when input and output have been accounted for in any completed action. It is the positive result of comparing what we gained to what we lost in the act of gaining it. If gains and losses are entirely monetary, profit is easy to calculate because it is a simple matter of subtracting one number

296

from the other. But in reality, both output and input are a mix of many different types of value that the actor has to evaluate the subjective worth of. If the resulting analysis is more positive than negative, the action was profitable and the choice equitable.

Resource

A resource is anything found in nature that, once acted upon intentionally, gains utility and value. Resources develop in nature according to the principles of physics and biology that govern their states of existence and transformation. Intentionally harvesting them and arranging them in such a way as to maximize their utility transforms them into commodities with human discretion (i.e., ownership) over how they are consumed.

Risk & Security

Risk is the measure of the probability of everything unwanted that can happen as the result of a choice. Some risks are known and predictable (such as a car breaking down on the way somewhere), and some are unknown and unpredictable (such as a freak tornado destroying a home in a location not known for tornadoes). No matter how much you know and can control about a situation, there is always some level of risk because something you did not know to expect can always go wrong.

Security is the measure of how well we can manage the risk inherent to all forms of wealth. It derives from our ability to adapt to changes that could otherwise destroy the order we've built into our lives that enables us to remain comfortable and pursue our goals. The better we understand our values, the better we can leverage our assets to acquire more of them as various forms of wealth. The better we understand the risks our wealth faces, the greater security we can build into our management of it (e.g., by diversifying our wealth into many unrelated forms or maintaining intentional redundancies of our most valuable and important assets).

Sales

Sales is the process of persuading someone that an exchange of costs for gains will be equitable according to their subjective assessment, resulting in profit for them. In a common buying scenario, sales requires convincing them that the money they pay for an asset will be worth its benefits and that it is a better source of value than their other options. Sales, in some form and to some degree, is necessary for every business model because people do not have perfect pre-existing knowledge of what they want (i.e., the demand), their options for acquiring it (i.e., the supply), and the confidence to act.

Satisfaction & Dissatisfaction

Satisfaction is the emotional state that results when conscious demands are acquired and their gains realized. Under theoretical conditions of absolute satisfaction, all choices would cease because there would be no goals to attempt to acquire. However, in practice, satisfaction is never absolute or permanent. We achieve specific states of satisfaction for fleeting amounts of time before the same demand reoccurs or a different demand takes its place at the top of our priorities to resolve. Hence, we are chronically strategizing and laboring in some form to reach yet another state of satisfaction. Whatever leads to a greater state of satisfaction is subjectively positive, and whatever leads to a lesser state of it is subjectively negative.

Dissatisfaction is the emotional state that motivates us to set goals and take actions toward accomplishing them. Dissatisfaction can be momentary and bodily in nature, such as hunger that is quickly satisfied by the consumption of food. It can also be persistent and psychological, such as a sense of existential meaninglessness that can only be satisfied over a lifetime of accomplishments. However, not all pain necessarily equates to dissatisfaction (just as not all pleasant experiences equate to satisfaction), as we can easily find the will to endure what is uncomfortable for a more satisfying purpose. The measure of dissatisfaction is always what motivates making choices to alleviate it.

Scarcity

Scarcity is the result of the demand of a given asset exceeding its supply. Though everything is scarce in an absolute sense, since the universe is comprised of a finite amount of physical resources, it is irrelevant to economics when supply so greatly exceeds demand that it is not worth the investment of the costs required to manage, strategize, and sell it for a profit (i.e., when it is a free good). Monetary price naturally rises as scarcity increases and falls as scarcity decreases, thereby encouraging greater discretion from buyers when less of an asset is available.

Skill

Skill is the application of knowledge through controlled physical actions and mastery of the mechanics of the body. Skill is the gateway through which intangible assets become tangible. The ability to read, write, or speak is a skill. The ability to throw a ball is a skill. The ability to swing a hammer or pull a saw is a skill. Knowledge in a vacuum without some kind of application via the body can have no effect upon tangible reality.

Speculation

Speculation is the act of acquiring an asset for the purpose of exchanging it with others who will value it more. This way, assets move through the hands of those who understand their value to those who demand it. Without speculation, sellers would be limited to offering their assets only to people who want to directly consume them, and buyers would only be able to acquire assets from those who directly manufacture them. Every middleman or reseller engages in speculation for the benefit of the economy. Speculators also help maintain supply when scarcity suddenly changes by acquiring assets before their supply drops and/or demand rises.

Strategy

Strategy is the deliberate arrangement of assets for the purpose of achieving goals. A working strategy depends upon an accurate understanding of cause-and-effect principles in reality as well as the assets that will play roles in the chain of causality. If we do not feel confident in our abilities to predict the outcomes of complex systems of goal achievement, we will never attempt to strategize beyond a basic level, which will make larger and longer-term goals impossible.

Supply & Demand

Market supply is the sum total of an asset that is accessible to human management and consumption. However objectively useful the asset may be, it means nothing from an economic perspective until there is subjective value attributed to it in the form of demand. This demand (or at least the speculative perception of it) makes the investment cost of harvesting the appropriate natural resources, refining them into commodities and goods, and managing the whole process equitable for entrepreneurs. The marketplace of consumers uses the perception of this supply of the assets as the basis for strategizing to accomplish their goals.

Market demand is the chronically shifting sum total of how consumers value a given asset. On the individual level, demand for food rises sharply when we haven't eaten for several hours, to the point that it might momentarily be more subjectively important than any other conscious demand, but it falls to near zero as soon as we eat enough to satisfy the dissatisfaction caused by our hunger. We are not entertained by the same things as adults that we were as children, and we are likely to discover new aspects of our demand the longer we live. Entrepreneurs must either attempt to anticipate existing market demand and meet it with what they supply or incite new demand for their assets.

Technology

Technology is anything invented for the purpose of helping someone accomplish a goal more efficiently or effectively. Better technology is a product of better education. A saw is a tool for improving the pursuit of the goal of cutting wood. Cars and roads are technology for improving the pursuit of the goal of rapid transportation. A printed book is technology for improving the pursuit of the goal of education. Even institutions like businesses are technology for improving the pursuit of the goal of exchanging wealth.

Utility & Disutility

Utility is the sum total of possible uses an asset has according to its physical properties and the natural constraints of reality. Our knowledge of any asset's utility increases with education. Oil had the same utility long before it became the primary source of energy in the Industrial Age, but we could not use it until we became educated and technologically advanced enough to do so.

Disutility is the objective negative effect a liability has upon the pursuit of one's goals. What is helpful for one person in one circumstance (and, therefore, would be considered an asset) might be quite unhelpful for someone else (and, therefore, be considered a liability) as they pursue different goals and require different conditions to acquire them. Some level of disutility must always be overcome in the pursuit of goals. Accordingly, the expected value of the goal must be worth the cost of overcoming the disutility according to the subjective evaluation of the individual.

Value

Value is the degree to which an asset appeals to an individual's subjective satisfaction. All concepts of value are arbitrary and unique to the individual perceiving them. Even among the objective needs we all share, such as the need to eat to survive, our priorities for fulfilling them will align with how we personally evaluate our priorities and what strategies for doing so will bring us the most subjective satisfaction. Subjective value is always the prime driver behind choices and actions because it is an emotional experience, whereas knowledge of objective utility is an intellectual one.

Waste

Waste is any byproduct of the production or consumption of wealth that lacks known or equitable utility. It is, in essence, whatever we consider not worth the costs of managing. What people have considered waste through history has shifted with their knowledge about how they can apply previously useless garbage as useful assets. What was once freely given away or disposed of can begin to be managed and exchanged by people who value it or at least understand its value. The more we know about how to tap into the inherent utility of physical things and apply it in valuable ways, the less waste we will produce. There will be less we cannot consume or exchange.

Wealth

Wealth is anything, tangible or intangible, that offers utility to the people who control (i.e., own) it. Wealth creates greater opportunities and options for pursuing our goals. All wealth can be categorized in a logical progression of importance as knowledge, skills, capital goods, consumption goods, commodities, and currencies. Wealth's forms are delineated by what people find valuable to consume. These assets are presented as products and services on the market by the entrepreneurs who produce or manage them.

www.ingramcontent.com/pod-product-compliance
Lightning Source LLC
Chambersburg PA
CBHW062116020426
42335CB00013B/988